DATE DUE

MAR 1 4 1997	

BRODART   Cat. No. 23-221

THE LEFT IN SEARCH OF A CENTER

Edited by Michael Crozier and Peter Murphy

University of Illinois Press • Urbana and Chicago

To the memory of Ferenc Fehér (1933–94)

This book had its genesis in the "Reason and Imagination in Modern Culture" conference, organized by the journal *Thesis Eleven* and held in Melbourne, Australia, in 1991. Original versions of several of the essays in this volume were first presented as papers at that conference.

Library of Congress Cataloging-in-Publication Data

The left in search of a center / edited by Michael Crozier and Peter Murphy.
p.   cm.
Includes bibliographical references and index.
ISBN 0-252-02199-1 (cloth : alk. paper). — ISBN 0-252-06497-6 (pbk. : alk. paper)
1. Postmodernism—Social aspects. 2. Post-communism.
3. Civilization, Western. 4. Democracy. 5. European federation.
I. Crozier, Michael, 1956– . II. Murphy, Peter, 1956–
HM73.L43   1996
303.4—dc20   95-16648
                                                    CIP

Contents

Introduction: Searching for the Civic Center
Michael Crozier and Peter Murphy • 1

1. The Status of Hope at the End of the Century
Ferenc Fehér • 31

2. From Rationalization to Reflexivity • Barry Smart • 43

3. *Inter putatorem et vastitatem:* The Ambivalences of the Garden Metaphor in Modernity • Michael Crozier • 64

4. Border Closures • Paul R. Harrison • 86

5. Power and Rationality: The Western Concept of Political Community • Barry Hindess • 103

6. Classicism, Modernism, and Pluralism • Peter Murphy • 118

7. To Think What We Are Doing: Reconsidering Citizenship and Philosophy • Gillian Robinson • 140

8. The Marxian Legacy and the Problem of Democracy
Dick Howard • 162

9. Libertarian Confederalism and Green Politics: A Perspective on European Unification • John Ely • 179

Contributors • 211

Index • 213

MICHAEL CROZIER AND PETER MURPHY

Introduction: Searching for the Civic Center

The years 1989 and 1990 were filled with great optimism and celebration because of the collapse of the sclerotic despotisms in Eastern Europe and the promise (then looking forward to 1992) of a united Western European Community, ready to put aside the rancorous national antagonisms of the past. As we write today, just half a decade later, that optimism has drained away and the bright anticipations have evaporated.

In the East, the collapse of communism has been something less than the triumph of liberal democracy that many commentators trumpeted at the time. This was predictable.[1] It was always difficult to imagine the imperial heartland of the old Soviet Union, with its roots in an autocratic and patrimonial past, learning the habits of either liberalism or democracy overnight. The strength of nationalists and conservatives—as well as the appeal of "strong" leadership—in Russia, Ukraine, Georgia, and elsewhere, flows naturally out of hundreds of years of servility, brutality, and acquiescence that have characterized governments and subjects alike throughout the Slavic world. The heritage of Orthodoxy, bureaucracy, and passivity is a harsh climate for any Western-style politics to flourish in. The "brotherhoods" of the nationalists, the "rule of strong authority" of the conservatives, has much more resonance east of the Carpathians than does Western-style pluralism or parliamentary debate.

The West was a dream of many of the intelligentsia who lived in the desperate latter days of the old Soviet Union, but it was a dream of plenty, of the very thing the Soviet system promised but could never deliver: material abundance. We might say that these "Westernizers" (the "reformers" and their supporters) projected communism's own (unrealizable) fantasy onto the West (for the West in this context read a liberalized marketplace plus, maybe, elections). Alas, the liberal West does not produce material abundance. Its institutions are—at best—a way of "rationally" managing scarcity, of distributing (limited) goods at a price. The realization that the West is not a place of effortless, costless abundance—that the teleimages of a consumer's paradise tell only part of the story—was born of the logical refusal of the West, and particularly of the United States, to open an unrestrained line of credit to Boris Yeltsin and his "reformers." That would simply have been manna from heaven, a false playing to the myth of a superpowerful god (the West) who could redeem the world's suffering with food, warmth, and succor aplenty.

The tragedy is that the Russians, Belorussians, Moldavians, and the rest suffer great deprivations as they attempt to dismantle the monstrous economics of the old communist system and find a replacement for it. Those who suffer desire consolation, or at least something that makes sense of that suffering. There is nothing more humanly intolerable than to suffer without that experience making some sense. Even Stalinism, with its incalculable horrors, would say to those whose souls it tortured: this is for the future of humankind. What can Yeltsin and his compatriots say? To intone liberal platitudes does not help them. Liberalism does not console; it is not redemptive. It simply says: God helps those who help themselves (or at least it said this before it jettisoned entirely any religious language). The nationalists and conservatives of the ex-Soviet Union say: all your sufferings are justified—they mean something—because those sufferings are a sacrifice for your beloved nation, your venerable patriarch; trust in strong leaders, because they will lead you out of chaos and torment; in their strength and determination lies a certainty that will (eventually) subdue all of the menacing ambivalences of the transition from communism. This is a discourse that is deeply embedded in Russian political culture, and it resonates broadly in Russian society, crossing the boundaries even between Slavophiles and Westernizers. The Yeltsin-style strong executive presidency continues the long historical tradition of a state with significant authoritarian features.

What can Westerners say or do about this? Very little, except perhaps to avoid harboring illusions about the transition from communism in the Slavic world. In this century, the West already has held too many illusions about the lands east of the Carpathians. Many of the West's keenest minds were suckered by the fatal illusion of hope writ large—as Ferenc Fehér puts it, in his essay in this volume. They were seduced by the romantic illusion of otherness incarnate, the longing for a world completely different from their own. Today, the best that we can hope for—the rational hope that we might harbor—is that the archaic patrimonialism of the old Soviet Empire will evolve into something that, in Western eyes, is a little less brutal, less cruel, less paternalistic. The promises of an absolute transcendence of what exists, of a leap into the abyss, are pledges without guarantees, as Fehér points out, and should be distrusted. Steady, incremental shifts are more admirable.

In the case of the Slavic world, the model for such an incremental transformation is just as likely to be the corporatist states of the Asian-Pacific Rim as it is Western nations. The Confucian ethos of those Asian countries, of course, is irrelevant to the Orthodox East. But there is something telling in the way the Japanese, Taiwanese, and others have adapted a culture of loyalty, ritualized conformity, and respect for authority to the demands of a modern industrialized society. The ex-Soviet societies of the Slavic world face a similar question: how do we (now) imagine a political community in the light of the (increasingly universal) promethean forces (industrial, cybernetic, communicative) unleashed by the genie of modernity? This is a question, of course, not just for the ex-communist states but for all states throughout the world. How is it possible to maintain a coherent political and social identity in the face of the *dynamis* of the modern world? Dynamis both produces meaning and erodes it. This is the paradox of modernity. The Japanese, Taiwanese, and South Koreans (and for all intents and purposes the Chinese mainland when the geriatrocrats finally relinquish power) have all adapted familial/hierarchical/loyalty/status structures—all of them meaning-generating—to the insistent demands of the dynamics of the modern world. Singapore and Hong Kong have gone one step further, adapting certain aspects of the city-state form—albeit paternalistically managed—to the roar of incessant modernization. Dynamis is the modern Caesar to whom all pay tribute. Those who do not suffer the ignominy of fossilization, of obsolescence.

The Soviet communists were obsolescent—grotesquely obsolescent. To educate great mathematicians and deny them computers is, in the eye of the Critical Tribunal of Modernity, senseless beyond belief. The creed of modernity is the belief in progress, development, dynamism, and rational change. Moderns draw meaning (of sorts) from that; it is their faith (of sorts). To court stagnation, to be content with the lumbering, accident-prone, rusting steam engine instead of the up-to-date superfast electric train is, for moderns, senseless. The Soviet communists bred stagnation, inertia, and paralysis. Nothing symbolized this more than the infamous distribution system. Nothing moved, nothing circulated, except at a snail's pace, around the old Empire. Red tape, queues, geriatric trucks and machines, dirt roads—all and more immobilized the system.

But what replaces the immobile state? A state of change? A modern state? The modern state, the modern economy and society, was originally a Western phenomenon. It came out of Western Europe and was transplanted across the Atlantic and Pacific to the settler societies of North America and Australasia. As the end of this century nears, and with it the end of the millennium, modernity is becoming increasingly a *global* phenomenon. While this is most starkly apparent in East Asia, all the way from São Paulo to Cairo there are signs that the enchantments of the modern are irresistible: instant communications, instant coffee, instant divorce. It is impossible to live anywhere today without, at the very least, making concessions to the modern. The catch, though, is the dissipation of meaning.

Modernity means a faster pace, greater flexibility, higher productivity, intensification of innovations, quicker delivery, and so on. It *cuts time*. It does this by an ever-refined *rationalization,* as Barry Smart emphasizes in his contribution to this volume. Moderns work constantly on *how* they do things. They figure out more efficient, clever, and streamlined ways of producing, orchestrating, and delivering. But delivering *what?* Modernity makes a virtue of impatience. It is a "hurry up" culture. What are we impatiently waiting for? That modernity can deliver smartly, with less waste, delay, and unnecessary baggage, is a good thing but not unambiguously so, if the rationalization lacks meaning. Modernity in itself is poor at producing meaning, at giving its denizens a sense of *why* they are doing what they are doing. Dynamism can be admired for its own sake (we need only think of the speed culture of the auto racers), but when experienced repeatedly it becomes wearing and tiresome. In the end, dynamic personalities will tend to "spend" whatever meaning they "accumulate" from their activities. The logic of innovation, progress, and development will turn out under these conditions to be illusory, as Smart puts it. For dynamism to be persistently meaningful, it needs a context, a foil, something to modulate it.

Modernity has always lived off the meaning-producing potentials of things that are not purely modern. For hundreds of years the prodigious (and sometimes fantastic) economic dynamics of modern capitalism fed off religion. The decisive role of Lutherans, Methodists, Baptists, and others in building a remorselessly expanding capitalism, and in creating rationalized methods of accounting and distribution, are well-known. Through the nineteenth and twentieth centuries the promise of capitalism, however, was that it could increasingly shed its religious aura; it could, in Dick Howard's terms, produce meaning immanently, out of its own processes of change.

The imperative of the modern economy, state, and society is to eliminate reliance on any "transcendental norms"—to repudiate any "transcendental signifier"—be it called god, tradition, heritage, locality, generational ties, community, nation, or whatever—anything that is an "enveloping whole" to which human actions might be subjected. The risk of this, as Ferenc Fehér points out, is spiritual desolation. What modern societies can and at times do produce is a bored, cynical, lifeless, despirited population: bored with fast food, cynical of politicians promising reforms they never deliver, despirited by shifting locality too many times, buffeted by the endless cycles of boom and recession, disappointed by the limited reality of their lives compared with the endless horizons, and overstimulated expectations, that modernity engenders. Boredom and cynicism generate a demand for escapism—for young people, in particular, to experiment with drugs, suicide, or nihilistic gestures (e.g., headbanging). The attempt by some to dignify this as a kind of "wild culture" fighting its way out of the grip of a rationalized, ordered world is, as Michael Crozier points out, unconvincing. Today most American inner cities are a disturbing testimony to the spiritual dislocation that can be provoked by the incessant demand of modernity to restructure and transform. Such maneuvers are intrinsic to its dynamism. But many psyches in modern societies cannot keep up with the pace of change. In the worst cases, they become the casualties of modern life—marginalized, segregated, ghettoized—they end up on desolation row.

The lesson of this is that dynamis is the first global culture (*in nuce*), but it needs something else, something to give it form, coherence, meaning; without that, its costs will outweigh its benefits. The successful modernizers in fact are those who can merge dynamis with another, more stable source of cultural identity. Consider the Japanese: they have merged a traditional ethos with a modern economy, with some intriguing results. For instance, the traditional Japanese minimalist aesthetic became the basis for the product miniaturization that was, in turn, the key to so much of the marketing success of Japanese corporations since the 1950s in the world economy. Yet Japan is not the West. So what is the "something else" that can in a Western context furnish the raison d'être for rationalization processes, that can restore or sustain meaning under conditions of rationalization? To answer this question, consider another question: what is it that distinguishes Western from Japanese society? One of the most important distinctions is the fact that Japanese society is highly consensual, while Western societies, in sharp contrast, are *conflict oriented*. First, this means that Westerners harbor, readily generate, and have a high tolerance for *oppositions*. Second, Western societies are predisposed to provide *public spaces* for the interplay of opposing social, economic, and political forces—including parliamentary and public broadcasting forums for opposing political forces, educational institutions for the conflict of ideas, and a publicly funded infrastructure for economic competitors. Third, Western societies tend to display high levels of *reflexivity* toward oppositional currents. This is exemplified by the existence of institutions and offices (such as constitutional and arbitration courts, the speakers of legislative assemblies, etc.) that are designed not for "taking sides" but for arbitrating differences and making impartial judgments. It is also represented, as Dick Howard emphasizes, by the classical American Madisonian ideal of simultaneous union and diversity in the state—the American Republic's "out of many, one"—an ideal that owes a substantial debt to the experience of the northern Renaissance city-states that John Ely examines and even more specifically to the Dutch republican distrust of dogmatic religiosity that Paul Harrison discusses and the corresponding search for a form of civic association freed from this dogmatism.

A reflexive attitude is also exemplified, as Barry Smart indicates, by the contemporary (postmodern) desire to recognize the other, to accept heterogeneity and differentiation, although this desire is often confused in the postmodern mind with a desire for absolute transcendence of one's own world in the direction of the other. In a civic world, different cultures and forms of life must live with each other in the spirit of equilibrium, not transcendence. Preparedness *both* to live in the midst of difference *and* to distinguish oneself from the other—through skillful display and playful competition—is deeply rooted in Western civilization. What makes it a civilization is its capacity to provide a link between different forms of life; what makes it unique as a civilization is that it links together conflicting forms of life via the public domain. In the terms of Gillian Robinson's Arendtian reading of this, the West is premised on an ethic that encourages a plurality of opinions as well as assertiveness and distinctiveness in action, deed, and perspective that in turn give those opinions their robust character. In short, what gives meaning in Western societies is public, agonistic life or civic engagement. From public sporting contests to scientific expositions, from theater festivals to commercial exhibitions, from the public lectures of writers and academics to the public drama of the courtroom, the denizens of Western societies find "the sense of things" through listening to, watching, judging, and participating in the spirited debates, friendly conflicts, challenging rivalries, skilled displays, and exhibitions of "excellence in performance" in the public domain.

This public complex notably declined in importance in Western societies during the 1980s. The power of the rationalizers tended to squeeze funding for public institutions and spaces of all kinds (public-private or public-state). Of course, some of the blame for this lies at the feet of many erstwhile "defenders" of the public domain, many of whom confuse the public domain with the welfare state and make the (disastrous) assumption that public institutions are "institutions of protection"—institutions for the protection of the weak by the strong (echoing age-old patrimonial thinking)—an assumption that the rationalizers proved devastating in assaulting. Sadly, so many of the current defenses of the public domain still carry echoes of the patrimonial idyll. It is not at all unusual to find antirationalizers citing the examples of the corporatist states of East Asia or Germany in arguments to restitute the public domain. But this buys into the tacit traditional-cum-authoritarian assumptions of those states that are not plausible for the majority of Westerners today.

• • •

The problems of rationalization cannot in all circumstances, and certainly not in the West, be solved by simply fusing modern dynamism with an overarching tradition. In the West at least, traditional symbols cannot provide a satisfactory basis for political community. Tradition means a fixed location for individuals, in relation to status, authority, and so on. It means belonging to an overarching community or status group and being tied to other status groups or communities via a chain of authority. Hierarchy draws people together into a meaningful whole. The community of church, work group, locality, and nation always implies at some point a hierarchy. The hierarchy may be patriarchal, one of status, or simply the precedence claimed by a "predestined" nation ("America First," the "greatness" of French civilization, etc.) vis-à-vis other nations or national groups.

Traditional, conservative gambits are popular when the strife of modernity reaches a crescendo, evident, for example, at the very end of the 1980s. The self-image of the eighties, much like the Roaring Twenties or the 1880s in the West, was marked by breathless and ebullient dynamism. Much of this was contrived, as Western states, corporations, and consumers opened seemingly endless lines of credit, borrowing furiously, with inflationary consequences in the price of both goods and money. Public, corporate, and private debt ballooned. When invested, that debt went into speculative holdings—junk bonds, futures, property—that were expected to increase in value over time because of inflation. The phoney dynamic of such a "boom" is nothing new. Nor is it surprising that when this kind of boom runs out of steam (self-generated steam) some of the people who lose jobs, investments, or are simply threatened by the downturn, will then seek refuge in a kind of conservatism.

A case in point is the support for Pat Buchanan's bid for the 1992 Republican presidential nomination, in challenge to George Bush. Yet the Buchananite invocation of "conservative values" appealed only to a relative minority of Americans (probably no more than 10 percent). The "religious right" alienated many Republicans with rhetoric that challenged modern liberal equality. Even for the Republican mainstream, modern equality—especially the equality of women—will not be forsaken, even for the promise of certainty. Images of hierarchy and strong authority produce meaning for fewer and fewer people in the West at the end of the century. Even mainstream churches (Anglicans, Episcopalians) have realized this as they do theological handstands in order to accept women into the priesthood and as they try to remove the image of God the Father. The imagery of anyone serving "higher" purposes or agencies, of subservience, is today ever more bereft of meaning. This process has been ongoing episodically for a very long time in Western societies and shows no sign of abating—quite the contrary.

Equality, however, is not without its own drawbacks. The problem with equality is not that it deprives people of a sure but subservient place in the world—a place in what was once called the Great Chain of Being. Rather, the problem is the often disorienting rat race that, as equals, we are invited to join. Equality most intelligibly means "equality of opportunity." Equals can—if they want, if they have the financial means, intelligence, interest, and concern—vote, buy and sell property, occupy executive offices, run for public office, and so on. Equals are not equal in their bank balances, contacts, what they can focus on, IQ, degree of concern about the world, or almost anything else. They are not equal in their profits from buying and selling, their accomplishments in administrating people or things, their effectiveness in garnering votes, or even in exercising their vote. Equality means that there is no "higher power" (class, sex, race) that makes decisions—good, bad, or indifferent—for you. Women make decisions alongside men, blacks alongside whites, Irish alongside English, and so on. They make good decisions and lousy decisions, inspired ones as well as insipid ones. The problem of equality is that there is no animating or contextualizing purpose behind the decisions that equals make.

The liberal draws life-meaning from being a *chooser* but that does not help make sense of the decisions the liberal makes unless those decisions contribute to "giving people greater choice." Equals cannot say: I'm doing this for God, or for my status group, or tribe, or chief, or out of loyalty to my corporation. They *may* be able to say: I am making this decision because it is the most rational one (cost-effective, efficient, methodical, smartest) that I can come up with. The meaning of my actions is that I am a *rational chooser.* My decisions contribute to making things go smoother, faster, cost less. This gives choices an air of substantive meaning even if the atmosphere is pretty thin.

This rational chooser line of argument was very popular in the 1980s. Margaret Thatcher led the way with an energetic program to rationalize the British state. Others, like the Hawke-Keating Labour administration in Australia, followed suit. Thatcherism represented the end of the welfare state experiment, which had tried to join a very old notion of a "sheltering canopy" with the imperatives of a modern rational state. It was always an uneasy marriage. The welfare state promised both "rational accounting"—in other words, budgeting processes that encouraged corporations and individual citizens to act rationally—*and* "protective shelters" for those who "couldn't keep up," including not just individuals who were sick or old but whole industries, management strata, able-bodied workers who were insulated from modernity's drive for rationalization. From the rationalizers' perspective, rorts, sweetheart deals, and feather bedding took hold in the welfare state. For example, for someone who was injured at work, "welfare" emphasized caring for them indefinitely in the hospital and then pensioning them after leaving hospital. By contrast for the rationalizer, the emphasis is on speeding recuperation and rehabilitation, so the person might return to productive employment. The welfare state encouraged a view of human action as one of securing resources from higher up (in companies, ministries, universities, etc.) rather than of rationalizing the use of resources. It encouraged the beneficiaries' rather than the rationalizers' view of the world, and the beneficiaries' view of the world is a very old one—for millennia people have looked to beneficent gods and kings to assuage life's vicissitudes. Thatcher's liberalized Conservative party went hunting for such impeccable Tory principles, while old-fashioned Tories like Edward Heath looked on helplessly from the sidelines, and the British Labour Party—unreflective defenders of the old welfare state—became electoral pariahs in all but the most devastated parts of Britain (like Scotland).

A majority of Britains embraced Thatcherism, in part because of the very apparent decline of British industry in comparison with the increasingly rationalized (modern) East Asian competition. In response to external pressures, rationalization became a growing force throughout the 1980s in all Western economies with significant pseudo-traditional elements. The *long-term* irony of the rationalization process is that it *does* generate economic growth (notwithstanding the ups and downs of the economic cycle) but at the cost of declining employment levels. Its outstanding feature is to produce more with less. Rationalized economies shed labor, especially unskilled labor, unless there are above average growth rates ("economic miracles") to compensate. The accompanying problem is that such rates cannot be sustained indefinitely. For this very reason, we have seen in the West in the last twenty years the disappearance of the Keynesian social standard of full employment. "Leading edge" growth is no longer typical of Western economies, and significant persisting levels of unemployment have emerged as a social fixture. The poorly educated and the low-skilled are especially vulnerable. This represents partly a return to the historical norm. It becomes more and more apparent that the industrial factory system created the ingredients to mop up large amounts of unskilled labor that had in the past only ever been, at most, semi-employed. Now postindustrialism (post-Fordism) has extinguished that demand. The result is the reappearance of a significant underclass—the permanent poor.

One key current departure from the historical norm, however, is the fact that businesses and governments are increasingly rationalizing middle management as well. The last decade has seen a quiet social revolution underway in Western societies, involving the radical pruning of the middle strata. The managers who have been retrenched were previously a kind of industrial-corporate or civil service cordon sanitaire that "filtered messages" up and down organizational hierarchies without performing any concrete productive function. They were a class beyond any meaningful productive measure. They served mainly to absorb and diffuse the tremors of change initiated from the boardroom or senior ministry levels and to smother both the dissatisfactions and initiatives of those underneath them. In some sense they did nothing, which was precisely their virtue, until it became a virtue no more.

The technicians and professionals that perform services for clients (who credential, counsel, program software, and draw up legal contracts for them) have, insofar as long-term trends are concerned, escaped the fate of the middle management drones, such that now the social desire to join the professional-technical class far exceeds the opportunities to do so. There is simply a limit to the number of lawyers, teachers, and accountants that any society needs. Governments of all stripes in the past decade paid a price for the emergence of the new unemployed. Electorates blamed governments for the phenomenon, the socialists in France as much as conservatives in Britain. But governments also court this blame when they pretend that normal rates of economic growth (fueled by the rationalization processes of mature economies) will (eventually) reduce unemployment to negligible levels when that will never happen. Over time the gap between expectation and reality has produced increasingly confused, exasperated, and cynical electorates. It has also entrenched a political unwillingness either to confront the new realities of persistent unemployment and underemployment or to put on the political agenda questions about what new forms of distribution (wealth, job, etc.) are required in order to cope with this new reality.

One of the basic lessons to be drawn from the experience of recent history is that the rationalization process, whatever may be its necessity, has many unintended (or unacknowledged) consequences. Its reason creates confusions, paradoxes, illogicalities. Consequently, no successful politician of a rationalist stripe has ever stayed in power on the basis of the rationalizing creed alone. Margaret Thatcher, for example, made much (effectively so) of what she took to be the virtues of the liberal economic actor (independence through personal effort, self-reliance, self-denial, and so on). The appeal to moral virtue played as much of a role in her electoral dominance as did her appeal to economic rationalism. She was not merely a rationalist but a liberal-rationalist. She was also skilled at invoking prerational images of "national glory," especially in the wake of the Falklands War. Ronald Reagan, even more so, spent much of the eighties trading in patriotism—making America feel good about itself again, proclaiming the United States as the greatest nation on earth. Underlying such rhetoric was the invocation of a "greater whole"—of something transcendent—that nurtures, shelters, and protects citizens against a threatening, intimidating world. In Australia, the rationalist Paul Keating was counterbalanced by the consensus figure Bob Hawke, the first personifying a rationalization of change, the second, a vague kind of community.

The share-market collapse of 1987, the world economic recession in 1990, the Persian Gulf War, the banking crisis, and the collapse of communism further revealed the weaknesses and paradoxes of the liberal rational view of political community and equally of its conservative alter ego. The economic downturn demonstrated that while states had (sort of) been "exercising restraint" over domestic expenditures, companies and individual consumers had been engaged in a credit-fueled orgy of speculation and spending. Few of the liberal rationalist virtues of self-discipline and self-restraint were in evidence. The allure of rapid gains seemed much more compelling than any old moralizing about waiting till you can afford to buy what you want. Modernity breeds impatience. Impatient consumers, bankers, CEOs make a lethal combination. Inflated property and stock values disguised the uncreditworthiness of borrowers.

When the bubble of illusion burst, so did the credibility of eighties-style rationalism and with it projects like that of full European integration—the ambition of Brussels's modernizers led by Jacques Delores to turn Europe into a single market, including a single currency market, to allow goods, finance, services, and people to flow quickly and conveniently around Europe without the obstacles of passports, customs, national currencies, or reserve banks. *Europe as a mobile state—* the repository of dynamis going into the next millennium: if in 1989 this was seemingly guaranteed, by 1992 significant parts of this idea of European Union were in trouble. The referendum for the Maastricht Treaty brought conservative anti-European Europeans out of their shells. Some of the Irish saw in an integrated European Law—and the European Commission on Human Rights—the specter of equality demolishing the patriarchal basis of Irish Catholicism. Many of the Danes feared the loss of their national identity if swamped by German goods and bossiness. The arch-liberal-rational modernizer Thatcher took fright at the bureaucratic-rational modernizers in Brussels and their challenge to the prerogatives of British sovereignty. French farmers feared the loss of the protective cocoon of their subsidies. Germany (in 1993) would not compromise in any measure its economic stability (low inflation) for the sake of making a common European currency mechanism work.

Nationalism emerged as an unexpected force, nowhere more spectacularly or more disturbingly than in Germany, where reunification of the German state meant a much more powerfully sentimental community of focus than Brussels's modernizers ever imagined. But "affection for nation" always implies insiders and outsiders—those who are superior, those who are inferior. The upsurge in Germany of racism against the guest workers (e.g., Turks, Vietnamese)—with its eerie echoes of the Nazi past—is the inevitable dark side of any powerful and deeply felt surge of national feeling. To find a reason for existence in a nation means that anyone who does not belong to that nation is at some level a threat to one's identity, and such perceived threats quickly turn to hatreds. This can be avoided where people love their constitution rather than simply their nation (which is typical of a lot of American and to some extent even of English patriotism). The constitutional order can embrace many different nationalities. But where one finds meaning in one's nation—its specific language, culture, and history—chauvinism and hostility to other nationalities will invariably follow in some form. (Moreover, because Germany's constitution was imposed on it after a defeat in war, it can never be an object of love. Thus, constitutional patriotism is impossible for the Germans.) Having a nationality and a strong national government to back it up is a hedge for many Germans against the failures and impositions of a rationalizing modernity. For older West Germans, it is a bulwark against memories of the inflationary chaos of the Weimar Republic. For former East Germans, it is a hedge against the inevitable depravations of the economic rationalization of the bankrupt industries of the communist East. Germany, not unlike Japan, has merged some deeply conservative motifs (captured in the rubric of economic security) with highly rationalized technologies and, like Japan, remains (whatever the imposed democracy) a status and authority conscious, corporatistically hierarchical, conformist, and, in crucial aspects, latently traditional society.

Reunified Germany is now a powerful reminder that Europe does not exist as an intelligible political entity. It remains, for all the talk, a customs union. Europe cannot act as a unified political force. Its paralysis in the face of the ethnic wars of the Balkans, triggered by the collapse of Yugoslavia, and Europe's more or less acquiescence in the face of the tribal-nationalist genocide on the borders of Europe (at the intersections of the Slavic, Turkish-Islamic, and European worlds) is telling. Europe cannot act politically because it is not a political entity. It remains a cohort of neighboring nation-states who have conceded relatively little of their sovereignty to the European idea and then mainly for economic reasons. A European political union is only possible, as John Ely argues, if Europe takes seriously the idea of a *federation* of states, instead of pursuing the idea of Europe as a surrogate *nation*-state (as the integrationists like to think of it) operating on the model of a ministerial government.

The federal model—whether we like to use the contemporary examples of the United States or Australia or (as Ely does) historical ones like the federative leagues of city-states during the European Renaissance—is the only really successful model of a *consensual* union of states. But politically the Europeans disdain the lessons of either the New World or their own past. Yet what they are left with is hardly edifying. Indeed, it is reasonable to suggest that the very idea of Europe remains under strain today. The reunification of Germany has implicitly called the idea of Europe into question. It has raised the prospect that Germany, as it did in the 1930s, will attempt to pursue a middle path between the Slavic East and Western Europe (a Western Europe still reliant on the Americans to provide whatever political and diplomatic unity of purpose it has). In this scenario, Germany will gradually expand its sphere of influence in Central Europe, exercising growing economic, diplomatic, and ultimately political influence over the Czech Republic, Croatia, Hungary, Austria, and quite possibly even Poland and Ukraine. As a consequence, Bulgaria, Romania, and Albania would be both isolated from the West and be even more likely to fall back on forms of governance from the Turkish-Islamic past. The reason for supposing all of this—apart from the lessons of history—is that Germany is only ambivalently a Western state. The popular antipathy to "Americanism"—still, in the twilight of the century, the leading spirit of the West—is both broad and deep in German society. There is a great temptation for Germans to look toward an integrated Central Europe to protect the deeply conservative ethos of its state—a conservatism that it relies on to produce meaning that the propulsive rationalization of the postwar German economy constantly strips away. For Germans, "Americanism," English liberalism, French romanticism, Italian licentiousness, and so on represent a threat to the precarious balance that they have established between a corporatist conservatism and a socially engineered business and industrial rationalism—in other words, the balance between security and dynamis.

• • •

Conservative images of a secure society continue a powerful half-life in modernity. By promising to protect Americans from the threats of communism, American conservatives made endless political capital during the cold war. The call to national security harnessed and mobilized the energies of large numbers of Americans during the twentieth century—so much so that their widespread and atypical loss of confidence and purposefulness in their society's future in the late eighties and early nineties must be partly attributable to (ironically) the *end* of the cold war. A "small government" Republican like Ronald Reagan—rhetorically committed to rationalizing government expenditures—in fact *expanded* spending on the military in the eighties (and in doing so quadrupled the American deficit). The appeal of this to both overtly conservative and more liberal Americans (not, of course, to the ultraliberals for whom freedom of choice is the only issue but to those moderate liberals who are interested in extending both the parameters of choice *and* efficiencies in government and business) was paradoxical but electorally rewarding. Reagan was a living contradiction—a deeply ironic contradiction that typified U.S. society as a whole. For

Americans, military might was properly deployed against communism in defense of a liberal order *and* an "open society." Security was pursued in the name of freedom and dynamism (choice and enterprise, liberalism and rationalism). (In Reagan's case this meant budgets that were—in practice, from a rationalist perspective, crazy—voodoo economics. In the same spirit, Thatcher's Falklands escapade would have bankrupted the British state if the Argentinians had not caved in almost immediately.)

The collapse of communism meant the end of the conservatives' chief platform. Where now is the threat to America and Americans that can mobilize conservative sentiment (a minority but energetic sentiment) in support of the liberal and rational-dynamic order? To insist, as Pat Buchanan conservatives did, that the family is threatened by liberal freedoms leaves conservatives out on a limb. The Gulf War barely halted George Bush's military cutbacks. While Saddam Hussein's despotism needed containment, the Kuwaiti royal family was hardly an endearing or consistent personification of a liberal or rational order that American and Western forces might want to defend without qualification. Again the paradox: tradition allies itself with modernity virtually everywhere in the Middle East, in a highly unstable combination. Saddam rules Iraq with ultramodern weapons and party-style organization yet with the bloodlust and brutality of an ancient tribal village clan-boss turned tyrant. Kuwaiti and Saudi ruling families, while lacking Saddam's grotesqueness, rest on traditional hierarchical and hieratic principles while financed by modern oil refineries. Large sections of the local populations in these countries distrust the compromise. Islamic fundamentalists maintain pressure for traditional (religiously sanctioned) authority. Where departure from this is greatest (as in Egypt) so is the strength of the fundamentalists. Iran demonstrated the extent of the instability of the equilibrium between tradition and modernity in the Middle East—indeed it is hardly an equilibrium at all, more a stitched together ad hoc arrangement, the contrivance of ruling elites precariously caught between Western liberal demands, the realities of modernization, and the consolation sought by their own lower classes in religion.

Notwithstanding what it calls its "vital interests" and however it might intervene from time to time militarily or diplomatically in particular conflicts, the West today, of course, can no more determine the destiny of the Islamic world than it can determine what happens in the Slavic world, "Confucian" East Asia, or the "Catholic-Baroque" world of the Philippines and Spanish-speaking Latin America. The era of global superpowers and their projection of a single world culture is dead.

We live, as postmodernists would say, in a world of multiple cultures. The postmodern generation (the generation of 1968) hit upon this in the course of demonstrating their moral outrage at the remnants of Western colonialism in Algeria and elsewhere. Anticolonialism was their formative political experience, and the conclusion they drew from it was that there is no universal ethos fit for the world as a whole. Western claims to represent the universal simply covered up for colonial domination.

The postmodern generation, attracted to the romantic otherness of Yemen, Algeria, and Colombia, postulated an ethos premised on respect for the other, for difference. Politically, this constitutes part sense and part nonsense. The sense of it is that the West is not a universal force. We cannot expect its norms and culture to rule the globe. Despite some silly prognoses following the collapse of communism, we cannot look forward to the triumph of liberalism across the globe. Neither Georgia nor Ukraine, let alone Pakistan or Malaysia, are about to connive with the march of universal history toward the global triumph of the liberal ideal. The political fallacy of the postmodernist, however, is that while major and irredeemable cultural divisions remain worldwide, the maxim of "respect for the other" is insufficient unless, first, that respect is *reciprocated*. Consider the example of the complaints of the Malay government directed toward Australia in the late 1980s about the "critical" way the Australian media portrays Malaysia. It is not enough for a state like Australia to understand the Islamic sensitivities of the Malays and their cultural discomfort with oppositional or contestatory politics, unless the Malays also understand the freewheeling and robust nature of Western, and especially New World, political culture. Respect and understanding must be *universal*, not just practiced by one side or the other. Second, it is also insufficient unless there are *bridges* between cultures that permit the resolution of disputes, expedite trade and exchange, facilitate the fixing of borders, and so on. Such bridges are universals of sorts, common languages that enable peaceful coexistence and fruitful exchange between otherwise very different cultures. The failure to erect such bridges promises the kind of cultural war that followed the disintegration of Yugoslavia where Slavic, Islamic, and Westernized factions confronted each other with what was simply blind and demonic hostility, without any real capacity to communicate or negotiate meaningfully.

This is not the place to discuss what such a common language might be (e.g., could it be the language of human rights, or something else?). But it is worth making the point that one language has de facto appeared increasingly common across the globe—the "modern" language of rationalization. This, it is important to stress, is not the language of liberalism even if liberalism at times allies with it. Liberalism (liberal equality), as Barry Hindess argues, is culturally specific. The language of the rationalizer, on the other hand, seems more and more adapted to disparate cultural contexts. The West—Europe via colonization in the nineteenth century and early twentieth century and America via its "influence" primarily in the twentieth century—exported one thing that has outlasted all the governors' mansions and trade offices: the genie of modernity, the electric ghost of dynamis.

The rest of the world now copes with this as best it can, in a variety of different ways. For some, it is apocalypse now—when modern machines bulldoze the house of tradition and leave behind only killing fields tilled by Sorbonne-educated maniacs: this is the lesson of Kampuchea. For some, it is the reassertion of virtually feudal tribal chiefs and clerical rulers (e.g., Afghanistan, Iran, Fiji). In other places, a military hierarchy replaces the purely patrimonial rule of princes: Indonesia. So it goes. As for the West? It now retreats to search its own soul, in no small measure because the relationship between conservatism and modernism remains a source of enduring tension in the West. As we near the end of the century, the choices for the West remain well etched: nationalism or liberalism, protectionism or free trade, hierarchy or equality. Yet there remains an important and resilient doubt that neither pole of orientation can provide the basis for political community in the West as we enter the twenty-first century. Neither can provide a meaningful order that will engage the energies of Westerners as a whole, renew their faith in their own world, and stop them from looking to other worlds, as so many have done in the course of this century. Just as they once were seduced by the mirages of the old Soviet Union, disenchanted Westerners now turn to the resurgent East Asian orbit or even to the radicalisms of Islam. This turning away from the West, or even the more prevalent signs of apathy and cynicism in Western publics, will not abate until the denizens of Western societies begin to reexamine the complex history of the West to identify other ways in which meaningful order and political community are formed aside from the promises of either a geriatric conservatism or a liberalized modernism.

• • •

The perception of profound fractures in the political imagination of the West is not entirely novel. In its long history of cross-cultural experiences and internal turmoils, the West has at times come to reflect on its self-identity in general and on its political forms in particular.

In the process, the political languages and traditions at its disposal have been traumatized, revitalized, transformed, even rendered redundant. In the context of modernity, this process is sharpened by the question of immanent sustainability. This is not to suggest that modern political imagination in toto has jettisoned redemptive or transcendental aspirations; indeed, in numerous cases, the contrary is true.

The efficacy of a political language rests not only on its ability to deliver an understanding of the basis of a political community but also on its capacity to "articulate" political action. In this sense, a political language may be a political ideology, but the reverse is not necessarily the case: there may well be a chasm between ideological understanding and political action, not to speak of articulated political action. In terms of political community, the disjunction between understanding and action can have debilitating effects on the vitality of political imagination; the community can experience simultaneously an incapacity to understand its predicament and an inability to project itself into political action. To this degree, the crisis or breakdown of a political language is at once bewilderment with the present and disorientation with regard to self-projection. Arguably this is what has happened in the late twentieth-century West. In this context, the bewilderment and disorientation, this double obscurity, is not simply restricted to the public political sphere sensu stricto but permeates the whole gamut of sociocultural life, to a greater or lesser extent.

If, on the one hand, we can speak of the dynamis of modernization, of rationalization, it would be misleading, on the other, to speak in the singular of a modern political discourse of the West. Liberalism, for example, has been tempered by the republican tradition quite apart from its traditional bête-noire conservatism; equally, Marxism, liberalism's superego, has been confronted with manifestations of its own totalitarian proclivities; and all, at different times, have put nationalism into their own service. Needless to say, all have had to contend not only with the relentlessness of modern rationalization but also with the gnarly issue of modern democracy and, it might be added, with varying degrees of disdain and enthusiasm. Consequently, it would be more accurate to describe the political language of the modern West as a complex of competing yet related discourses and ideologies.

In the short interregnum since 1989, there has come a brief triumphal rhapsody from certain sectors in the West on the victory of liberalism and capitalism over communism, of freedom over oppression, of abundance over scarcity; indeed, for Francis Fukuyama, the fall of communism marked the end of history, the end of humanity's ideological evolution, and the triumph of Western liberalism. The irony in these utterances soon became apparent as the dark clouds of economic recession descended on the Western economies with concomitant social and political realities. The issue to note in this context, however, is not so much the political-economic vicissitudes as the political language of the West coming home to roost—not that it had ever actually left. What is involved here is not the differences but the commonalities between the competing discourses in the West: in short, their shared cultural semantic. While 1989 can be taken as a significant historical nodal point in the contemporary epoch, the issue of the shared cultural semantic of the West has come into sharp relief over the last twenty or so years.

Among the key moments of this semantic, two themes can initially be highlighted: industrialism and social labor. At least since the mid-nineteenth century, industrialization has been championed by both the workers' movement and industrialists as the road to social progress. Although as social actors these two groups have, on the whole, emphasized their opposition to each other's ideology and interests, they nevertheless have had a common belief and confidence in the merits of industrial modernization.

In Alain Touraine's account of industrial society, this common cultural model has been the field upon which the issue of the social organization of labor has been contested between the workers' movement and industrialists. Further, Touraine identifies this social conflict as decisive in the "production" of industrial society because of its centrality in the generation of "the cultural, moral, and cognitive categories through which the society understands itself."[2] Moreover, it is in this sense that the cultural patterns of industrial society are not the outcome of capitalistic domination, pure and simple, but of social conflict and its emergent compromises. In terms of utopian horizons, the dynamism of industrial commerce offered ever new possibilities for the liberal personality to flourish; equally, the workers' movement in no manner rejected industrialization, simply the capitalistic direction of this process. This leads us to the second theme of social labor or, more precisely, the potentials of a society based on social labor.[3]

To the degree that social conflict was focused on the appropriation of "abstract labor," future orientations were unsurprisingly concentrated on the sphere of production and, in the case of socialists, on the liberation of labor from alien control. One of the most famous instances of the latter was the Marxist utopia of the free association of independent producers: individuals' appropriation of the totality of the productive forces in order to achieve self-activity, that is, to become complete individuals unencumbered by natural limitations. Broadly then, whether in terms of liberal individualism or socialism, industrial society generated future expectations on the basis of its mode of self-production. In addition, the dynamis of the industrializing process, and the more general rationalization of social life, engendered the voices of conservatism and backward-looking communalism, voices concerned with or frightened by the breakdown (or rapid transformation) of community and traditions. In this instance, the promise of social progress via rationalization was treated with suspicion, if not as a process of dehumanization. Nevertheless, these dissenting voices could not avoid speaking in modern tones as the dynamis continually questioned the unquestionable of their position; the postulate of a static social organism could not be sustained as counterfactual in the face of modern rationalization's penetration into all spheres of social life. Consequently, such voices could only offer either a cautionary warning to proceed with hesitation and avoid enthusiasm or utopias decontextualized from the sociohistorical realities and thus rendered substantially mute.

A third theme that accompanies industrialism and the modern functional division of labor is the issue of modern democracy; what is actually meant by the idea of democracy is, however, rather more variegated. While just about all of the major political ideologies in the modern West have laid a claim to democracy, on the whole it has tended to be filtered through the more fundamental cultural and philosophical ideals of each of these discourses. Thus, it has only received ideological life within the competing ideologies and consequently has been fleshed out in diverse ways; nearly all these ideologies pay some homage to democracy but for quite different reasons.[4] Liberalism only came to embrace democracy after it was convinced that democracy would best enhance its primary value of liberty; a democratic constitutional polity could offer the striving individual the necessary latitude for enterprise, a latitude in which the individual has the right to choose among options and things and enjoys the promise of opportunity. In this scenario, the democratic constitution demarcates the limits beyond which the state must not intrude upon the liberty of the individual.

Conservatism hedged its bets on the issue by the postulate of responsible representative democracy. In the face of modernization, conservatism's primary concern for the integrity of the social organism was seen as best protected by those inculcated with the values and long-standing traditions of the community. The elected were not so much to give voice to the electors as to articulate "good sense" in the interests of the community as a whole; in the hands of such leaders, the constitutional state would ensure the maintenance of society's time-honored values and traditions.

In general, socialism has tended to deal with the issue of democracy in a derivative manner. While several incarnations of socialism have dabbled with the notion of direct democracy, two other more influential tendencies can be isolated. First, we can identify a socialism engrossed with equality, in which democracy came to be equated with economic democracy where the fundamental right is to an equal share of society's goods and resources. Second, there is a socialism bedazzled by the promise of a more rational society: in this instance, democracy is expected to wither as society becomes the administration of things, as political conflict is displaced by impersonal—hence "fair"—technical management. In both cases, democracy is at best a means to overcome the alienation of labor; at worst, it is considered an impediment to industrial growth. As a consequence, social democracy as ideology came to be preoccupied with public ownership, the relief and elimination of need, and the administrative rule of the state. In the wake of the modern party system, social democracy endorsed democratic sovereignty so that no one party could monopolize power in the modern state, thus ensuring against a decline into patrimonialism and its necessary corollaries of partiality and inefficient and nonrational administration.

Bolshevism, precisely because of its preoccupations with hyper-rationalism and productivism, claimed to bypass this "bourgeois" democracy. As a consequence, and not without a debt to the authoritarian traditions of former Russian modernizers, the totalitarian character of Soviet industrial modernization was by no means an aberration or distortion of the original Bolshevik project. Equally, the rhetoric of the "people's democracy" thinly papered over the irrationalities, inefficiencies, and patrimonialism generated by this experiment. More to the West, the phenomenon of authoritarian corporatism in Fascist Italy, Nazi Germany, and Falangist Spain found no need to resort to a rhetoric of democracy, preferring the rallying cry of the nation or "the people" and thus engaging in a form of modernization that attempted to veto differentiation at, we might add, enormous human cost.

By contrast, in the post–World War II era in the West and in parts of Asia, corporatist arrangements of labor, capital, and the state have been cast in democratic terms, though with greater deference to modernization and economic well-being than to political citizenship. In these arrangements, conflict is understood as anathema to successful modernization, and the resolution of the interests of the major power players and their constituencies is seen as in everyone's interests. Accordingly, the conflict and differentiation generated by modernization is supposedly captured and domesticated into a rational-administrative vortex of just outcomes for all, thus avoiding any disruption to the modernizing process itself. This management of conflict presumes its democratic character on the assumption that it has the rational ability to identify and contain all of the possible dimensions of conflict. Where corporatist arrangements are linked to democratic sovereignty, the electoral process becomes largely a review of the management capacities of the contenders.

• • •

For a socialism, liberalism, or conservatism that makes some appeal to democracy, the notion of democratic citizenship is more or less dependent upon more primary values of the specific discourse. Unlike these ideologies, yet also having varying influence on them, the modern civic or republican ideal places prime value on citizenship per se and, over time, on democratic citizenship in particular. Citizenship, as a civic ideal, has always had a *double meaning*. On the one hand, it has signified the duties of office and responsibilities for the building and maintaining of public facilities (roads, theaters, etc.). On the other hand, it has signified participation in public contests, dramas, competitions. In modernity, citizenship in the first sense has been largely displaced by the workings of the sovereign, bureaucratic state. Citizenship in the second sense, although more successfully maintained, has been put under pressure by the growth of the demands of private life. The decline of citizenship in the first sense was undoubtedly connected with the fact that citizenship classically, as Barry Hindess reminds us, was exclusive rather than inclusive. The modern bureaucratic rational state—the modern nation-state—offered a universal, if vastly watered down, kind of citizenship.

In modernity, republican sympathizers have never been able to formulate a convincing alternative to bureaucratic office and fiscal systems (which is not to say that a convincing model is inconceivable). Nonetheless, the civic ideal has persisted via the continuing interest in the existence of a wide range of public spaces, forums, and theaters— domains that have become, over the course of the last two hundred years, increasingly accessible to all. Citizenship in this second sense not only overcomes the privation of individual existence but also engenders a viable and energetic res publica and offers the chance for people to participate simultaneously in the shaping of both their individual persona and destiny and society's character and fate. Such citizenship means the appearance and participation of people in public domains at all levels—from parliaments, councils, and town meetings to literary and artistic forums, from commercial and technological exhibitions to public parks, gardens, cafes, and promenades. Here, democracy becomes absorbed on a normative level rather than as a mere means to an end.

A democratic civic polity is neither a backdrop for individual restlessness nor an insurance policy for impersonal rational administration; rather, it is the space for, and product of, the exertion, contestation, and participation of human subjects, in public domains including those beyond the purely political. In this polity, the citizen is not simply the abstract individual whose social bonds rest on either voluntary contractual agreements or a set of universalistic rights, nor is this citizen merely a concrete subject embedded in a preestablished social order. More to the point, in this polity individuals only truly become citizens by appearing, acting, and distinguishing themselves in the public domain. In this sense, the "constitution" of a civic society is at once the ongoing product of its citizens and the bounds it has set for itself that arise out of the demands and responsibilities of a public life.

The successive reformulation of the republican and civic ideal affected ambiguously the political language of the modern West. On the one hand, it offered a contribution to the search for a political form both appropriate to the modernizing process and that would reinvest that process with meaning. This was a political form that drew strength, rather than dismay, from its capacity to acknowledge differentiation and conflict as part and parcel of social life.[5] Public life was constituted by the spirited, and sometimes dramatic, encounters between different, contending forces in the public domain. The public space drew these forces together and gave different schools of artists, gardeners, or scientists, for example, the chance to display their excellences, to pursue friendly rivalries, and to exchange knowledge. Their activities filled out the public domain. But *public encounter* can easily be displaced by *private drive.* Consequently, the Aristotelian and humanist antecedents of the modern reformulations of the civic ideal carried with them not only the fundamental understanding of the human subject as *zoon politikon* but also a suspicion, if not an outright condemnation, of the rentier and entrepreneur as the epitome of corruption. As J. G. A. Pocock's work highlights, the attempts to portray the capitalistic *homo economicus*—the driving figure of economic modernization—as the exemplar of modern citizenship were dogged, perhaps even to this day, by this republican suspicion.[6] Ironically, where liberalism endeavored to circumvent the problem by privatizing the individual, socialism sought to socialize homo economicus. In the American experience with its strong republican moment, the difference between citizen and entrepreneur has tended to remain distinct though possibly embodied in the same person. More generally, the distinction between civic-mindedness and self-interest has retained a level of cogency in the political language of the West even with the appearance of the professional politician.

Beyond this, the modern civic ideal has cut its swath across the major modern ideologies of the West by its insistence upon the question of the *political*—the res publica, the public thing—as an antidote to the excesses and often banality of the modernizing process. The degree to which it has been able to successfully raise this question has depended on whether the contingency spawned by the modern dynamis is convincingly displaced or not by the promise of dynamis, however projected. It is not by chance, so to speak, that in the last twenty odd years there has been a renewed intellectual interest in the civic ideal and more broadly in the issue of the political, for contingency has once again become an important trope in the political language of the West. In its wake, there have been attempts to revitalize conservatism's secure society, to reinvigorate the promise of further liberal modernization, even to "democratize" a socialist vision, yet each stumbles over its own past, leaving the general atmosphere inert. Mastery of the dynamis is no longer wholeheartedly and unquestionably believed, and the desirability of such mastery has itself been placed in doubt, especially after the disastrous Soviet experience. Moreover, industrialism and the functional division of labor, which played such a crucial role in the development of the modern ideologies, have undergone major transformations—what some have described as the emergence of postindustrial society. In their attempts to come to grips with these transformations, liberals, socialists, and conservatives tend to recall the categories and assumptions generated in industrial society, proffering accounts that, once subjected to critical scrutiny, do not stand up to the test of phenomenological adequacy. In regard to utopian energies, this recourse to the potentials of a society based on social labor, above all else, misses the point that the power of abstract labor to give form and structure to society is diminishing.[7] This is indicative of both the success and subsequent decline of the postwar Keynesian compromise: the promise of full employment was also a normalization of consumption—of both consumer goods and state services—in short, a decentering of the work-centered way of life.

The equation of citizenship with worker (and a male worker at that) can no longer be sustained given the new "public-ness" or visibility of women, ethnic groups, youth, the retired, and so on. The postulate of the abstract individual (or worker), theoretically problematic to begin with, becomes ever more difficult to embrace given the increasing complexity and diversity of society. Thus in this light, liberalism and social democracy are caught in a conundrum: while they maintain a productivist anthropology, contemporary society's self-production tends to impede, if not thwart, their attempts to conflate this anthropology with a notion of citizenship. A similar fate befalls conservatism in that the reality of social diversity belies its fundamental emphasis on the need for cultural homogeneity. In this sense, the hitherto prevailing ideologies of the West remain perplexed. What the civic or republican ideal has to offer in this scenario is the image of a public life as the telos for, and corrective to, an otherwise aimless process of modernization.

The civic ideal has a complex lineage. Arising in the ancient Mediterranean city-states, its influence was extraordinarily persistent in the Mediterranean littoral, surviving empires, barbarian invasions, and church and seigneurial opposition. Eventually reborn in the upsurge of city life during the Italian Renaissance, the civic ideal's influence spread to the free cities of Northern Europe. It fed into English politics after the failure of seventeenth-century absolutism and it affected, in certain crucial respects, the shape of the eighteenth-century English Constitution and its tethering of royal power. French admirers of the English Constitution, including Montesquieu, drew influential intellectual lessons from this experience, while the American settlers across the Atlantic drew some practical lessons and turned the civic idealism of eighteenth-century Augustan culture against the power of the English Crown as well as against the machinations of Britain's empire building in the Atlantic.

The many formulations of the civic ideal, from Roman to Renaissance republicanism and to English Whigs' borrowing from this tradition, were reworked by the Americans as they searched to establish the foundations of the first modern republic. The civic ideal has constantly been reinvented. Through many permutations, it has appeared on the stage of history wearing many different masks. The exhaustion of our current ideologies suggests that the civic ideal is worth returning to in the hope that we may be able to extricate ourselves from the tired impasses of past decades. The "dialogues" of socialism, liberalism, and conservatism have become a broken record. They repeat themselves as clichés, with fading relevance to the actual—and serious—conditions of our times. The collapse of communism is an extreme example of the failure of all the great ideologies. They simply no longer speak meaningfully to the citizens of Western states.

Meanwhile, the romantic sideshow of postmodernism has been a distraction for jaded minds that has played effectively to our tacit awareness of the exhaustion of the grand narratives, but it has been unable to offer anything *constructive* to shore up the ballast in the leaking ship of the West. Indeed, the worst of the postmodernists want to dance on what they think is the coffin of the West. Exhaustion, however, should not be mistaken for extinction—far from it. The history of the West is partly the history of expansion, then exhaustion, and then revitalization—*re-naissance*. This, above all, is what the West most needs: the spirit of renaissance. Such renaissance has always been associated with the civic ideal and city life—the life both of the citizen (*cive*) and of *civ*-ilization—that the civic ideal nurtures and promotes, along with the edifice of republican offices and state structures that are built on its foundations. The symbol of an energetic and good-tempered Western society over the centuries has been the lively, festive, and well-proportioned city center, welcoming to strangers, proud of its aging patina, simultaneously anarchic and businesslike, rowdy and respectful. (Of course, governments have often sought to monumentalize city centers and make them pompous. But usually, somehow, the civilizing instinct of the inhabitants absorbs and dissipates even these grand designs.) In contrast, a telling symptom of the disorientation and loss of confidence in Western societies has been the fascination of the postmodern generation with "decentering" and the ill-tempered and puritanical politics that have accompanied this. A revitalization of the civic idea, and its symposiac delight in life, and a new willingness of moderns and postmoderns to enter into the public spaces and places of their societies, without rancor or resentment, seems crucial if the storms of the late twentieth century are to be weathered and our leaking ship steered to a hospitable anchorage.

The heritage of the civic paradigm resonates in many of the perspectives and arguments raised in this volume. Michael Crozier, invoking the eighteenth-century landscape garden as a moment in the English tradition of *civitas* and as a counterpoise to the postmodern advocates of romantic wilderness, raises questions about the appropriateness of wilderness as a social model, while Ferenc Fehér reflects ruefully on modernity's propensity to turn the city into a jungle, underlining the point that any renaissance of the West will require a revitalization and a remoralization of city life. Crozier suggests that the contemporary counterposition of freedom from the constraints of cultivation, fringe-dwelling, and wilderness to the modern disciplinary state with its supposed networks of control and its sense of itself as a severe garden pruner obsessively weeding and trimming society is a false polarity and implies a false choice, ignoring as it does the rich history of civilized urbanism and artful landscape gardening that developed as part of the civic heritage. Fehér makes the point that whereas at its height the classical culture of the Mediterranean polis inculcated a respect for limits—and correspondingly registered the absence of extravagant hopes and fears (hope and fear writ large)—the future bound dynamis of modern culture constantly stimulates both hopes of crossing the horizon and horrors of the unknown over the horizon, leaving its denizens prey to irrational and destructive fantasies. Associated as it is with growth and progress, with the abandonment of all obsolete tastes, with taking sides with the new, with being impatient with the unconquerable thing in itself, the drive of modernity becomes illusory, Fehér observes, when the hope to transcend particular barriers has been transformed into the hope of mastering the infinite (i.e., when it is transformed into the hope of humankind for self-deification). For human beings, the belief that one is a god can only lead to destructive or violent consequences. On the other hand, to recognize one's humanity is to recognize and accept limits, and this was something that those who inhabited the world of the polis understood. Can our feelings for limits return? Fehér wonders whether modernity can ever know rational hope, or whether its dreams of the future will always turn into nightmares.

Barry Smart takes up the suggestion of Ferenc Fehér and Agnes Heller[8] that the contingency of modern personalities can be transformed into a destiny, as a way of addressing these questions. The view that contingency can be transformed into destiny is a view that originates in the Stoicism of the Hellenistic polis, and it supposes that even when the social context encourages irrationality, individuals can still behave rationally. Moderns may be buffeted by the perpetual oscillations of the roller coaster of modernity, but they can (if we accept the paradox) *choose* to act *consistently* or rationally. Among the array of possibilities that modernity offers, they can still choose themselves as moral and decent beings and in doing so redeem reason in the face of the denuded rationality of modernity, or its lapses into grotesque irrationalities.

A more skeptical view of the ideal of the autonomous, rational personality is proffered by Barry Hindess, who sees that ideal often confounded—not so much by the temptation of the sublime as by the particularistic determinations of culture and ethnicity that resolutely persist in the modern world. The figure of reason is confounded by the prerational attachments and affections that grow out of particularistic cultures and ethnicities. The citizen of the polis who is capable of self-rule—of *acting consistently,* moderately—is a figure of reason. In a different but parallel vein, the figure of reason in modern times is the rationalistic protaganist of the nation-state who pursues the project of *making laws and practices consistent*—in other words, homogeneous—within the state, in opposition to the welter of localist affiliations and arbitrary arrangements of premodern, patrimonial societies. The late twentieth-century revivals of strong ethnic identifications and of movements based on them ("the politics of identity") remind us of the recurrent failures of modern rationalism, and its nation building, to provide a satisfying sense of political community or to fully sublimate prerational drives. Further, this begs the question of whether the classical city might not have offered a better home for reason than the modern, sovereign, and rational bureaucratic nation-state.

We see both the classical and modern notions of reason coalesce in the interesting case of Baruch Spinoza. Paul Harrison draws lessons from the history of the Dutch Republic and its efforts to overcome social divisions by detaching religion from politics, and from the way in which the thought of Spinoza, one of its great residents, at the same time echoed traditional republican concerns that city and state life should institute balances—of affect against affect, power against power, and so on. Harrison observes how Spinoza adapted the contractual language of seventeenth-century liberalism and absolutism to this cause and how this contractualism ultimately led Spinoza away from the cosmopolitanism of the Renaissance city toward a kind of early nationalism, a metaphor for the shift that occurred in European politics in the wake of the Renaissance away from civic and federalist models of politics to sovereign and nationalist kinds of politics.

John Ely also examines the lessons of Northern European republicanism, exploring the ideas of federal integration (particularly the notions of confederation) that developed during the Renaissance as federations of free cities evolved in Northern Germany, the Netherlands, Switzerland, and Northern Italy. Ely argues that such federative ideas provide an important model for European integration today that promises a much smoother path to a European Union than the nation-state model that shackles so much political thinking in contemporary Europe, not just in the case of those opposed to unification but also those in favor of it.

Barry Hindess reflects on how the impetus of globalization and the multiplication of cultures and ethnicities in Western states is, from a practical standpoint, eroding the efficacy of the nation-state. Communication, travel, and commerce cross more and more borders. The increasingly rapid circulation of people, ideas, and goods disrupts the homogeneity so crucial to the nation-state. In this context, Hindess questions the continuing viability of the model of the modern sovereign state and the theories of power associated with it. At the same time, he questions whether the republican tradition and its assumptions about citizenship can take account of the realities of cultural heterogeneity. He suggests that both Greek and Roman citizens identified with a common culture, which was exemplified by the myth popularized in Periclean Athens that all citizens shared a common ancestry, making it virtually impossible for resident aliens to become citizens.

Peter Murphy, somewhat in contrast, suggests that the classical city tended toward complex rather than common origins, symbolized in the image of the crossroads. (In light of this reading the readiness of Cleisthenes' Athens to permit aliens to become citizens can be counterposed to the experience of Periclean Athens.) Murphy assumes that the classical city in ascendancy—the touchstone of the civic ideal—was characterized by increasing levels of social fluidity and differentiation, public contestation and activity (although in decline was capable of falling back into communalism). Citizenship in the sense of officeholding was restricted and often closed in a caste-like manner. But this was offset by an unprecedented and extraordinary appetite for public building, festivals, and performances that generated meaning for citizens and noncitizens alike and the memory of which over the centuries has made good the meaning-deficits of many generations of Westerners. Murphy argues that with the liberal ideal of free choice and the romantic ideal of self-determination, so influential in modernity but proving less and less able to provide Westerners today with a sense of purpose and meaning, perhaps a reworking of the older ideals of civility (like the prudential striking of a balance or equilibrium between the divergent forces in the city and the state) can fill a lot of the cracks, the weathered and eroded cement of meaning, that we see in the current facade of the West. Murphy points to Hannah Arendt, who drew heavily on both the Mediterranean civic ethos and on the experience of the early American republic, as an exemplar of someone who refused to join the standard lineup of ideologists, as either a conservative or romantic, liberal or socialist. As she said, she fell between all chairs.

Gillian Robinson's essay reflects on the significance of Arendt's view of moral conscience for citizenship and, in doing so, reminds us of both the complexity of the idea of the citizen and the inappropriateness of efforts to reduce the citizen (in the liberal view) to the voter or (in the pragmatic view) to the ideal speaker. Citizenship is an expression of a form of life (that the liberal or pragmatic vivisectionist proceeds to cut up): the life of city-dwellers who are lovers of public life, cosmopolitan in attitude, civilized in their conduct of agonistic pursuits, and republican in politics. In the past two hundred years, that form of life has been marginalized by the modern dynamis and the forces of bureaucratization, centralization, and corporatization that it employs in the name and service of ceaseless and formless change, expansion, accumulation, and often devastation.

To reassert a humanistic and tolerant civic ethos that embodies respect for pluralism, balance, equilibrium, and measure seems, at the end of the century, more than timely. Of course, we can tap into such an ethos in many different ways. We can look—as Dick Howard does— at American republicanism and its Madisonian and Jeffersonian incarnations. We can also look to Northern European Renaissance cities, the Whiggish English sympathizers of the civitas, the experience of the Mediterranean polis, the twentieth-century republicans like Arendt or Pocock, large modern federal republics, or small historical city-states. None of these will tell us exactly what we can or should do in the here and now. Their problems, their dilemmas, their possibilities are not the same as ours. But we can think in their spirit. We can draw lessons from their examples. The rest we must do for ourselves.

Notes

1. See the remarks of Peter Murphy in "Transition to What?" *Policy* (Sydney) 8, no. 2 (1992): 41–43.

2. Kevin McDonald, "The Unmaking of the Labour Movement," *Social Alternatives* 6, no. 4 (1987): 13. Cf. Alain Touraine, *The Self-Production of Society* (Chicago: University of Chicago Press, 1977), and the special issue of *Thesis Eleven* (vol. 38, 1994) on Touraine's social theory.

3. See Jürgen Habermas, *The New Conservatism* (Cambridge, Mass.: MIT Press, 1989), 48–70.

4. Peter Murphy, "Socialism and Democracy," *Thesis Eleven* 26 (1990): 54–56.

5. See especially, Niccolò Machiavelli, *Discourses* (edited and introduced by Bernard Crick [Harmondsworth: Penguin, 1983]). See also, Johann P. Arnason, "The Theory of Modernity and the Problematic of Democracy," in *Between Totalitarianism and Postmodernity*, ed. Peter Beilharz, Gillian Robinson, and John Rundell (Cambridge, Mass.: MIT Press, 1992), 42–43.

6. J. G. A. Pocock, *The Machiavellian Moment* (Princeton, N.J.: Princeton University Press, 1975).

7. For instance, the indicators for economic recovery in the 1990s, politicians' rhetoric aside, are no longer necessarily linked to a return to meaningful levels of full employment.

8. See, for instance, Agnes Heller and Ferenc Fehér, *The Postmodern Political Condition* (Cambridge: Polity Press, 1988); Heller, *A Philosophy of Morals* (Oxford: Blackwell, 1990).

FERENC FEHÉR

The Status of Hope at the End of the Century

At the dawn of the modern age, hope sank to the nadir of its prestige, and on it, Baruch Spinoza handed down the verdict of classic rationalism, allowing no appeal. Hope is prior to knowledge, the frame of mind of the "not-yet-conscious," a figment of imagination, not a product of reason.[1] While in Christian times hope had been cherished as a well-grounded moral feeling qua the *creatura's* trust in good tidings, in our promised salvation—in a promise that could not deceive us[2]—in the subsequent era of rationalism, hope was no longer a bearer of any certitude. Before the tribunal of *ratio*, hope was proven guilty of incoherence, of being a coward and shying away from that reality whose knowledge alone can grant us certainty; finally, it was proven guilty of being "merely subjective." The polemic was at once epistemological and ethical in nature. Also invoked against hope was the age-old maxim of the Stoics and Epicureans, the maxim of dismissing the shadow cast by death: carpe diem. As rationalism had correctly envisioned, hope had been normally coupled with fear; yet fear was not only deemed unmanly, it was also a state in which the use of our rational faculties was limited. As long as we fear and hope, we cannot know, it was surmised, because we are cognitively paralyzed. As long as we fear and hope, we are slaves of our passions and imagination, as well as of the higher authority that had made us a promise and that, in exchange, keeps us in bondage. Johann Wolfgang von Goethe happily joined in Spinoza's verdict, and, in the second part of *Faust*, he set both fear and hope in the pillory.[3]

No one knew more acutely than the greatest philosopher of hope,

Ernst Bloch, that at the heart of all radical utopias, there lay hope, the subjective drive for that which we have never achieved. Hope, which was not yet reality, often sought respectability by donning the utopian garb, the costume of reality beyond reality. But this age-old story reached a peculiar stage in modern society, as this society appeared in an emancipated form after the French Revolution. The New World was the offspring of inventive imagination, but it was run on the basis of laws—yet people lived shackled to laws. Many of them longed for a newer Atlantis, beyond laws. What the hope of radical utopia promised them was a "second salvation," not hope prior to knowledge but one beyond calculus, planning, and laws—hope that transcended a completely mastered objectivity.

In this century, the most significant debate between the philosophies of hope and antihope is the encounter between Ernst Bloch and Martin Heidegger. Heidegger's emphasis on horizon drastically curtails the whole domain of future or "beyond." The world of being-here lies within the horizon; hoping for its transcendence is a sign of inferiority. In Heidegger, it is heroic *Entschlossenheit*, Friedrich Nietzsche's heritage, that takes the place of hope. Bloch offers a sharp and sociologically unjust rejoinder to Heidegger's position: "But at least as suspicious as the immaturity (fanaticism) of the undeveloped utopian function is the widespread and ripe old platitude of the way-of-the-world philistine, of the blinkered empiricist whose world is far from being a stage, in short, the confederacy in which the fat bourgeois and the shallow practicist have always not only rejected outright the anticipatory, but despised it." Bloch quotes Heidegger: "'In wishes existence projects its being into possibilities which not only remain unseized when provided, but whose fulfilment is not even considered or expected(!). On the contrary: the predominance of being-in-advance-of-oneself in the mode of mere wishing entails a failure to understand factual possibilities. . . . Wishing is an existential modification of comprehending self-projection which, addicted to thrownness, merely continues to indulge in possibilities.'" Bloch then adds: "This sort of thing, purely applied to immature anticipating, unquestionably sounds like a eunuch accusing the infant Hercules of impotence. . . . The point of contact between dreams and life, without which dreams only yield abstract utopia, life only triviality, is given in the utopian capacity which is set on its feet and connected to the Real-Possible."[4] The encounter is, in fact, a stalemate.

Bloch rightly points to the sterility of Heidegger's rejection of anticipatory dynamics in toto. The horizon is not a fixed firmament; it is shifted and pushed forward continuously, by every step we take, and the anticipatory drive, often ignorant or dismissive of "factual potentials," is one of the major forces pushing the horizon ahead.[5] On his part, Heidegger would easily spot the vestiges of old metaphysics in Bloch. Behind the whole potpourri of dreams, daydreams, projections, and fantasies, a metaphysical protagonist lurks in Bloch's philosophy: hope writ large, a principle that homogenizes the disparate and dispersed acts of longing, hoping, and dreaming throughout history.

This is not meant as a vilification of Bloch's thesis. Crucial dimensions of the philosophy of praxis have been unearthed by "the principle of Hope," dimensions that remained hidden, even suppressed, in the more "scientific" version of this theory. Hope is free from the fetishism of laws because it is a marginal and eccentric agent. It is not, however, an antipode of the conscious. It presses incessantly to become conscious and manifest itself (and having reached its self-defeating goal, it loses its constitutive quality). Due to its marginality and not-yet-conscious character, hope can become (more than "science") the guide of praxis. Hope is less than certitude because the identity of certitude is unambivalent while hope is the progenitor of many certitudes in the making. Hope's surplus expresses a crucial, and at least rationally, never fully accountable aspect of rationality, that circumstance in which we always harbor hidden intellectual reserves that cannot be fathomed by reason or mobilized by hope alone.

Late modernity marked the high tide of hope. Apocalyptic and redemptive modernism, its worldviews and artworks, drove the concept "hope" to the peak of its more recent career. But with postmodernism, this dynamic came to a standstill, and hope waning seems to have returned to that point on the nadir where it had been at the time of classic rationalism. The contrast between the modern and the postmodern is not one of hope versus hopelessness. The postmodern niches in the modern world are not asylums of lost illusions. Hopes (in the plural) keep the world going no less than earlier; yet hope writ large, Bloch's metaphysical protagonist, has lost its powerful appeal for many reasons.

First, it is related to a promise without which it is not even prerational; it has no body, no frame, no substance: it is an empty fantasy. At the same time, those who hope cannot be the source of hope's promises, because the promise must be given from an Archimedean point, fixed above and beyond the human domain, in order to have the slightest authority. The transcendent promises of political-historical hope have been completely discredited in the century of the Holocaust, the Gulag, and ethnic cleansing. Second, the concept of unified hope, homogenizing the disparate acts of longing, dreaming, projecting, imagining, and fantasizing, is inseparable from universal history, a narrative that is crumbling in front of us, dissolving into an agglomerate of discourses. Hope is not a less demanding taskmaster than the laws of history because it feels fulfilled and satisfied only when it impresses its one and only stamp on the world. And the world of the postmoderns wants to bear not one but several stamps. Third, hope writ large is the principle of the absolute negation of that which exists. Hope cannot enter into compromise with the prevailing order of things without being compromised itself, for hope is otherness incarnate. We may hope for slight improvements in our worldly business, but we act in the sign of hope only if we long for a world that is completely different from ours. The modern cult of hope, unlike its Christian predecessor, is a radical one. To postmoderns, however, the promise of the absolute transcendence of that which exists is a leap into the abyss, an irresponsible pledge without a guarantee, an attempt to cross the horizon that can only be an act of lunacy.

Hope and fear, both writ large, have been traditionally linked to one another. Fear is the *horror vacui* within the same syndrome where hope stands as the promise of being filled, of becoming plenum. Fear, in this metaphysical sense, is just as homogenized a concept as hope: it is a concept that merges all the particular fears accompanying the way of all flesh. The best-known philosophical name of this specter was angst, the favorite ghost of the generation preceding the postmodernist wave.[6] The deliberate philosophical emptiness of fear qua angst is conducive to embracing hope. But the postmoderns' overarching feeling is of coming home, rather than of finding the world completely devoid of meaning (which is the feeling par excellence that guides us to fear). Discarding fear, the negative metaphysical protagonist, suggests by implication the rejection of hope. In this sense, hope is better off jettisoned, for—concerning the great and costly attempts at transcending the present in our age—it has been observed continually that in them hope and fear have indistinguishably merged, and both of them have proven to be bad advisers. Hope encouraged irresponsible experiments conducted on living, suffering beings. Fears of freedom, of having an opinion of our own, of finding the world a vacuum that has to be filled with the ingredients of free action—all of these invariably trigger unrestrained brutality that would sooner destroy the world than find a sober accommodation in it.

Can any culture survive without hope? More precisely, can a world lastingly exist and generate cultural energies in which hopes are not backed by a promise and where they have no political character? There is no need to answer the question hypothetically; it will suffice to point to classic Greek culture in order to give a direct reply. The golden age of

Hellas was a unique moment in cultural history partly because it was familiar with hopes and fears (plural), like every other period, but not with hope or fear in the singular. An archaic age can be retrospectively excavated in this culture where a great hope and a great fear cast their shadows over the Hellenic origins. But hope came to glorious fulfillment with the free city of Athens, with its constitution and citizens, its philosophy and tragedy, with the harmony between humans and the deities who were embodiments of beauty and measure, as well as of the merger of human and divine qualities. As hope abounded and came to fruition, fear of relapsing into the animal world, the world of brutes, slaves, and barbarians, the fear of endlessly repeating the mad reveling of the feast of Kronos, subsided. Fulfillment and internal security, amid recurrent catastrophes, formed the equilibrium that in turn shaped the substrate of the classic Greek world. This is why the only philosopher of our day who is Greek, Cornelius Castoriadis, rejects so categorically both hope and fear. Perhaps this is why, for him, the history of philosophy ends with, and the story of rationalized theology begins, with Plato, in whose thought the vision of the Pamphilian Er, a mystic almost pre-Christian figure of hope, already made its appearance.

Classic Greek culture was such an exceptionally self-sufficient universe that the idea of crossing the horizon was seldom present. There was nothing in the outer spaces that could have tempted the Greek to embark on such a foolhardy enterprise, nor could any thereafter lure him who lived together with his anthropomorphic gods in harmony and awareness of the only difference between him and the gods, immortality. Hence the principles of hope and fear were absent from the culture of Athens. By contrast, modernity has always been a future-bound trip. The horizon for the moderns was a fortress to be taken, a ribbon to be cut and left behind, with perhaps the exception of Hegel's philosophy. In Hegel, the present was absolute. By the homecoming of the world spirit, the present contains, in the form of recollection, the whole of past history, truth as a whole. Nothing beyond totality is worth exploration. Instead of transcendence, we can possess the entirety of the past, including hope, by recalling all hopes of bygone ages. But apart from this unique episode, almost the whole of modernity's culture has been tuned on the hope of crossing the horizon. At some point, this obsession with future and transcendence (in other words, dialectic) had to be brought to a standstill.

The monumental act of stopping the obsessive cycle of dialectic happened in the memorable years of 1989–91, the last ones of this century. Having been saturated with the petty details of a predominantly epigonistic politics and with the flare-up of tribalism in the region where the epochal change occurred, observers have not yet gained the necessary distance to grasp the irreversible consequences of this turn. Yet, it is no exaggeration to say that both the reason and the imagination of modernity will never be the same after the deluge.

The communist experiment that ran haughtily counter to the whole of recorded history now transpires as a complete catalogue of the pathologies of modernity. It was the carnival of a reckless political imagination and typically modern experiments with statecraft and social engineering, under the guidance of hope unbound masquerading as supreme science; it was an experiment where no concern was shown for the guinea pigs used in the social laboratory. It was an exercise in the philosophy of praxis where theory had the audacity of prescribing a direction to ordinary or "empirical" life. It was an anthropological revolution based on the exalted idea of human deification in which the whole filth of old history, slave labor included, returned with a vengeance. It was an adventure of science supreme that was arrogated to the role of a new religion of a political-metaphysical sort, a religion in which Friedrich Nietzsche's heart pulsated, for its only successful deed was the massive expulsion of Christian conscience and commiseration. It challenged every form of social organization in which moderns, as well as premoderns, have ever lived, without being able to supply a single new enduring solution. It was obsessed with transforming nature, while it poisoned and destroyed nature more brutally than any profit-centered form of industrialization could have. It corrupted our vocabulary by inventing terms in which freedom stood for tyranny, reeducation meant camps behind barbed wire, enlightenment was tantamount to brainwashing, humanism prescribed ruthlessness to enemies' children, and loyalty demanded the betrayal of family. The invention of New Speech, in which both specimens of the same monstrous species merged into one, did not provide language for unhindered communication but instead a so-called "dialectic" for concealing one's ulterior motives. The Great Experiment has discredited the planning and designing spirit of modernity to such an extent that it will probably be decades before moderns will be able to recapture the vigor of social engineering. The collapse of this truly cancerous outgrowth of modernity spelled a strong taboo on hoping for an absolute transcendence of the present. For, as long as it still had a spirit, the totalitarian world was truly kept going by hope and fear.

What is this modernity shorn of hope? Modernity without hope can be self-complacent, heroic, bored, paralyzed, and finally self-reliant. Bloch unjustly accused Heidegger of giving voice to self-complacent modernity, that particular type which draws the most philistine conclusion from the recent taboo of hoping for absolute transcendence. The devotees of self-complacent modernity echo Alexander Pope about all being well that is. For them, anticipatory dreaming and hoping is a subversive pastime; they suggest instead that we cultivate our gardens as a hobby. By stifling its own imagination and blunting the critical edge of its spirit, conceited modernity also curtails its reason. It leaves out of consideration the crucial fact that modernity has always been, and will remain, a "dissatisfied society"[7] that feeds on tensions and negations and cannot subsist without them.

What Heidegger in fact recommends is "heroic" modernity. It is a position of resolve vis-à-vis being-toward-death, our ultimate situation that cannot be avoided, suspended, or overcome by hope of any kind. Nor can resolve (entschlossenheit) be reduced either to a simple memento mori or a recommendation for a Stoic stance. We would not need Heidegger's philosophy for either of these. More profoundly, resolve and being-toward-death signal the potential demise of our culture, the only frame in which we can imagine and think not only our life but also our death. Heroic modernity is a stance of high culture that never ceases generating cultural surplus, notwithstanding the absence of hope from it. It is also a pagan type of modernity that is not only short of hope but also solidarity, emancipation, and many other values with which the obsolete humanism has endowed us. In opting for heroic modernity as our culture and in rescinding hope in the very same culture, we would abandon half of what is now our culture.

Bored modernity sees the world devoid of hope as a great stage on which the same ceremony is performed in a ritual of endless repetition. This is the position of "the end of history," based on two clear insights. First, its advocates see modernity arriving at the terminus of the project history, a universalist narrative, by abandoning the treacherous hopes of absolute transcendence. Second, the thesis of bored modernity echoes the Hegelian wisdom that the reduction of modernity's dangerous hopes of transcendence also implies the diminishing of grandeur. But this also means that after the end of history, politics will also end by becoming a politics of consumption. This is, in fact, a position of intensive self-querying. The poet of antiquity stated with proud dignity: *tantae molis erat Romanam condere gentem*, and the bare statement of the completed genesis was at once the highest praise. But the human being of bored modernity, casting a glance at its own world, asks in its soliloquies whether it was worthwhile. Tedium is a sign of internal incertitude that is a dubious state of mind for the generation of cultural surplus.

Paralyzed modernity is desperate. It hopes for hope, but it has lost, or never acquired, the capacity of anticipatory thinking, feeling, and imagining. Modernity dwells in a philosophically old-fashioned world of subject and object. It is aware of itself as subject insofar as it hopes. It is equally aware of what is "outside"—that which it calls objectivity, a world of alien things that the subject never made or mastered. If there is still a niche of modernity in which Georg Lukács's and Theodor Adorno's favorite terms, reification and fetishization, are meaningful and in vogue, it is paralyzed modernity. But at this point, hope turns into mystical visions, into longing of a kind that opens the gate for the new poison of our civilization: narcotic drugs.

Self-reliant modernity is not identical with self-complacent modernity; it has different reasons for relinquishing hope writ large. Self-reliant modernity is not at all content with what its participant members can see in the world. The critical edge of its thinking has not been blunted by the idolization of what exists and what should be thoroughly rearranged, not even once and for all, but again and again. Self-reliant modernity has rather acquiesced in the contention that we are living in a dissatisfied world and that there is no absolute transcendence of either the dissatisfaction or the complexity and tensions of modernity out of which dissatisfaction arises. It is our present human condition to make as much sense of the complex, tense, and dissatisfied world as we can, to create as much autonomy and social justice in it as possible without destroying it in a social experiment, without making futile and dangerous attempts to cut the blue ribbon and cross the horizon. Hope writ large, utopia's fundamental principle, is banned from self-reliant modernity or, more precisely, its denizens turn away from it. This gesture is simple and devoid of tedium, despair, heroism, or false superiority. It is the gesture of those dwelling in self-reliant modernity who are in no need of transcendent principles of a political-metaphysical kind for setting their house in order. Amid a wave of religious resurrection, self-reliant modernity is perhaps the only happily secularized domain within modernity. This is the attitude of the postmoderns.

As philosophy is indeed our age expressed in thoughts (as Hegel contended), a change of philosophy's attitude toward hope seems appropriate after 1989, the end of this century. Throughout the second half of the twentieth century, the mainstream of philosophy was divided between favoring either self-complacent or desperate modernity with regard to hope. In one of the major philosophical streams, hope was simply dismissed because of its association with utopia, as unsatisfactorily rational and potentially venomous (although rationality itself was, rightly, demoted from an absolute to a relative status). This was Karl Popper's attitude, which contained more than a grain of the superiority of ratio that he otherwise theoretically condemned.

By contrast, Herbert Marcuse put an excessive premium on the mystical hopes of desperate modernity, from which the philosopher expected both cultural and philosophical energies to rise. His gesture was highly influential and, at the same time, profoundly problematic. If we travel back in imagination to the New Left culture of the 1960s, we can see Marcuse's electrifying, vision-generating impact on a considerable part of it but also the moral indifference that has been instilled by his preference for mystical, and often even drug-promoted, hopes. In contrast, there is no need for a plea on behalf of the single salutary approach, of self-reliant modernity, nor is there need for an exclusive preference for reason vis-à-vis imagination, or the other way around. Reason and imagination must move together for the philosophical constellation to change. Instead, certain types of hope should be tentatively abandoned and a particular hope embraced.

There are three major pernicious hopes of modernity: the illusory-destructive, the self-deifying, and the self-contradictory. Illusory-destructive hope is that of crossing the horizon, of absolute transcendence. Its roots have already been detected, by Karl Mannheim among others, in the never completed secularization of modernity, in the preserved vestiges of messianism that stubbornly resisted the Enlightenment.[8] But there is a crucial contemporary source of this type of hope; moreover, it is only when growing out of modern roots that it becomes both illusory and destructive. Thus far, modernity has been closely associated with growth and progress, with the abandonment of all obsolete tastes, pushing back nature's barriers, taking sides with the new (of all kinds and in all areas), and being impatient with the unconquerable thing in itself. This aggressive drive becomes illusory when the hope to transcend particular barriers has been transformed into the hope of mastering the infinite; and it becomes destructive when the lives of all those participating in the experiment will be treated as a mere launching pad from which we could catapult ourselves beyond the horizon.

At the same time, this vain and costly attempt has been identified with human greatness in modernity at a time when anything less than mastering the social and natural universe was a sign of mediocrity. But masters of the universe are normally called gods, and this is why the illusory-destructive hope can be termed, in another configuration, humankind's hope of self-deification. Schubert's motif of *"wir sind selber Goetter"* is inseparable from modernity, perhaps because the illusory postulate of absolute secularization was coupled with the equally illusory postulate of absolute autonomy. Emancipation from servitude under transcendental powers, laying the foundations of the modern and "artificial" world on our own rational and imaginative faculties, fragile and limited as they are, is one thing. Attempting to eradicate from modernity both the memory of gods and the longing of many for the Thereafter, looking for rational certainty where there can be none and, in frustration, making the attempt to put deified Man on the pedestal of gods, is another thing. The hope of human deification is the religious hope of a problematically secularized civilization.

The self-contradictory hope is the hope of paradise on earth, regardless of its materialistic or idealistic orchestration or of whether the substrate of the earthly paradise is absolute affluence or complete, faultless moral goodness. Both are traditional hopes of humanity, yet they have been loaded with a new problematic in recent times, because the imagination of modernity—rightly blamed by Heidegger for being shaped by technological patterns—cannot accept anything short of the "ultimate solution." But no technological standards can be applied precisely to the major problem of dissatisfied society, because the ultimate solution of the problem eliminates the problem itself and with it also the complexity of a world that cannot live without the problem. There is an answer to many facets of the "social question," but there is no answer to the social question as such, because it is the essence of modernity to transform certain issues into social ones. This simply means that certain grievances of life, which earlier counted as normal, albeit negative, constituents of the human condition, have now been transformed into issues waiting for a political solution, and there is no telling in advance if further constituents of the human condition will become social issues in the future. Similarly, the hope of a morally perfect world would eliminate the one and only "moral progress" we have made with modernity, the contingent freedom of modern individuals who have to make ethical choices, thus destining their personalities morally. The imaginary fulfillment of the self-contradictory hope of moral perfection would mean the end of morality as we know it.

What can be done with the pernicious hopes of modernity? Making them taboos, particularly the once politically potent hope of absolute transcendence, would curtail the autonomy of modernity; such repression could result in a neurosis of culture, no less than repressions cause neuroses in individual persons. Moreover, the pernicious hopes can only be banned from the public use of reason, that is, from the political discourse, by social pressures but not from "the imaginary institution of society." Metaphorically speaking, a psychoanalytic self-treatment of modernity is called for. There is more in the metaphor than meets the eye, for it is typical childhood traumas from which a still young modernity suffers. The modern world was born amid violent primal scenes of political, industrial, and cultural revolutions that it tried to sublimate. But just as with all sublimation processes, a considerable part of the traumatic memories remained operative, and they burst to the surface by discharging destructive and self-deifying hopes. A balanced discourse that makes no concessions to the suppressed violent desires (destructive or self-destructive) of traumatic modernity, but that does not simply censor them, may be the first step toward eliminating the traumatic hopes.

What can we rationally hope for? Already Immanuel Kant raised the question of what we can know, do, and hope for. In dealing with hopes, Kant used no qualification. Humans can hope for literally everything: human perfection, the immortality of the soul, or grasping the goal of the universe. Reason has no censorship role in this regard, or else humankind's autonomy would be dangerously curtailed. But there is a special "rational" kind of hope that should even be favored. We hope rationally for something we have no knowledge of because it is beyond our time and space horizon but about which we would like to gain knowledge. In the case of rational hopes, hope stands for the mobilization of our energies, for the readiness to invest them into tasks the fulfillment of which may or may not guide us toward the sought-for objective but about which, it can be stated with some certainty, they will not mislead us. The particular hope that is not hope writ large, not a metaphysical hero, but more than mere subjective longing, desiring, imagining, and fantasizing, is the hope for the survival of our culture. The memento mori encapsulated in "Can modernity survive?" has been made publicly. Hoping for the survival of our culture is not illicit or irrational. It is not the hope of immortality but of longevity. In this hope, we wish our own world a long and happy life.

Notes

1. Baruch Spinoza, *Ethics* (London: Dent, 1989).

2. See the best characterization of Paul's rendering of the role of hope in the Christian's life in Rudolf Bultmann, *Theology of the New Testament* (London: SCM Press, 1952), 320–23.

3. *Klugheit:* "Zwei der groessten Menschenfeinde, / Furcht und Hoffnung, angekettet, / Halt ich ab von der Gemeinde; / Platz gemacht! ihr seid gerettet." Johann Wolfgang von Goethe, *Faust*, in Fuenf Akten, Erster Akt, Weitlaufiger Saal, Berliner Ausgabe, *Dramatische Dichtungen*, vol. 4 (rpt. Berlin: Aufbau, 1965), 327.

4. Ernst Bloch, *The Principle of Hope*, trans. Neville Plaice, Stephen Plaice, and Paul Knight (1959; rpt. Cambridge, Mass.: MIT Press, 1986), 1:145–46.

5. The curtailment of the anticipatory dynamic by Heidegger's emphasis on the horizon is a fact, although he never ceased to emphasize that "everything begins with the future." Moreover, Heidegger even criticized Sigmund Freud for introducing a casual, past-oriented story of the psyche while, according to Heidegger, we are a project, that is, future-bound beings (*Zollikoner Seminare* [Frankfurt am Main: V. Klostermann, 1987]).

6. See the characterization of the "existentialist generation" as well as of the role of angst in their cultural movement in Agnes Heller and Ferenc Fehér, "Existentialism, Alienation, Postmodernism: Cultural Movements as Vehicles of Change in the Patterns of Everyday Life," in *The Postmodern Political Condition* (Cambridge: Polity Press, 1988).

7. The analysis of the problematic of dissatisfied society can be found in Agnes Heller, "Dissatisfied Society," in her *The Power of Shame* (London: Routledge and Kegan Paul, 1933) and in Heller and Fehér, "On Being Satisfied in a Dissatisfied Society," in *Postmodern Political Condition*.

8. Karl Mannheim, "The Utopian Mentality," in *Ideology and Utopia: An Introduction to the Sociology of Knowledge*, sec. 4 (1929; rpt. London: Routledge and Kegan Paul, 1976).

BARRY SMART

From Rationalization to Reflexivity

2 Writing at the beginning of the twentieth century, Max Weber believed that the "fate of our time" was characterized "by rationalization, intellectualization, and above all, by the 'disenchantment of the world.'"[1] Although times have changed, few would disagree that the global diffusion of modern Western forms of reason has induced a disenchantment of the world. What that might involve, how the process of disenchantment described by Weber might now be interpreted, and what its consequences have been appears to be a matter of some debate. In any event, the globalization of modernity and Western rationality constitutes merely one narrative, albeit a powerful one. Traditional communities and forms of life have indeed been dislocated, disturbed, and disorganized by the corrosive consequences of modern rationalities, by the impact of modernity upon traditional customs, practices, and beliefs. But in Weber's work there is another narrative present in a vestigial form that has recently received a much more explicit articulation, namely a disenchantment *with* modernity, in one form expressed as a "postmodern" reenchantment of the world.

Modernity has increasingly become subject to its own "heretical imperative,"[2] vulnerable to the recognition of "inconvenient facts," identification of unfulfilled promises, and continuing existence of problems and dangers, if not exacerbated risks and threats. To what extent this critical condition constitutes a consequence of the development of modernity alone, represents an effect of the resistance, regeneration, or reconstitution of traditional forms of life, and/or signifies an articulation of traditional and modern forms in various complex and unanticipated ways is an issue currently exercising the postmodern imagination.

• • •

The question of the fate of humanity under conditions of modernity is at the center of Weber's work. For him the "problematic of the modern mode of life—disenchanted, rationalized, disciplined"—precipitated a process of depersonalization affecting all aspects of human life, in particular undercutting the possibility for an ethical conduct of life. The more the modern world is rationalized the less is the likelihood of our being able to live in an ethically interpretable manner. The "opacity of the world in which we are 'placed' to ethical interpretation is the 'fate' with which Weber's work struggles."[3] The consequences (costs) of the dissolution of personal and ethical relations, synonymous with traditional forms of life, constitute the central theme of Weber's exploration of the impact of modern reason on social conditions and human experiences.

The given, unconscious, and thus unquestioned "unity" of the premodern world has been sundered by the dividing practices of modern reason. The development of modern purposively rational conceptions of the world has led to the relegation of religion and belief to the realm of the irrational. Weber comments that this has become "more the case the further the purposive type of rationalization has progressed."[4] The consequences of modern reason have subsequently become even more pronounced, the costs and benefits a matter of continuing debate, and the misgivings tentatively articulated by Weber have been amplified and elaborated. Precisely when the modern age commenced remains a matter of contention, with bids ranging from the fourth century and Augustine's reconstitution of a philosophy of progress to the eighteenth-century Enlightenment and the advent of a "tradition of reason," a tradition that Weber implies overstated the scope and potential of reason, which promised more than could conceivably be delivered and ultimately contributed to the development of a "charisma of reason."[5] This charisma has been on the wane for some time.

In Weber's fragmented sociological reflections on modern reason and its consequences, embryonic traces of the doubts and questions that have been developed in deliberations over the existence of a postmodern condition first received sociological expression. From the outset Weber is cautious about Western rationality, concerned to point to its limits and limitations and "to show the tensions that existed in the relations between the processes of rationalization as they existed, and still continue to do so."[6] Specifically, we might note the recurring difficulty that rational and methodical forms of life have had in satisfactorily answering questions about "ultimate presuppositions," foundations, or grounds—the continuing problem of meaning in a disenchanted modern world. There is an accumulation of signs that the modern pursuit of mastery over all things (through the continual refinement of calculating and purposive forms of rationality) seems destined to remain unfinished, incomplete, and frustrated. Increasing rationalization has not led to an increased general awareness of the conditions under which we live our lives or to an enhancement of personal autonomy. On the contrary, increasing differentiation of fields of knowledge and an associated growth of specialists and professionals has precipitated an increase in dependence. Moreover, if the aim has been to submit all forms of life to calculation and control it is now clear that significant features of the social conditions we encounter remain incalculable and beyond external control. To that extent, the modern world is less than completely disenchanted and modern subjects have yet to be reduced to the status of "rational" objects.

For Weber, it is clearly a moot point whether the process of rationalization that has been a feature of occidental culture and the "'progress' to which science belongs as a link and motive force" has any meaning "beyond the purely practical and technical."[7] The constant revolutionizing and disturbance of all social relations, and the uncertainty and turmoil that constitute a necessary corollary of modernity, represent for Marx and Engels the price of progress, a down payment required to create the preconditions appropriate for a postcapitalist resolution of the social question.[8] Weber, in contrast, considers the endless flux and turmoil associated with modernity, the constant transformation of culture, ideas, knowledge, prospects, possibilities, and problems, as the source of the meaninglessness to which modern existence is increasingly subject. Modernity simultaneously creates the promise and possibility, perhaps even a fleeting experience, of satisfaction, but it is driven by an endless, endemic dissatisfaction that diminishes the experience and meaning of existence. As Weber remarks, "the individual life of civilized man, placed into an infinite 'progress' . . . placed in the midst of the continuous enrichment of culture by ideas, knowledge and problems . . . catches only the most minute part of what the life of the spirit brings forth ever anew, and . . . as such is meaningless." Scientific rationality promised more but has simply offered "artificial abstractions" that are unable to "teach us anything about the *meaning* of the world."[9]

Weber was considering the consequences of modern conditions in a context in which the routines of everyday life were challenging religion.

At the risk of oversimplifying the contrast, the context in which I am attempting to explore the articulation of modern rationalities and post-modern imaginations is one in which there is an increasing disenchant-ment with modernity, exemplified in particular by the challenge mount-ed by regenerated and reaffirmed religious systems of belief and by the apparent anomalous presence of postmodern conditions. Many old gods have indeed ascended from their prematurely designated graves, but they are not all disenchanted, nor do they necessarily assume the form of impersonal forces as "they strive to gain power over our lives and again . . . resume their eternal struggle with one another."[10] Refusing to accept the relativizing consequences of modernity, the fundamentalist turn evident in each of the three monotheisms (Christianity, Judaism, and Islam) has promoted resistance to modern forms of life. Whether the religious movements thought to have been left behind by moderni-ty have become the avant-garde of postmodernity is open to question.[11] Less controversial is their contribution to the debate over the limits and limitations of modernity and associated possible emergence of a mood or condition of postmodernity.

The resurrection of the sacred as a sphere of experience pertinent to modern forms of life, as a counter to the nihilism of the modern world and the "vision of reason that brought this world into being," certainly constitutes a part of the postmodern condition.[12] The tension between religion and intellectual knowledge identified by Weber as a component of modernity persists, but the relation of forces has changed. Science continues to encounter claims that the social world is a meaningful and ethically oriented cosmos, but it is no longer so easy to consign intellectual approaches that pursue the meaning of occurrences, or prioritize "interpretive" over "legislative" reason, to the realm of the "irrational." That dividing practice is no longer sustain-able. Weber clearly had a sense of the difficulties that were likely to arise:

> Science has created this cosmos of natural causality and has seemed unable to answer with certainty the question of its own ultimate pre-suppositions. Nevertheless science, in the name of "intellectual in-tegrity," has come forward with the claim of representing the only possible form of a reasoned view of the world. The intellect, like all culture values, has created an aristocracy based on the possession of rational culture and independent of all personal ethical qualities of man. . . . Worldly man has regarded this possession of culture as the highest good. In addition to the burden of ethical guilt, however, something has adhered to this cultural value which was bound to

depreciate it with still greater finality, namely senselessness—if this cultural value is to be judged in terms of its own standards.[13]

Weber challenges the idea that science represents the only reasoned view of the world. Rationalism means "very different things," and the processes of rationalization of conduct can assume varied forms. It is clear that the rationalization of worldviews could develop in a number of different ways and need not lead to a reduction of religious views of the world and "a corresponding increase in instrumentally rational forms of conduct graded by modern 'value-free' science."[14] As I have suggested above, religious worldviews have not disappeared; on the contrary, they continue to exert an influence on the course of social development. A comparable conclusion is implied in Ernest Gellner's comments on the limits of modern reason, notably that "rationality dependent on the division of labor has transformed our world, but will never reach those all-embracing, inherently multi-strand choices between incommensurate alternatives."[15] Insofar as that is the case, the modern project is destined to remain perpetually unfinished, its realization continually frustrated by "residual" and "irrational" forms that obstruct its quest for order.[16]

Rather than an inexorably ascendant or progressively rational social order, designed according to the cumulative wisdoms of post–Enlightenment Western civilization, we inhabit a social world that has become increasingly disoriented and disturbed by the knowledge that it is "committed to practising a rationality that is unfortunately crisscrossed by intrinsic dangers." The effects of bewilderment, and experiences of vertigo induced by the "revolving door of rationality . . . its necessity . . . indispensability, and . . . intrinsic dangers,"[17] may lead us to pursue more vigorously the receding promise of modernity. But it may also occasion a reconsideration of modern reason and inadvertently, or otherwise, provide scope for the nourishment of a "postmodern" imagination.

• • •

Inaugurated by Nietzsche and elaborated by Weber, concern about modernity and its consequences has become increasingly prominent and is now pervasive. Nietzsche wondered where our modern world belonged, "to exhaustion or ascent?"[18] The question continues to haunt us, albeit in a more aggravated context in which exhaustion, environmentally and experientially speaking, appears to have reached a more advanced stage. Indeed, it might be argued, following Anthony Giddens,[19] that we are increasingly overwhelmed by questions where once we considered ourselves to be in possession of answers and solutions. It is this process of questioning modern resolutions that has been diagnosed as symptomatic of the existence of a postmodern condition, the argument being that modernity only becomes "visible . . . from the moment in which . . . the mechanism of modernity distances itself from us."[20] As will become clear below, the idea that a critical analytical understanding of modernity requires, or assumes, the existence of a condition of postmodernity is open to dispute.

The question of modernity and its consequences is effectively a question of the post-Enlightenment development of Western civilization and the rationalizing project with which it has been articulated. Since the eighteenth century there has been a prominent assumption that increasing rationality is conducive to the promotion of order and control, achievement of enhanced levels of social understanding, moral progress, justice, and human happiness. The pursuit of order, promotion of calculability, fabrication and celebration of the new, and faith in progress have been identified as pivotal features of modernity. The project of modernity, however, has become the focus of increasing critical reflection in the course of the twentieth century. The benefits and securities deemed virtually synonymous with the development of modernity have become matters of doubt and the possibility of their realization, if not their desirability, the subject of question and criticism as faith in the doctrine of progress has dissipated.

What are we to make of these developments? As modernity has become subject to critical analysis, to its own heretical imperative, so in turn its sacred idols have been profaned, its "prejudices and opinions . . . swept away."[21] We are no longer so easily deceived or led astray by the illusory logic of innovation, development, and progress.[22] Exemplified in its strongest form by Jürgen Habermas, one response to this has been to argue that we now encounter a strategic choice, either "hold fast to the intentions of the Enlightenment . . . or . . . give up the project of modernity as lost." Habermas is intent on defending the project of modernity from antimodern and postmodern criticisms, positions that are conceived to rob "a modernity at variance with itself of its rational content and its perspective on the future."[23] In particular, Habermas seeks to preserve the primacy of modern reason by contributing to the development of an understanding of the world that may claim to have identified universal structures of human existence and norms for human action, thereby claiming universal validity.[24]

Acknowledging the existence of a series of social, cultural, and political problems that have arisen with modernity, Thomas McCarthy argues that there is a "need to subject these phenomena to careful analysis if we wish to avoid a precipitate abandonment of the achievements of modernity. What is called for, it might be argued, is an enlightenment suspicion of enlightenment, a reasoned critique of Western rationalism."[25] There can be few, if any, major objections to this argument. The question is whether an enlightenment suspicion of modern Western reason and its claims can be found in Habermas's attempt to uphold and complete the project of modernity. Where enlightened suspicion and reasoned critique is present in his work, it is directed almost entirely at the pathological consequences of "capitalist modernization."

In contrast to the alternatives constituted by Habermas of either attempting to live up to the Enlightenment's promise or abandoning the project of modernity, a third possibility embodied in a range of other analyses is evident. In a series of diverse studies—exploring the history of modern rationalities (Michel Foucault), the politics of modern and postmodern conditions (Agnes Heller and Ferenc Fehér), the (post)modern experience (and problem) of living with contingency and ambivalence (Zygmunt Bauman), and the complex consequences of, and possible alternatives to, modernity (Anthony Giddens)—the question of the Enlightenment and the project of modernity is approached, with varying degrees of explicitness, more openly, critically, and imaginatively than is possible within a project whose parameters are fixed from the outset by a felt need to defend and promote modern reason. Beyond significant differences in style, orientation, and focus, what each of the third category of analyses share is an evident willingness to address the possibility that the pursuit of order and control, promotion of calculability, affirmation of the new, preoccupation with progress, and other features intrinsic to modernity are necessarily articulated with a simultaneously constituted range of other experiences and conditions that are conceived negatively, as problems—namely, the risk of chaos, the persistent presence of chance or threat of indeterminacy, the increasing incidence of ephemerality, and its alterego, the seemingly inexorable growth of dissatisfaction.

One implication of this is that those conditions are not so much remedial "abnormal" effects of a particular historical perversion of modernity, of its "pathological" capitalist form, as consequences of the complex practices, institutional dimensions, and associated experiences inaugurated within Western Europe approximately two hundred years ago and subsequently dispersed via a process of globalization. In brief, they constitute consequences of modernity per se, that is, of the only historically existing form known to us, "modernity as a brand-new experiment . . . that is, still in its period of trial and (grave) error"[26]—and in question.

Opening the question of modernity and its consequences does not inexorably force us to make a choice between either endorsement or betrayal of the Enlightenment. We can refuse Habermas's gambit. As Foucault reminds us, it is not a matter of "either accept the Enlightenment and remain within the tradition of its rationalism . . . or . . . criticize the Enlightenment and then try to escape from its principles of rationality."[27] We can contribute to the making of our history, but we also know, after Karl Marx, that we cannot do so under circumstances of our own choosing. Whether we are drawn to the light or hide ourselves in the shadows, we remain, to a certain extent at least, both subjects of and subject to the Enlightenment. Thus, one aspect of the question is our connection to the Enlightenment, an aspect I will pursue, albeit briefly, through Foucault's work.

In a sense, the connection is already embodied in the very exercise on which I have embarked, namely a recognition of the possibility of an interrogation of the present. One way of understanding our continuing indebtedness to the Enlightenment is in terms of our perpetual and necessary return to the question of the present—as Foucault puts it: "What is my present? What is the meaning of the present? . . . Such is, it seems to me, the substance of this new interrogation on modernity."[28] But to say that our connection to the Enlightenment is embodied in the continuing presence, if not necessity, of a critical ontology of the present is to fast-forward to the conclusion. How does Foucault get there? He argues that a number of paradoxes have led us back to the question of Enlightenment. Modern reason makes universal claims yet has developed in contingency; it constitutes a reason whose "autonomy of structures carries with itself the history of dogmatisms and despotisms."

The question of Enlightenment has returned for three key reasons: (1) the increasing importance assumed by scientific and technical rationality in social, economic, and political life and an associated concern about the uneven consequences of this, (2) the growing realization that a socioeconomic revolution cannot deliver on its promise to conclude, as Marx wrote, the "history of all hitherto existing society," and (3) because postcolonial populations have begun to "ask the West what rights its culture, its science, its social organization and finally its rationality itself could have to laying claim to a universal validity."[29] It is the articulation of such questions that has allowed analysts to speculate about the steady accretion of postmodern forms of life. But that is not Foucault's declared position, notwithstanding David Hoy's powerful argument to the contrary.[30]

Acknowledging that modernity as a question has a history, Foucault comments that it is no longer necessary to pose it in terms of an "axis with two poles, antiquity and modernity." Rather than conceive of modernity as an epoch "preceded by a more or less naive or archaic premodernity and followed by an enigmatic and troubling 'postmodernity,'" modernity may more appropriately be envisaged as an *attitude*, a way of relating to contemporary reality. This involves much more than an accommodation to the disruptions, discontinuities, and forms of perpetual motion intrinsic to modern life. It is not "simply a form of relationship to the present, it is also a mode of relationship that has to be established with oneself." For Foucault this represents a critical orientation to the present, a critical analysis that reflects upon the limits within which our forms of knowledge, social practices, and modes of subjectivity are constituted, an analysis that transgressively asks: "In what is given to us as universal, necessary, obligatory, what place is occupied by whatever is singular, contingent, and the product of arbitrary constraints?"[31] Giddens identifies precisely this characteristic of critical reflexivity as symptomatic of the fact that we are living through a period of "high" or "radicalized modernity."

Whereas Foucault is unwilling to refer to modernity as an epoch, or era, suggesting instead that it is more appropriate to explore the various ways in which "the attitude of modernity, ever since its formation, has found itself struggling with attitudes of 'countermodernity,'" the other analyses considered here simultaneously incorporate into their critical ontologies of the present a consideration of the structures and experiences synonymous with modern forms of life, as well as the prospects that might arise with the emergence of a condition of postmodernity.

• • •

The consequences of modernity are manifold and far from exhausted, for modernity has by no means run its course. The consequences discussed follow from the way in which modernity is conceptualized. For Foucault, as noted above, modernity is an attitude, a way of relating to ourselves, others, and the conditions of existence we encounter, reproduce, and transform. The prevalence of a critically questioning, reflexive orientation (or modern attitude) toward the present is evident in the identification of more and more areas of our existence as subject to "the influence of history," an influence that "introduces discontinuity into our very being,"[32] one that renders existence open to being different. Such an attitude does not imply, or guarantee, a progressive or positive outcome, a resolution of prevailing problems and difficulties, or the constitution of a "higher" form of life—rather it seems to represent for Foucault the way we are, the way in which we increasingly experience the complex processes that constitute and reconstitute our existence. Implicit in such a notion are the characteristics of ambivalence, contingency, and reflexivity integral to the other analyses of modernity and its consequences (to be examined below).

If we accept modernity as a form of relationship to the present that was inaugurated with the Enlightenment, then we may argue that analytically it continues to represent a relative novelty, that it is "still an abstraction in the early phase of the process of 'concretization.'" The interrogation of modernity, the recognition that yesterday's "modern" resolutions are frequently the source of today's modern problems, and the realization that the passage of time and (what is often conceived to be its corollary) the quantitative accumulation of information and knowledge are not able to render modern conditions more transparent (because they simultaneously represent a form of interference with the conditions themselves) have been identified as symptoms of a "postmodern historical consciousness,"[33] of "the passage of modernity to its postmodern stage"[34] and, in contrast, of a "radicalizing of modernity" which indicates that "we have entered a period of high modernity."[35]

It would be misleading to make too much, at this stage, of the contrasting terms employed to describe the continuing transformation of modernity, for there is a substantial degree of common ground between the respective positions. For example, modernity is regarded as a "double-edged phenomenon" (Giddens), simultaneously a source of benefits and costs, satisfactions and dissatisfactions, securities and risks, opportunities and limitations. Modernity appears like a roller coaster fueled by perpetual oscillations between promised, and for some occasionally, briefly realized moments, perhaps even "significant niches of satisfaction" (Heller and Fehér), and more sustained periods and experiences of discontent and dissatisfaction. Modernity presents itself as order, but its necessary corollary is disorder or chaos. In brief, "existence is modern insofar as it contains the *alternative* of order and chaos . . . [for] the negativity of chaos is a product of order's self-constitution: its side-effect" (Bauman).

In premodern societies the contingency associated with the general condition of human existence—"every person is thrown into a particular world by the accident of birth"—is experienced as fate. With modernity, our relationship to our conditions of existence, our time and place, is transformed. An acceptance of fate is displaced by experience of the contingent character of the contexts in which we find ourselves: "It is not only being 'here' or 'there' that is conceived as contingent, so too is *the individual's relation* to a particular place and time as a mere

'context.' . . . Put simply, from a modern point of view, particular social arrangements and institutions can just as well exist as *not* exist. The
world into which people are born is no longer seen as having been
decreed by fate but as an agglomerate of possibilities."[36]

In a world that claims to be able to offer an increasing range of choices, one potential choice, at least, has to be excluded, namely the possibility of putting an end to the contingent character of modern existence. Modernity appears to require us to live with contingency, to cope
with or reconcile ourselves to conditions that, while pretending to
order, regulation, and necessity-by-design must, in some far from final
instance, admit the persisting presence of contingency. Contingent
existence is experienced as "existence devoid of certainty."[37] The problem is how to respond to the presence and threat of uncertainty. In the
absence of any safe orderly havens offering shelter from the turbulence
of uncertainty, what are our options? Certainly not a reinvigorated
attempt to complete the modern project, which would surely deliver
more of the same. One proposed alternative is to try to "eliminate
contingency by transforming it into destiny."[38] This seems to require
us to regard the actualization of some of the diverse possibilities that
have constituted the various contexts in which we have lived and reflected upon our existence as *optimal outcomes* embodied in and secured
through our choices and actions. Such a strategy may relieve the anxiety frequently associated with an awareness of the extent to which
our existence has been subject to contingency. It may indeed allow us
to feel that we have made a mark, left a trace, on the world in which
we live. But any feelings of satisfaction—within what remains, after
all, not only a dissatisfied society but in many respects an unsatisfactory one as well—ought perhaps to be tempered by the possibility that
marks may be removed and traces erased.

If it is the pursuit of self-determination in cooperation with others
that "best allows the transformation of our contingency into destiny,"
it is necessary to recognize that such a strategy will not so much eliminate contingency as offer, at best, momentary relief from it, as self and
others act to shape their destiny and then reflect upon their participation in the actualization of one of the available possibilities. The exercise of self-determination requires degrees of openness, options, and
possibilities, indeterminacy concerning present and future conduct. In
short, the absence of certainty constitutes the space in which self and
others can make their marks or leave their traces. The diverse contexts
and fluctuating circumstances in which we find ourselves, and may
attempt to (re)constitute ourselves as subjects, as selves able to recognize and take advantage of the potential for self-determination made

possible by the absence of necessity, are themselves subject to contingency. It is the contingent character of aspects of the present in which we act that offers the possibility of self-determination. Insofar as this is the case, we should seek not the elimination of contingency but the constitution of the conditions in which it becomes possible for people to exercise self-determination in the face of contingency. This task begins with an acceptance of contingency as an intrinsic feature of both the modern self and modern society. Accepting "that certainty is not to be,"[39] that we live in and with contingency, does not represent a loss, for the promises of certainty were from the outset unrealizable. It is the question of how we cope with the consequences of living with contingency that has simultaneously troubled modern sensibilities and stimulated postmodern imaginations.

Modernity has a number of paradoxical features and consequences that encompass both local and global dimensions and now appear to permeate virtually all aspects of our existence. And, given the pervasiveness of modern institutions, the extent to which we are able to exercise self-determination is likely to remain circumscribed and problematic, a matter of contest, struggle, and difficulty. Reflecting on the difficulties of trying to cope with the "juggernaut of modernity," Giddens remarks that "so long as the institutions of modernity endure, we shall never be able to control completely either the path or the pace of the journey. In turn, we shall never be able to feel entirely secure, because the terrain across which it runs is fraught with risks of high consequence. Feelings of ontological security and existential anxiety will coexist in ambivalence."[40]

The persistent problem of a lack of control—exemplified by the continuing irreverent disorder of things that it was once assumed would submit to the organized designs and orderly formations of legislative reason—contributes to the growing ambivalence identified as a corollary of modernity. Contingency, ambivalence, and a seemingly inexhaustible capacity to transform seductive prospects for satisfaction into frustrating experiences of dissatisfaction appears to be bound up with modernity, synonymous with its existence. Dissatisfaction, uncertainty, disorder, and failure effectively promote, or revitalize, the quest for order, control, and satisfaction. Consequently, problems or difficulties of this order are taken to signify the need for further extensions or enhancements of modern practices or, more ambitiously, a mission to retrieve the rational promise of modernity from its historical perversion.

With the extension of the practice of reflexivity to modernity itself, the assumption that problems and difficulties will be alleviated, if not resolved, through a revision of the modern formula, has been challenged. But what does the process of interrogation to which modernity has become increasingly subject signify? As Zygmunt Bauman asks, is "the fading of self-deception, a final fulfillment, emancipation, or the end of modernity?" Does it represent a radicalization of modernity, or is it more appropriate to consider it a symptom of a postmodern turn?

• • •

If there are respects in which these positions present a range of comparable observations on modernity and its consequences, there are simultaneously clear indications that substantial degrees of difference exist over the question of an appropriate conceptual designation for the social, cultural, and political conditions that now prevail and to which our analyses must respond. For two of the positions (Foucault and Giddens), modernity continues to be an appropriate designation for the present. But whereas Foucault's observation—namely, that our analytic efforts should be directed toward trying to "find out how the attitude of modernity, ever since its formation, has found itself struggling with attitudes of 'countermodernity'"—effectively constitutes a dismissal of the notion of the postmodern (as of little relevance for an understanding of contemporary conditions), Giddens, while arguing strongly that the conditions we encounter represent the consequences of a process of "radicalization of modernity," also entertains the idea of a possible future postmodern order or system.

In contrast there are other analyses of modernity and its consequences that suggest it has become necessary to generate, or deploy, a conception of the postmodern in order to develop an adequate understanding of contemporary conditions. Accordingly, we can find references to an emerging "social, political and cultural configuration" of postmodernity,[41] "the rise of postmodernist cultural forms" articulated with the development of "more flexible modes of capital accumulation,"[42] the appearance of "unmistakable trends of postmodern politics," and new problems and possibilities, constraints, choices, and responsibilities illuminated by the "postmodern" identification of the limits and limitations of modernity. I will confine my comments here to the postmodern responses to modern conditions and their consequences outlined in the related works of Heller and Fehér on postmodern politics and Bauman on the task of coping with the postmodern challenge.

In both cases, postmodernity is presented as a way of relating to modernity, literally a consequence of its consequences, a response to the broken promises, buried hopes, and attendant dilemmas that must be faced without the solace of anticipated, if not guaranteed, future resolutions. It is not that nothing can be done, that present problems are conceived to be necessarily impervious to future resolutions, but that problems do not admit of quick technical fixes, nor can there be one final solution to the dilemmas and difficulties encountered in social life. Accordingly, postmodernity is described as "not a new era" and as "in every respect parasitic on modernity; it lives and feeds on its achievements and on its dilemmas,"[43] and again as

> no more (but no less either) than the modern mind taking a long, attentive and sober look at itself, at its condition and its past works, not fully liking what it sees and sensing the urge to change. Postmodernity is modernity coming of age . . . looking at itself at a distance rather than from inside, making a full inventory of its gains and losses. . . . Postmodernity is modernity coming to terms with its own impossibility; a self-monitoring modernity, one that consciously discards what it was once unconsciously doing.[44]

The portrayal of postmodernity as a form of historical consciousness, mentality, or attitude leaves room for considering the question of the respects in which postmodern ways of relating to the world are formed and embodied in social life (and may also contribute to its restructuring). It has been suggested that the postmodern political condition is premised on the demise of "grand narratives" and an associated abandonment of redemptive forms of politics, a political and cultural campaign against ethnocentrism and its corollary, an "acceptance of the plurality of cultures and discourses." In terms of one prominent, increasingly challenged, yet not quite totally abandoned form of redemptive politics—socialism—it is hard to dispute that "as a 'new formation' transcending modernity [it] is a conceptual mythology." Rather than constituting a new social space, socialism presents a rearrangement of the furniture of modernity as the solution to all social issues and problems. The complex histories of the societies of "actually existing socialism" have taught us that the institutional changes that socialism might be able to deliver will not resolve all social issues, and this hard lesson has contributed to the erosion of its grand narrative status. Given the devaluation of socialism as the imaginary, alternative, progressive form of life to a capitalist modernity (and the corollary, an extensive and intensive proliferation of postmodern political conditions, premised on pluralism, and manifest, for example, in relations of indifference between cultures, unauthentic celebrations of otherness, and either a total denial, or a relativization, of universals), the question of what ties are "still capable of holding our world together"[45] must be addressed.

A comparable response to the taxing challenges of living with contingency, with facing up to postmodern conditions—in cooperation with and in consideration of others, in ways that might allow us to take advantage of, as well as cope with, the opportunities, threats, risks, and dangers they simultaneously embody—informs Bauman's series of critical reflections on modernity and its consequences. He identifies postmodern conditions in a wide range of contexts and responses in contemporary social, cultural, political, and economic life. Intellectual disaffection with the modern project's goal of rationally engineering the good life, associated doubts about the feasibility, desirability, and relevance of global projects, in a context where there are now recognized to be a plurality of cultures and discourses articulated with new, transient forms of local-global relations, a shift in the relative significance of relations of repression and seduction in the reproduction of "systemic control and social integration,"[46] and experience of fragmentation and dislocation of both identity and community, arising from an acceleration of communications, an overproduction of cultural products, information, and meanings, and coupled with an absence or discrediting of reliable reference points, secure standards, stable criteria, fixed forms, accepted authorities, guarantees, foundations, and so on, are all manifestations of a complex condition of postmodernity.[47] The irretrievable loss of trust in the project of modernity and its ability to manage, enhance, and ultimately fulfill human potential raises the prospect of restoring (more) responsibility to human agency. "Having been trained to live in necessity, we . . . [now find] ourselves living in contingency."[48] If we are to limit or avoid a paralyzing nostalgia for the lost promise of modernity, if postmodern conditions are to be received and experienced as providing opportunities, in short turned to individual and collective advantage, then it is necessary to respond positively, with imagination, to the prospect of living without guarantees and with contingency and ambivalence.

· · ·

The prospect of living without certainty or necessity may cause us to respond with fear, anxiety, and insecurity, but it also allows us to live with imagination and responsibility. Contrary to the reflex responses of critics who have equated postmodernity with a reactionary or conservative form of politics,[49] there is no singular, predetermined, or necessary postmodern political agenda. Irritatingly for those who require their targets to declare themselves either for or against, it is increasingly evident that postmodernity presents "a double face like Janus,"[50] in effect constituting a site for political possibilities, rather than a distinctive political strategy.

Potentially everything is up for grabs in a political game constituted under postmodern conditions: the game is specified and the rules improvised as the game proceeds; the positions and sides constituted and reconstituted as the game itself is transformed; and the end, if end there can be, is indeterminate. Such a scandal of indeterminacy has licensed the idea that postmodernity necessarily means "everything goes." But if under conditions of postmodernity anything may go, it is not the case that any- or everything does go, has to go, or has to be accepted. The fear of anything goes, of a chaos of (in)difference, arises in the context of an apparent loss of the prospect of order, certainty, and security. As I have already suggested, in practice little has been lost, for the promise of order, certainty, and security associated with the advent of modernity is necessarily articulated with the threat of chaos, indeterminacy, and risk. Anything goes may also be taken as a somewhat inflated invitation to contribute to the realization of some possibilities rather than others, an indication that "things can be changed, fragile as they are, held together more by contingencies than by necessities, more by the arbitrary than by the obvious, more by complex but transitory historical contingency than by inevitable anthropological constraints."[51] In short, anything goes is an invitation to move beyond fate—"a feeling that things will take their own course anyway . . . [a feeling that] reappears at the core of a world which is supposedly taking rational control of its own affairs"[52]—and an invitation to assume responsibility with others for the shaping of our destiny.

If the debate about postmodernity commences with a conception of the paradox intrinsic to modernity, it does not end there. Rather, it extends to questions of "new forms of subjectivity . . . [and] practices of the self in a postmodern world,"[53] alternative forms of postmodern politics, and the shape a future postmodern social order might assume. I am not convinced that too much is to be gained from trying to arbitrate among the contending claims that our present reveals a continuing engagement between attitudes of "modernity" and "countermodernity" (Foucault), the presence of a "period of high modernity" (Giddens), the ending of modernity (Vattimo) and consequent possibility of "understanding . . . it as an historical whole" (Levin), or finally the potential for achieving temporal and spatial distance from modernity, by dwelling in, or facing up to, "postmodernity" (Heller and Fehér; Bauman). Each of these positions offers tools for understanding and provides a perspective on our present, a basis from which we might proceed to assume responsibility and take advantage of the scope for autonomy that exists under (post)modern conditions. Each analysis delineates the limits of modern reason and draws attention to the necessity of exercising imagination in order to cope with the difficulties and take advantage of the opportunities we encounter. Whether it is Foucault's notion of an "aesthetics of existence" and the associated idea of politics as an ethics, Heller and Fehér's contention that we may be able to transform our lives from contingency into destiny by satisfying the need for self-determination, Bauman's caution concerning the need to nurture solidarity to counter the tendency "for postmodern tolerance to degenerate into the selfishness of the rich and powerful," or the somewhat different "futuristic" conception of postmodernity outlined by Giddens, namely an institutionally complex system that represents a "movement 'beyond' modernity," the forms of subjectivity and community, the social relations and practices that are likely to emerge, remain necessarily indeterminate and beyond the scope of orderly modern designs.

Postmodernity as a chance of modernity or a more modest modernity, an inherently reflexive modernity, is synonymous with the acceptance of difference and dissension. It necessitates acceptance of the "the heterogeneity of dissensions"[54] as the only consensus likely to succeed and/or be sustainable, accommodation to the transient and fluctuating character of communal forms of life in and through which people constitute identities, simulate belonging, and pursue freedoms, and endorsement of the differences of others as a necessary condition for the preservation of one's own difference. To realize the implicitly progressive potential of postmodernity, however, tolerance of difference alone is not enough, support and defense of the differences of others is required. In short, solidarity has to be constituted amidst and for difference. The unanswered question at the heart of the postmodern political agenda is how to make common cause, to constitute a form of solidarity, while preserving and enhancing differences.

● ● ●

The present situation is one in which there exists a pervasive and irresistible questioning of the modern institutions, practices, and forms of rationality that have eroded or displaced traditional forms, a thoroughgoing reflexivity, which leaves us with more questions than answers and, in consequence, a conviction that modern knowledge does not so much precipitate an accumulation of certitudes as a proliferation of doubts. In brief, more knowledge has not meant less ignorance, for "the growth of knowledge expands the field of ignorance."[55] There is, in short, no privileged narrative to which we can now turn to resolve the problems and paradoxes we encounter.

If the forms of difference and diversity we encounter are to become something more than simply opportunities for, or consequences of, marketplace-constituted individualized lifestyles, if tolerance is to receive expression communally and solidaristically, rather than through privatized indifference, then it is necessary to encourage consideration of alternative possibilities, to imagine different ways of coping with and/ or responding to prevailing and future circumstances. In short, it is necessary to cultivate "new political visions, new visions of the body politic,"[56] and/or "a radical imaginary"[57] that simultaneously relativize and problematize existing social practices and conditions and thereby open up the prospect, not of the realization of a social blueprint, a Utopian design, but of the possibility of changing things, of transforming prevailing forms of life for the better.

One conceivable response to such comments is that "the postmodern political condition is tremendously ill at ease with Utopianism of even a non-Messianic type."[58] An unease concerning utopias is understandable and warranted. But if we are to avoid resigning ourselves to our postmodern fate, it is necessary to reconstitute utopias rather than abandon them. In short, we need to generate visions of postmodern possibilities. Bauman's call for "solidarity" concerning the defense of difference—and all that it implies in terms of a postmodern political agenda and associated articulation of individuals in communities—represents one implicit version. Giddens's identification of the contours of a possible future postmodern order, post-scarcity, multilayered democratic participation, demilitarization, and humanization of technology constitutes another more explicit version. Openly embracing the idea of utopias as necessary to the constitution of preferable postmodern futures, Giddens argues that, given the counterfactual character of modernity, "a rigid division between 'realistic' and utopian thought is uncalled for" (hence the promotion of models of "utopian realism"). This view receives some endorsement from Heller and Fehér's comment that their proposal for a "radicalization of democracy" (necessary for the realization of appropriate forms of self-determination) may appear utopian, but "the association of Utopian with unfeasibility is completely unjustifiable."

To alleviate the threat of postmodern conditions and promote the opportunities simultaneously associated with them, to achieve an acceptable and appropriate articulation of forms of diversity with "communally chosen and communally serviced forms of life,"[59] will require tolerance and solidarity. But imagination will also be needed to create the forms of communal life conducive to the preservation and enhancement of diversity. The interrogative character of modern reason, the undermining of answers and displacement of "solutions" by a radically questioning form of life, simultaneously necessitates the constitution of analytic and existential practices that dare to think and/or imagine the as yet unthought and unexperienced, that dare to imagine the forms of life that might be reflexively constituted through continuing processes of (post)modernization. If we are looking for a designation for such practices of the imagination, for the various attempts to exercise upon one's self and others practices that might contribute to the constitution of new forms of thought, new ways of relating to self and others and, hence, through the complex reflexive circularity of social life, to new forms of the social, with their own attendant securities and risks, delights, dangers, promises, and problems, "postmodern" seems, for the time being at least, appropriate. Insofar as we find ourselves living with, if not at the limits of, modernity, modern reason must be reconstituted, and to that end it has become necessary to nourish the postmodern imagination.

Notes

1. Max Weber, *From Max Weber*, ed. H. H. Gerth and C. Wright Mills (London: Routledge and Kegan Paul, 1970), 155.
2. Peter Berger, *The Heretical Imperative: Contemporary Possibilities of Religious Affirmation* (New York: Anchor, 1980).
3. Wilhelm Hennis, *Max Weber: Essays in Reconstruction* (London: Allen and Unwin, 1988), 102.
4. Weber, *From Max Weber*, 281.
5. Sam Whimster and Scott Lash, eds., *Max Weber, Rationality and Modernity* (London: Allen and Unwin, 1987), 10.
6. Johannes Weiss, "On the Irreversibility of Western Rationalisation and Max Weber's Alleged Fatalism," in *Max Weber*, ed. Whimster and Lash.
7. Weber, *From Max Weber*, 139.
8. Agnes Heller and Ferenc Fehér, *The Postmodern Political Condition* (Cambridge: Polity Press, 1988).
9. Weber, *From Max Weber*, 139–42.
10. Ibid., 149.
11. Jonathan Sacks, *The Persistence of Faith* (London: Weidenfeld and Nicholson, 1991).
12. D. M. Levin, *The Opening of Vision: Nihilism and the Postmodern Situation* (London: Routledge, 1988).
13. Weber, *From Max Weber*, 355.
14. Whimster and Lash, *Max Weber*, 38.
15. Ernest Gellner, *Plough, Sword and Book: The Structure of Human History* (London: Collins Harvell, 1988).
16. Zygmunt Bauman, *Modernity and Ambivalence* (Cambridge: Polity Press, 1991).

17. Michel Foucault, "Space, Knowledge and Power: An Interview," *Skyline* (March 1982): 16–20.

18. Friedrich Nietszche, *The Will to Power* (rpt. New York: Vintage, 1968), 48.

19. Anthony Giddens, *The Consequences of Modernity* (Cambridge: Polity Press, 1990).

20. Gianni Vattimo, *The End of Modernity: Nihilism and Hermeneutics in Postmodern Culture* (Cambridge: Polity Press, 1988).

21. Karl Marx and Friedrich Engels, *The Communist Manifesto* (1848; rpt. Harmondsworth: Penguin, 1968).

22. Nietzsche, *Will to Power*, 55.

23. Jürgen Habermas, *The Theory of Communicative Action*, vol. 2 (Cambridge: Polity Press, 1987), 326–27, 396.

24. Hubert L. Dreyfus and Paul Rabinow, "What is Maturity? Habermas and Foucault on 'What Is Enlightenment?'" in *Foucault: A Critical Reader*, ed. David C. Hoy (Oxford: Blackwell, 1986).

25. Thomas McCarthy, "Translator's Introduction," in *The Theory of Communicative Action*, vol. 1, by Habermas (London: Heinemann, 1984), v–vi.

26. Heller, *Can Modernity Survive?* (Cambridge: Polity Press, 1990), 4.

27. Foucault, "What Is Enlightenment?" in *The Foucault Reader*, ed. Paul Rabinow (Harmondsworth: Penguin Books, 1986), 43.

28. Foucault, "Kant on Enlightenment and Revolution," *Economy and Society* 15, no. 1 (1986): 90.

29. Foucault, "Introduction," in *On the Normal and the Pathological*, by George Canguilhem (London: D. Reidel, 1978), xii.

30. David Hoy, "Foucault: Modern or Postmodern?" in *After Foucault: Humanistic Knowledge, Postmodern Challenges*, ed. J. Arac (New Brunswick, N.J.: Rutgers University Press, 1988).

31. See Foucault, "Kant on Enlightenment and Revolution," 90; Foucault, "What Is Enlightenment?" 39–45.

32. Foucault, "Nietzsche, Genealogy, History," in *Language, Counter-Memory, Practice: Selected Essays and Interviews by Michel Foucault*, ed. D. F. Bouchard (Oxford: Blackwell, 1977), 153–54.

33. Heller, *Can Modernity Survive?* 4–6.

34. Bauman, *Modernity and Ambivalence*, 244.

35. Giddens, *Consequences of Modernity*, 52–176.

36. Heller and Fehér, *Postmodern Political Condition*, 15–17 (emphasis in original).

37. Bauman, *Modernity and Ambivalence*, 236.

38. Heller and Fehér, *Postmodern Political Condition*, 26.

39. Bauman, *Modernity and Ambivalence*, 244.

40. Giddens, *Consequences of Modernity*, 139.

41. Roy Boyne and Ali Rattansi, eds., *Postmodernism and Society* (London: Macmillan, 1990), 9.

42. David Harvey, *The Condition of Postmodernity: An Enquiry into the Origins of Cultural Change* (Oxford: Blackwell, 1989), vii.

43. Heller and Fehér, *Postmodern Political Condition,* 10–11.

44. Bauman, *Modernity and Ambivalence,* 272.

45. Ibid., 12.

46. Bauman, "Sociology and Postmodernity," *Sociological Review* 36, no. 4 (1988): 809.

47. Bauman, *Legislators and Interpreters: On Modernity, Post-Modernity and Intellectuals* (Cambridge: Polity Press, 1987); see also his *Modernity and Ambivalence.*

48. Bauman, *Modernity and Ambivalence,* 234.

49. Habermas, "Modernity versus Postmodernity," *New German Critique* 22 (1981); Alex Callinicos, *Against Postmodernism: A Marxist Critique* (Cambridge: Polity Press, 1989).

50. Heller and Fehér, *Postmodern Political Condition,* 7.

51. Foucault, "Is It Really Important to Think?" *Philosophy and Social Criticism* 9, no. 1 (1982): 35.

52. Giddens, *Consequences of Modernity,* 133.

53. Levin, *Opening of Vision,* 20.

54. Bauman, *Modernity and Ambivalence,* 251.

55. Ibid., 244.

56. Levin, *Opening of Vision,* 338.

57. Ernesto Laclau and Chantal Mouffe, *Hegemony and Socialist Strategy: Towards a Radical Democratic Politics* (London: Verso, 1985), 190.

58. Heller and Fehér, *Postmodern Political Condition,* 4.

59. Bauman, *Modernity and Ambivalence,* 273.

MICHAEL CROZIER

Inter putatorem et vastitatem:
The Ambivalences of the Garden
Metaphor in Modernity

In book 14 of *Metamorphoses,* Ovid recounts the tale of Pomona's encounter with Vertumnus. Pomona, the goddess of fruits, is more than happy to spend her days nurturing her orchard. We are told that by means of skillful pruning and grafting, she cultivates beautiful blossoms that bear the most luscious fruit. She has no passion for things beyond her orchard, for "wild" nature, for rivers and woods. Nor do affairs of the heart have any attraction for her. Her self-sufficient felicity resides solely in her carefully tended orchard. As if to ensure this, she has fenced herself in to ward off her numerous rustic suitors who attempt, with little success, to woo her.

Even Vertumnus, god of the seasons and Pomona's greatest admirer, though a master of disguise, could not find a way to her heart. Then one day he dons the appearance of an old woman. In this form he gains access to Pomona's "well-kept gardens" and her ear. Initially, the old woman beckons her to consider an elm tree that is draped with a serpentine vine in full fruit, and asks: of what interest would the tree be without the vine and vice versa? Focusing on this image of natural symbiosis, she then questions Pomona as to why she is unmoved by its example in her shunning of marriage. Pomona remains silent. The old woman persists, praising her own alter-ego, his virtues and singular love for Pomona's heart. But the attempt at seduction through fable does not end here. The old woman also relates the story of the humble Iphis and his passion for the hard-hearted princess Anaxarete. To every one of Iphis's advances, Anaxarete responded with disdain and mockery, even cruelty. Finally, he conceded defeat and challenged her to consider his love for her by taking his own life. As Iphis's funeral procession passed Anaxarete's house, she looked out the window. On seeing his body, the stone that had occupied her heart for so long took possession of her whole being such that she could no longer move, transfixing her outward gaze forever. The old woman warns Pomona to take heed of this story lest her unyielding pride be like a frost that shrivels the early spring bud. Still Pomona remains unmoved. Suddenly, in frustration, Vertumnus the god resumes his own youthful luminescent form but there is no need to impose himself. Pomona is overcome by his beauty and submits to a passion as great as his.[1]

Ovid's tale, like numerous other love stories, is set in a garden, but the form of Pomona's garden is not an insignificant backdrop. It is indicative of the pruning mentality, of the *putator* herself. As the verbal form of putator (*putare*) suggests, Pomona's pruning and trimming activities reflect her thinking processes. She is not just indifferent to the chaos, to the *vastitas* beyond her garden, but also feels threatened by it. The only way she knows how to deal with this threat is to enclose herself. Not even the old woman's parables of natural harmony or human cruelty can bridge Pomona's defense. However, once confronted by the miraculous luminescence of the very embodiment of change, of contingency, inside the garden, Pomona's mind is "ravaged" (*vastare*) and she is overcome with passion.[2] In this chapter, I will explore this relationship between the garden-pruner and its part in the life of modernity.

• • •

The idea of *garden* is nearly a human universal, almost an ontological fact of the human condition. Its reach extends across the range of human cultures from the sedentary to the nomadic. Often a focus for utopian and metaphysical visions,[3] the garden idea not only allows insights into the "imaginary" of a culture but can also act as a means by which a culture can explore its own imaginary. The garden idea can be the object for interpretation or the interpretive procedure itself— or both: it can be meaning full and/or meaning generating. As metaphor[4] for, or mediator of, "Nature," the garden idea at the most general level can be seen as a form in which a culture expresses *and* constitutes its understanding of the natural and human world. As a consequence, the hermeneutical richness of the garden idea also brings with it certain interpretive hazards.

Anecdotally, just about everyone seems to have at least some point of contact with the garden idea, although far fewer with gardening per se. It is as though the metaphor invokes an historical-anthropological inquisitiveness, however fleeting. Yet aside from the voluminous words spoken and written on things broadly horticultural, the literature on the garden form quite often remains in a descriptive-cum-aesthetic mode or merely uses the garden as a means by which to reiterate a specific paradigm of social reproduction.[5] A popular contemporary procedure in this latter vein seems to be the reduction of the garden to a "colonizing" exercise either in terms of humankind's domination over nature[6] or as a simple reflection of asymmetrical property relations,[7] or both.[8] Undoubtedly, the question of power is involved in the garden idea but this sort of interpretive reduction is somewhat more questionable. The appeal of this approach seems to reside in its one-dimensional character. The ability to extend its interpretive grasp across history, *especially* European history, offers a sociohistorical account that can locate, at any point in time, the "powerful" and the "powerless," the configuration of which is understood as directly analogous to the present. Couched in these terms, this power paradigm treats historical and sociological nuances as mere grist for the mill. In the ever-expanding space of its universe, there is always constraining power at the center. To use the language of Zygmunt Bauman,[9] the *interpreter* and her love of decolonized boundlessness seems, in this instance, more than compromised with the *legislator* and his disciplining ambitions; she seems more than ready to "graft and prune" history to her own ends.

I have no desire to implicate Bauman's more recent work[10] with all of the above observations. Nevertheless, in his endeavors to formulate a sociological theory of postmodernity there is a tendency to bundle modernity into an era characterized in Foucauldian terms.[11] There is more here than simply an effort to construct an historical contrast to the new situation of postmodernity. It could be conjectured that the postmodern interpreter's sense of being on the "outside" of modernity is highly dependent on certain categories of the "inside." My primary intention is not to present an analysis of Bauman's work. Rather I wish to take off from the "horticultural" moment in his theorization in order to elucidate the ambivalences of the garden metaphor. First, I will outline Bauman's use of Ernest Gellner's contrast between wild cultures and garden cultures.

• • •

According to Gellner, the emergence of modern industrial societies out of agrarian-based societies can be captured in botanical terms as the transformation of wild cultures into cultivated or garden cultures. The notion of wild cultures refers to systems of cultural reproduction that are self-generating. By contrast, garden cultures are understood to reproduce themselves across time by relying upon "conscious design, supervision, [and] surveillance." For Gellner, the appearance of garden cultures marks the birth of European nationalism.[12]

Bauman's appropriation of Gellner's contrast has a broader agenda than simply a concern with the rise of the modern nation-state. Arguably, this becomes the implicit preoccupation of Bauman's attempt to give a general account of modernity. Following Gellner, Bauman understands the emergence of modernity as a process in which wild cultures were transformed into garden cultures. By their very nature, garden cultures construe the "wilderness" beyond the garden fence as the other, as the realm of meaninglessness, yet as such also potentially pliable. The gardener's pruning and grafting techniques are essential for the reproduction and growth of a culture unable to tend for itself. Bauman contrasts this image of the gardener with the "naturalness" of the gamekeeper who inhabits wild culture. The gamekeeper image embodies an appeal to a form of reciprocity, rather than dichotomization, vis-à-vis the natural world. Whereas the gardener *watches over* his carefully tended patch with a commanding gaze, the gamekeeper is *embedded* in a complex set of dense relationships over which she has limited control. Bauman translates this imagery directly into the sphere of social integration. While in the wild culture of the gamekeeper, there was a certain level of reciprocal surveillance, in garden culture surveillance becomes unidirectional, "grounded in an asymmetry of control," where there is a sharp distinction between the watcher and the watched.[13]

In Bauman's rendition, the modern state takes the historical stage as a *gardening state*. In order to establish and secure its supremacy, the state required the clear demarcation between inside and outside. It therefore put into effect its "closure-exclusion" mode of operation. Subjected to these maneuvers, wild culture was purged and delegitimized, changing the former carriers of the old culture to mere raw materials for the cultural gardeners.[14] Bauman locates the historical origins of this gardening onslaught in the breakdown of communal control in the early modern period. The appearance of "masterless men" heralded a new social situation that was both expanding and fluid. The "visibility" of these men was no longer guaranteed by the reciprocal surveillance of the wild culture. This new threat to cultural cohesion thus produced a new agent—the gardening state—that undertook the task of restoring social visibility.[15]

According to Bauman, the period extending from the Reformation to the era of the Jacobins was above all a time in which the rural and urban classes were subjected to unprecedented levels of political repression and persecution. The fissures opened by the failure of community control were rapidly filled by the new garden-state practices that implemented a program for the complete transformation of social conformity into a uniform and universally binding cultural model. Popular traditions and local festivals, for example, had to be weeded out because they were anathema to the well-kept garden and its contrived order. Bauman therefore interprets the uninterrupted line of persecution he draws through this period as a campaign to totally dispossess and culturally disarm the popular masses.

The triumph of garden culture came about with its installation of an artificial mechanism that automatically dealt with the problem of weeds and turned them into indistinguishable yet manageable lawns. This mechanism, according to Bauman, was the Panopticon. Its "trick" of unidirectional surveillance introduced two far-reaching innovations. First, it facilitated the separation of conduct from motives, enabling the calculus of human behavior to dispense with the problem of will. As a consequence, habits could be sustained externally thereby reducing, if not eliminating, the need for coercion. Second, it erased individual differences among the "watched" by the imposition of a universal behavioral routine: qualitative variety was replaced by quantifiable uniformity. Yet this tabula rasa of indifferent human material also generated the need for the specialist-cum-educator to attend to the pastoral care of the lawn. Precisely because of this, education became "an irremovable constituent of power," the possession of knowledge being nothing but power.[16] Taking the French Revolution as the culmination of the Age of Reason and Enlightenment, Bauman proposes that educational theory was *the* theory of society, a complete design; education "stood for the concept, and the practice, of a managed society."[17]

For Bauman, the seeming paradox of the Enlightenment project between the rule of ideas and surveillance-based discipline is resolved by tracing the whole endeavor to the crisis of the early modern period. The sixteenth-century revival in skepticism was indicative of the new uncertainties of the time. It had arisen in response to both the collapse of the Catholic Church's monopoly on truth and the discovery of comparative cultures. The "republic of letters" replied to this situation by seeking a new certainty based upon a generalization of their own way of life. Reason portrayed as a civilizing process was cast against all relativity and the plurality of ways of life; civility as the supreme cosmopolitan virtue was set above the mores of local traditions. In this sense, Bauman characterizes the concept of civilization as a "proselytizing crusade waged by men of knowledge against vestiges of wild culture."[18] The notion of culture was reshaped through its farming associations into a master metaphor that enervated "the new mechanisms of social reproduction." Once this was operationalized, the new certainty became grounded in the alliance of power and knowledge: "political order and true knowledge [were] blended into a design for *certainty*."[19] The morass of skepticism could be avoided as long as this alliance was honored.[20]

During the nineteenth century this alliance between the intellectual and the state began to show signs of stress. In one way, the stress was the outcome of the alliance's "success": as the gardening state grew, the conceiver of its design began to diminish in stature and the gardener's commanding role was categorically recast into a theory of history. On the other hand, the alliance turned into a battle over who was more appropriate to administer society: the expert with his scientific laws of society or the political practitioner. The social scientist, no longer satisfied with making power more knowledgeable à la enlightened despotism, now sought to make knowledge powerful. However, the pretender to the throne had missed his chance: the time of ideas had passed as panoptical social reproduction became firmly established.[21] Toward the end of the nineteenth century, the Faustian price paid by the intellectual was becoming apparent. Having tasted the power of garden designing, legislator-educators were being pushed out into the undifferentiated pastures of their own making. Here, they could air their gardening aspirations, though increasingly with a sense of pessimism, or merely exercise a specialized expertise that traded in information rather than knowledge. The garden had become a prison of history for modern intellectuals, their only window on modernity being that of insiders—a self-referential and self-validating vision, still caught in the *prism of certainty* of the originary garden project.[22]

That is, until yesterday. The new era of postmodernity indicates to Bauman a gradual relinquishment by intellectuals of their legislative ambitions, replaced by an interpretive disposition. Bauman claims that what is distinctive about this new role and the postmodern period generally is the abandonment of the search for certainty in recognition of its futility. In its place there is the task of how to live "under conditions of permanent and incurable uncertainty."[23] Purged of the insiders' demeanor, postmodern interpreters view modernity as a closed object with a beginning and end.[24] Bauman argues that in the postmodernist debate this realization of modernity's demise is a fundamental, if not the fundamental, element in the self-awareness of Western society. By closing the historical garden gate on modernity, the possible tenability of Western consciousness can be contemplated. From a postmodern perspective, Bauman states that the episode of modernity was, "more than anything else, the era of certainty."[25] This new insightfulness must not be misconstrued vis-à-vis the asymmetry of power. The crisis of intellectuals' self-confidence and lack of operational "sites" indicates to Bauman that while the reproduction of *authority* has become redundant, power systems persist. There is no demand for intellectuals, only for specialists to service the new power and control technologies.

Bauman's considerations on intellectuals as legislators are not simply a recounting of past glories and subsequent decline. Rather, they dovetail into his broader theorization on the postmodern condition:

> Postmodernity may be interpreted as . . . fully developed modernity; . . . as modernity conscious of its *true nature*. . . . The most conspicuous features of the post-modern condition—*institutionalized pluralism, variety, contingency and ambivalence*—have been all turned out by the modern society in ever increasing volumes; yet they were produced, so to speak, *"by the way,"* at a time when the institutions of modernity . . . struggled for universality, homogeneity, monotony *and* clarity. . . . [The] postmodern condition can be therefore described, *on the one hand,* as modernity emancipated from false consciousness; *on the other,* as a new type of social condition marked by the overt institutionalisation of the characteristics which modernity—in its designs and managerial practices—set about to eliminate and, failing that, tried to conceal.[26]

Bauman takes these differences as sufficient justification for the formulation of a distinctive sociological theory of postmodernity—a theory that would make a decisive break "with the concepts and metaphors of the models of modernity and lift itself out of the mental frame in which they had been conceived." According to Bauman, the mindset to be transcended is modernity's vision of history and its master metaphor of movement with a direction.

In its place, Bauman suggests that the image of Brownian motion is an apt metaphor for movement in the postmodern condition: here there is constant mobility and change without the directional imperative of cause and effect. Bauman broadens the metaphor by taking theoretical sustenance from contemporary research in mathematics and in particular from what is commonly called chaos theory. He intimates the similarities between his characterization of the postmodern *habitat* as a complex system and chaos theory's exploration of complexity. Bauman draws attention to two aspects highlighted in chaos theory's differentiation of complex systems from mechanical systems: first, complex systems are unpredictable, and second, "they are not controlled by statistically significant factors." This provides a clear departure from the mechanical model assumed by modern sociology.[27] To the extent that the postmodern habitat is a system, it is a nonmechanical system and as such unassessable in terms of functionality or dysfunctionality. The statistical gymnastics of modern sociology are rendered mute given the disjuncture of significance and number. Consequently, Bauman describes the postmodern habitat as a "space of chaos and chronic indeterminacy" in which meaning-claims are constantly contested and hence continuously *ambivalent*. Moreover, no matter what state the habitat assumes, its appearance remains equally *contingent*. Similarly, this fluidity means that the self-identity of the agent is no longer bound up with her "life-project," but rather with the incessant and directionless activity of *self-constitution*, the only constant being the human body and hence the centrality of *body cultivation*.[28] Overall, Bauman regards this metaphor shift as having positive connotations at least for the theoretical self-understanding of contemporary Western societies, even if the current forms of panoptic and market manipulation also thrive in its sway.

• • •

Without engaging in a thorough appraisal of Bauman's "nonlinear" sociology, there are certain aspects that immediately catch our critical eye, and none more important than the use of gardening as the generative metaphor of modernity. Gardening culture is held as the key to modern state formation and its eradication of wild culture. The various philosophical and historical aspects of modernity are funneled back into the phenomenon of state building, such that the pruning and grafting of the garden modernizers seemingly exhausts the cultural imaginary of modernity. What immediately raises suspicion is the admixture in the metaphor itself of the architectonic and the horticultural. Of course, the gardening metaphor introduces a stronger sense of growth, and thus ongoing dynamism,[29] that the monumentalism of a building metaphor may be less likely to suggest. Nevertheless, we do not necessarily have to be inhabitants of the postmodern flux to notice the mixture or permit its possibility. Yet we should have at least a certain type of "modern" perspective to take heed of its "oddity." This is not merely the pedantry of a modern vivisectionist or the eccentricity of a particular national culture. The Kant of the *Critique of Judgement* would most certainly have registered the incongruity just as much as Horace Walpole would have, and Jean-Jacques Rousseau even more so. This perception of oddity lies not so much in the blending of the two moments as in their absolute conflation: the garden is understood as more or less equivalent to architecture. On a substantive historical level, André Le Nôtre's creations at Versailles for the Sun King were undoubtedly of the same ilk as the efforts of a Charles Perrault or Jean-Baptiste Colbert, all indulging a certain Baroque Cartesianism. Yet neither this architectural gardening nor the smaller "topiarized" Dutch gardens captured the imagination of the century of Enlightenment. What did send this century into *furor hortensis* was the appearance of the English landscape garden. One of the decisive aspects that emerged with the development of this new form was, as Kant noted, the clear differentiation of garden art from the strictures of architectural rule and technique.[30] Pruning and grafting were, for the time being, returned to the orchardist.

Needless to say, Bauman's account does not include this incongruity in his generative metaphor: gardening, just like architecture, is simply subsumed under the all-embracing umbrella of instrumental, Cartesian rationality. There is an obvious advantage for Bauman's argument in this conflation. An uninterrupted trail flows from the radial plan of the Versailles palace and its gardens to Jeremy Bentham's panoptical conception of the model prison. It would seem that Bauman himself has engaged in a bit of trimming and pruning on his garden metaphor in order to topiarize a complete picture of modernity. In other words, Bauman's use of the garden metaphor falls short of its claim: it does not reveal a garden *culture*, merely an approach to power that is designated, somewhat inappropriately it would seem, as "gardening" in general. Bauman leads us up a particular garden path and impresses upon us not only that this is the only path through the garden but also that its straightness is indicative of the garden itself. The pruning and trimming necessary to keep this path clear is regarded as symptomatic of garden activity per se, the assumption being that the garden is unambiguously focused on this one path. Presumably, this is why the legislator-pruners did not notice the ever-increasing volumes of pluralism, variety, contingency, and ambivalence accumulating by the wayside of the well-kept edges of the linear path. All of this may capture very well the specific gardening ambitions of the legislator as putator, but it is quite another matter to assume that these ambitions exhausted all of the *conscious* activities in the garden, as well as all the possible forms of the overall garden itself. In this sense, Bauman's postmodern interpreter, supposedly sensitive to nonlinear complexity, has appropriated holus-bolus the putator's own version of the modern garden and reiterated it into an enclosed picture of the sociohistorical actuality of modernity. *The* modern garden thus becomes Versailles writ large in the Panopticon, with the slippage into the purely architectonic letting the modern putative cat out of a postmodernist bag—a slippage, nonetheless, that goes unnoticed in a paradigm that subsumes all "gardening" into the unadulterated exercise of asymmetrical power.

This points to a problem in Bauman's overall theorization vis-à-vis its interpretive self-understanding. The unleashing of complex interpretation is supposedly achieved by transcending the modern mindset and its master metaphor. Suddenly, in this new open frame of mind, the epoch of modernity is revealed, with crystal clarity, as above all the era of certainty. Apparently, the new mode of interpretation can still be singularly resolute about some things, especially by proclaiming historical rupture. Whatever else, it would appear that for Bauman's new interpreter the category of complexity is not so much an interpretive category as a descriptive one. At best, this is hermeneutically naive for it makes no pretense even at "playfulness." The naïveté arises in a confusion of postmodernity as a new interpretive mode with postmodernity as "modernity emancipated from false consciousness." The description of the new social conditions as postmodern can be set aside here.

The terms "false consciousness" or, Bauman's other phrase, modernity's "true nature" grate in the postmodern ear with the sounds of metanarrative. On the one hand, Bauman recommends the adoption of the metaphor of Brownian motion that unbinds time, especially the constraining impact of the past, yet on the other hand, he seems able to achieve this only by actually constraining the past into a highly determined one-dimensional construct.

A brief glance at twentieth-century physics and chaos theory not only casts some critical light on such a procedure but also suggests a way beyond its limitations. Consider the notion of *effective dimension,* which attempts to make explicit the interpretive process involved in relating mathematical sets and natural objects. Although the representation of physical objects should, strictly speaking, be in three-dimensional shapes, physicists opt to conceive of them as being "in effect" of dimensions 0, 1, 2, 3, and so on. For instance, the description of a thread requires that "the theories relating to sets of dimension 1 or 3 must be modified by corrective terms." Deciding which is the better geometrical model can only occur after the fact according to the criterion of minimal correction. Therefore, effective dimension sensitizes the physicist to his own theoretical disposition such that questions of approximation and degree of resolution cannot be avoided.

To clarify this notion we can draw on the example of a ball of thick thread that, according to Benoit Mandelbrot, "possesses (in latent fashion) several distinct effective dimensions." Assuming the ball has a diameter of ten centimeters and the thread a diameter of one millimeter, Mandelbrot relates the almost Penelopian story as follows:

> To an observer placed far away, the ball appears as a zero-dimensional figure: a point. . . . As seen from a distance of 10 cm resolution the ball of thread is a three-dimensional figure. At 10 mm, it is a mess of one dimensional threads. At 0.1 mm, each thread becomes a column and the whole becomes a three-dimensional figure again. At 0.01 mm, each column dissolves into fibres, and the ball again becomes one-dimensional, and so on, with the dimension crossing over repeatedly from one value to another. When the ball is represented by a finite number of atomlike pinpoints, it becomes zero-dimensional again.[31]

Parenthetically, Mandelbrot notes that this interpretive "effect" is not the exclusive insight of those in the twentieth century: in a contemplative vein, medieval philosophers and Blaise Pascal (among others) touched upon it in their assertion "that on a cosmic scale our whole world is but a point!" Mandelbrot *does claim* that his fractal geometry of nature adds something new. In the above example, the shift from one dimension to another is couched in discrete terms, that is, in the language of mathematical topology where dimension is *always an integer.* In Mandelbrot's new geometry "certain ill-defined transitions between zones of well-defined dimension are reinterpreted as being fractal zones." To simplify for our purposes, the fractal geometry "allows the value of effective dimension to be a fraction" thus supplying an interpretive language to deal with zones between topological dimension. For instance, where the language of mathematical topology reduces the coastlines of all islands to a circle (and hence one-dimension), the notion of fractal dimension tends to distinguish between the coastlines of different islands. According to Mandelbrot, the differences "in fractal dimension express differences in a *nontopological aspect of form*," which he calls "fractal form." Nevertheless, he indicates that most "problems of real interest combine fractal and topological features in increasingly subtle fashion."[32] It would appear then that, in some ways, contemporary mathematics has not touched Bauman's sociological theory of postmodernity.[33] The notions of effective dimension and fractal dimension are not merely descriptive modes to deal with complex systems but, more importantly, they are self-reflective interpretive languages of form that enable *new* insights into old just as much as new problems. A straightforward topological approach may still suffice yet be complemented or replaced by the use of fractals, depending on the formulation of the problem.

It should be stressed, however, that for the working physicist the criterion of mathematical adequacy still remains. This is often forgotten in the enthusiasm with which a number of postmoderns have embraced chaos theory. Bedazzled by the computer-generated images of Mandelbrot's fractals, they appear not to have taken the time to *read* the text. Whatever else, this enthusiasm indicates a readiness to embrace the image of chaos. In this mindset, the mathematical investigation of complex natural systems is received with an extreme form of *naive realism:* nature itself is assumed to be chaotic in actuality and hence beyond the grasp of human conceptual thought. For someone like Mandelbrot, fractal geometry is not concerned with chaotic *formlessness*—quite the contrary. The endeavor is to *give form* to complex systems. While the colorful images generated by this new mathematics have caught aesthetic attention,[34] especially the illustrations of Mandelbrot's treatise, the central task is not artistic. Any suggestion of a new *poetic* mathematics is promptly dismissed, by a normally self-effusive Mandelbrot, as a "superficial impression."[35] Fractal geometry remains a mathematics of mapping even if simplicity is no longer the prime generative value.

There is no need to overburden an analysis of Bauman's theorization with mathematics; to do so might very well entail pitfalls. Nevertheless, to the extent that Bauman takes on the stated task of "mapping" modernity in its entirety, the new mathematics can hint at some of the interpretive hazards that may be involved in this type of procedure. In the present context, this can be briefly alluded to by reference to the ball of thread example. Bauman binds off modernity by putting a ring or circle around it, supposedly because it has a clear beginning and end. Immediately, the map takes on a topological dimension equal to one. The assumption of one-dimensionality is then confirmed by the exclusive paradigm of power that is then confirmed by the metaphor of movement with a direction, finally reconfirming the initial topological choice. In short, the hermeneutical circle in operation here is a tête-à-tête between Bauman and a *single* thread—something akin to his paradigmatic garden path—that he claims captures the *whole* ball, the whole garden. Consequently, Bauman's narrow topological procedure was bound to end up with a topiarized image of modernity.

This all appears as a rather circuitous route to highlight certain limitations of Bauman's one-dimensional paradigm of social reproduction. Nonetheless, aside from Bauman's own invocation of chaos theory, the enthusiasm of its broader reception can be deflected back on Bauman's contrast between wild and garden cultures. Buried in this contrast is a particular notion of wilderness.

• • •

According to Bauman, the premodern perception of the world lacked "an idea of the mutability of human characteristics."[36] Although there was a recognition of the diversity among humans and their ways of life, such diversity did not appear to present a challenge nor invoke a need for explanation. Parallel to the genetic understanding of local social differentiation, broader differences were merely regarded as a part of the overall "naturalness" of creation, preordained and immutable. Therefore, the premodern cosmos, even with its observed distinctions and diversity, "presented itself as a stable, harmonious construction" that was otherwise beyond human manipulation and transformation. As a result, political rule was never conceived as being a "managerial problem." In these coexisting wild cultures, only things, not human bodies, were the object of efforts at human control. The way of life of the powerful remained distinct from that of the ruled, and it was never viewed as the model to be followed by the latter. Indeed, there was never a *conscious* attempt by the powerful to transform the modes of life of their subjects, if for no other reason than the inability to conceive of ways of life as an "object" open to manipulation.

The focus of this caricature seems to be primarily the European Middle Ages. The sixteenth century and the Pyrrhonian crisis[37] are cited as the pivotal point between the demise of wild cultures and the emergence of the universalizing garden culture. The caricature and its dating may serve merely as an heuristic device for Bauman's more central concern with a characterization of modernity. Nevertheless, the imagery it invokes raises several questions, especially regarding its affinities with the *modern* romantic tradition of lionizing rustic simplicity. The self-referential modern cage that Bauman wishes to transcend seems to return again here such that the *outsider's* view appears to be somewhat tinged by the perspective of a modernist *insider.*

A few brief remarks will suggest the nature of the problem. In a manner, the argument requires a construct of *untamed localism.* Bauman's conscious intent is to formulate a contrast to the cultivation of modernity. The supposed historical counterfactual mobilized is the image of medieval localism in which human beings tend to behave as inhabitants of nature, rather than as disciplining gardeners. This is an image of wilderness, of vastitas, where there is freedom from the constraints of cultivation, where the mind being unencumbered by the concept can experience vastare—the "ravaging" of the mind—where the complexity of nature is quite happily encountered "chaotically" and where an individual can be absorbed into the marvelous. The reverberations of this image in the eighteenth-century English landscape garden[38] and in modern romanticism[39] are almost deafening. This is not the initial point of contention that can be brought to bear on Bauman's use of the notion of wild culture. The religious resonance of the image invokes its source for the medieval West. And the strict etymological rendering of vastitas as "desert-wilderness" indicates its historical-geographical origins in the Middle East. As Jacques Le Goff observes, "The desert-wilderness, whether real or imagined, has played an important role in the major religions of Europe and Asia: Judaism, Islam, and Christianity." Le Goff offers a convenient overview of the image and its impact on the medieval West.[40] He notes that, quite often, the desert-wilderness came to represent "values opposed to those of the city." Nevertheless, and especially in the Bible, the desert as "both a symbol and an historico-geographical reality" is somewhat ambivalent: it could be the location of the chaotic other as well as the place through which humans reach God. Drawing on this tradition, the beginnings of Christian monasticism in the fourth century were set in a "desert epic." Le Goff draws attention to Athanasius's *Life of Antony* and St. Jerome's *Life of Paul* as the foundational "desert" texts of the Christian eremitical tradition, both Roman Catholic and Orthodox. In these works the theme of desert solitude and harshness was linked with a paradisaical familiarity with wild animals. However, the desert was also the home of demons, and it was through the anchorite's struggle with them that he found God.

In the West, the symbol of desert gave way to the differing geographical situation such that the idea of solitude was incorporated into the image of the forest. Since neolithic times, the forest, like the desert, had engendered an interplay between material and spiritual realities. It both embodied humans' legendary fears and demarcated the limits of profane cultivation from its sacred interior. During the Middle Ages, the warriors attempted to turn the forest into their private hunting grounds. According to Le Goff, however, the warrior also had to share the forest with the eremite and the forest laborer. Although each performed a different role, all "went to the forest to behave as men of nature, fleeing the world of culture in every sense of the word."[41]

In this vein, the medieval forest-wilderness was not merely a refuge for pagan cults, hermits, and social outcasts but also a useful resource containing precious game, food, and fuel. Therefore, in the medieval imagination there was both an attraction and a repulsion to the forest. The ferocious-looking forest dweller captures this ambivalence: his "savage" or "primitive" appearance could invoke fear, but at the same time he could be the supplier of the forest's fruits or, as in the case of the eremite, the holder of wise council, especially for the common folk. Le Goff adds that the forest dweller was regarded not merely as a guest but as the master of the forest who had tamed its wildness. He was an "ambiguous mediator" between savagery and cultivation. In this sense, the forest was not "wholly wild or isolated"; rather it was a place "on the extreme fringes of society."[42] While a distinction can be drawn between the forest-wilderness and organized society in the medieval Western mindset, the relationship was by no means uncomplicated. It should also be emphasized that while the Middle Ages waned, "the ideology of the desert" did not, a recent manifestation being certain contemporary forms of political ecology.[43]

Bauman's caricature of the Middle Ages as wild culture need not be read in an overly literal sense to be equated with this ideology of the desert. To the extent that the inner realm of the wilderness was the desired destination of the individual fleeing the cultivation of society, the description of this social formation's culture as wild seems decidedly inappropriate. Further, while these cultures no doubt drew on time-honored local traditions, the importance of the Judeo-Christian tradition and its reworking of local customs cannot be underestimated.[44] In other words, there was an integration of localism with a universalism. While this may not have produced national or regional power blocs during the medieval period, neither does it mean necessarily that social integration on a city or even village level was any less "cultivated."[45]

What appears to be at work in Bauman's argument is a narrow conception of culture that is basically a notion of ideology subjected to the parameters of the power paradigm. This leads to a theoretical "trick" similar to the Whiggish tradition of prolepsis. In Bauman's account of modern gardening culture, ideology and power tend to become indistinguishable in the unfolding of the power/knowledge vortex. Therefore, if power and knowledge are reasonably distinct, then so also are power and ideology, thus releasing "culture as ideology" into a state of relative wildness.[46] On a substantive level, this makes the social fringe-dwelling ideology of the desert-wilderness a perfect contrast for an argument primarily concerned with characterizing modernity as garden cultivation. The trouble is that while it may bind this particular image of modernity, it remains largely internal to its own primary focus and argument, that is, modernity sensu stricto. Therefore, on both theoretical and substantive historical scores, it remains less than adequate in unraveling the cultural imaginary of the Middle Ages. Moreover, the contrasting image it invokes is, or at least was, dear to the heart of modernity itself, a fact systematically banished to the wayside in Bauman's account for the sake of absolutizing the power paradigm.

Significantly, one of the originary sites in which modernity actually explored images of wilderness was the garden, in particular the eighteenth-century English landscape garden.

• • •

The natural history of the English landscape garden is comparatively short. From the early efforts of Sir John Vanbrugh, Charles Bridgeman, William Kent, and James Gibbs to the widespread "improvements" of Capability Brown, this history is more or less confined to the eighteenth century. Nonetheless, in an age lacking the speed of contemporary communications, this garden idea and its form spread like wildfire and with a matching passion not just across England but Western Europe generally. While its origins and evolution are complex, the demise of its furor can be attributed to two factors. First, from the strict viewpoint of garden design, Brown had taken the idea to such a point where it became subject to an immanent critique: in his relentless pursuit of informality, the garden was reduced to an empty cliché of rolling lawns punctuated by clumps of trees. This "studied elimination of design elements"[47] took the liberation of the garden from architecture to its logical conclusion. At the same time, it not only induced boredom among many of Brown's contemporaries but also turned attention from the landscape park toward "the natural capabilities of the countryside" beyond.[48] This latter aspect indicates the more general reason for the decline. The bounds of the naturalistic garden could no longer contain the elements it had nurtured, the images of variety, surprise, ambivalence, and informality, in short, images of wildness. To paraphrase Horace Walpole's famous comment, the whole of nature had become garden[49] and, we might add, at the expense of the landscape garden's self-identity.

At this point, garden *form* went into what would now be called a postmodern condition, in which a plurality of forms emerged, referencing themselves with a free association from garden history, and even beyond. These new garden forms can tell us a lot about fashions, but that is not necessarily all they can communicate. That, however, is another story. The other side of the present tale is the escape of the eighteenth-century's garden *idea* into the world. This is not simply about the romantics' flight into the wilderness of the sublime, or the frontiersmen's decampment from society into the solitude of the sunset. These are but instances of a specific aspect of the garden idea and therefore partial. The counterpoint to this aspect in the actual gardens was the classical form of the Palladian villa. Nonetheless, even this contrast of the architectonic and the horticultural, of classicism and romanticism, of the putator and vastitas, still does not exhaust the idea. Of further note is the innovation that at once circumscribed the garden *and* allowed it to flee its own bounds; this was the "ha-ha." It enabled the dismantling of the medieval garden wall by replacing it with a sheer sunken ditch, thus opening the garden view—something akin to Leon Battista Alberti's *finestra aperta,* yet not architectonically framed.

To use the language of Mandelbrot, this innovation can be described as a fractal dimension of the eighteenth-century garden idea. It suggests a nontopological dimension that is subsumed by neither the putator nor vastitas; it is truly between these two dimensions and not betwixt them. The double-sidedness of the garden idea hermeneutic comes into full play here. For the eighteenth century, this new dimension enabled an exploration of its own imaginary: by confronting the infinite universe without fear or fervor, it could contemplate what limits, if any, it wished to draw for its own self-constitution. Access to this new dimension impacted upon, among other things, questions of personality formation, the rise of modern aesthetics, and forms of political discourse. Consider the century's two great revolutions: whereas the topological Jacobins were so dazzled by vastitas that they became putators with a vengeance,[50] the American republicans delved into the fractal dimension of the same imaginary, the republicans being an example of what Hannah Arendt[51] took to be the modern enactment of the *political:* the political self-constitution of an "open" society. This new dimension opened a space, a *possibility* for the *modern* political exploration of freedom—a protovalue deeply embedded in the imaginary of the West. Now relieved of the self-imposed fear of the outside, of contingency, the constitutional "walls" of the polis *could* be transformed into truly human bounds. In this space, and true to the imaginary, power is approached in a reciprocal *political* mode, a completely different form of power conceptualization than that of Bauman's architectural gardener.

The unleashing of the eighteenth-century garden idea *into* the world proffers this new fractal space, in all its complexity, yet without eulogizing wilderness or banking on the certainty of the architectonic garden. Its promise is not certitude but that "freedom" could be more than merely the solitude of the wilderness stroller.

Notes

1. Ovid, *Metamorphoses,* trans. by Mary M. Innes (Harmondsworth: Penguin Classics, 1986), 4:328–32. See also Alexander Pope, "Vertumnus and Pomo-

na," in *Pope: Poetical Works*, ed. Herbert Davis, intro. by Pat Rogers (Oxford: Oxford University Press, 1983), 205–8.

2. Cf. Charles Paul Segal, *Landscape in Ovid's Metamorphoses*, Hermes, vol. 23 (Weisbaden: Franz Steiner Verlag, 1969), 68–70.

3. See Richard Heinberg, *Memories and Visions of Paradise: Exploring the Universal Myth of a Lost Golden Age* (Wellingborough: Aquarian Press, 1990); Don Ihde, *Technology and the Lifeworld: From Garden to Earth* (Bloomington and Indianapolis: Indiana University Press, 1990), esp. 11–20; Charles W. Moore, William J. Mitchell, and William Turnbull, Jr., *The Poetics of Gardens* (Cambridge, Mass.: MIT Press, 1988).

4. See, for example, J. Mordaunt Crook, "Between Art and Nature: Landscape as a Metaphor of Mind," *Times Literary Supplement*, July 5, 1991, 14.

5. In the last decade or so, and following the work of H. F. Clark, Christopher Hussey, and Nikolaus Pevsner, journals such as *Garden History* and the *Journal of Garden History* have endeavored to remedy this malaise. A recent collection that highlights the multifacetedness of gardens is Mark Francis and Randolf T. Hester, Jr., eds., *The Meaning of Gardens* (Cambridge: Mass., MIT Press, 1990). On the interdisciplinary nature of garden history, see Morris R. Brownell, "Bursting Prospect: British Garden History Now," *Eighteenth-Century Life* (Special Issue on British and American Gardens, coedited by Robert P. Maccubbin and Peter Martin) 8, no. 2 (1983): 5–18. In the same issue, see Kenneth Woodbridge, "The Nomenclature of Style in Garden History," 19–25. See also Denise Le Dantec and Jean-Pierre Le Dantec, *Reading the French Garden: Story and History,* trans. Jessica Levine (Cambridge, Mass.: MIT Press, 1990); Monique Mosser and Georges Teyssot, eds., *The History of Garden Design* (Cambridge, Mass.: MIT Press, 1991).

6. See, e.g., Marc Treib, "Power Plays: The Garden as Pet," in *Meaning of Gardens*, ed. Francis and Hester, 86–93. Treib's approach, like several in this vein, is heavily indebted to the work of the human geographer Yi-Fu Tuan and his particular power paradigm. For a short introduction to this paradigm, see Yi-Fu Tuan, "Moral Ambiguity in Architecture," *Landscape* 27, no. 3 (1983): 11–17. For a gender version of this approach, see Carole Fabricant, "Binding and Dressing Nature's Loose Tresses: The Ideology of Augustan Landscape Design," *Studies in Eighteenth-Century Culture* 8 (1979): 109–35.

7. See, e.g., John Barrell, *The Idea of Landscape and the Sense of Place, 1730–1840* (Cambridge: Cambridge University Press, 1972), Barrell, *The Dark Side of the Landscape* (Cambridge: Cambridge University Press, 1985); Ann Bermingham, *Landscape and Ideology: The English Rustic Tradition, 1740–1860* (London: Thames and Hudson, 1987); Robert Williams, "Rural Economy and the Antique in the English Landscape Garden," *Journal of Garden History* 7, no. 1 (1987): 73–96.

8. See Carole Fabricant, "The Aesthetics and Politics of Landscape in the Eighteenth Century," in *Studies in Eighteenth-Century British Art and Aesthetics,* ed. Ralph Cohen (Berkeley: University of California Press, 1985), 49–81.

9. Zygmunt Bauman, *Legislators and Interpreters: On Modernity, Post-Modernity and Intellectuals* (Cambridge: Polity Press, 1989).

10. In addition to ibid., reference is also made to Bauman's *Modernity and Ambivalence* (Cambridge: Polity Press, 1991) and "A Sociological Theory of Postmodernity," *Thesis Eleven* 29 (1991): 33–46.

11. That is, the Foucault of *Discipline and Punish* (Harmondsworth: Penguin, 1979).

12. Ernest Gellner, *Nations and Nationalism* (Oxford: Basil Blackwell, 1983), 50–52.

13. Bauman, *Legislators and Interpreters*, 45–46.

14. Ibid., 58; Bauman, *Modernity and Ambivalence*, 20–24.

15. Bauman, *Legislators and Interpreters*, 39–44.

16. Ibid., 46–49.

17. Ibid., 69–71.

18. Ibid., 93.

19. Bauman, *Modernity and Ambivalence*, 233.

20. Bauman, *Legislators and Interpreters*, 94–95.

21. Ibid., 105–9.

22. Ibid., 116.

23. Ibid., 120.

24. Ibid., 116–17.

25. Ibid., 119.

26. Bauman, "Sociological Theory," 33–34 (emphasis added).

27. A question arises here as to whether Bauman would consider Niklas Luhmann's investigations into the *inherent complexity* of modernity as "modern sociology." See Luhmann, *The Differentiation of Society* (New York: Columbia University Press, 1982).

28. Bauman, "Sociological Theory," 38.

29. Cf. F. A. Hayek's use of the gardening metaphor apropos the growth of a liberal society, in *The Road to Serfdom* (Chicago: University of Chicago Press, 1944), 18.

30. Immanuel Kant, *The Critique of Judgement*, trans. James Creed Meredith (Oxford: Clarendon Press, 1978), pt. 1, bk. 2, 186–87; Jean-Jacques Rousseau, *La Nouvelle Héloïse or the New Julie*, trans. Judith McDowell (1761; rpt. University Park: Pennsylvania State University Press, 1968), pt. 4, letter 11, 304–15; Horace Walpole, *The History of the Modern Taste in Gardening* and *Journals of Visits to Country Seats* (New York and London: Garland Reprint Series, vol. 18, 1982); Edmund Burke, *A Philosophical Enquiry into the Origins of Our Ideas of the Sublime and Beautiful*, ed. and intro. James T. Boulton (Notre Dame: University of Notre Dame Press, 1968), pt. 3, sec. 4, 100–101.

Early in the seventeenth century Henry Wotton, no doubt under the influence of sixteenth-century Italian gardens, expressed an inclination on this separation: "First, I must note a certain contrarietie betweene *building* and *gardening*: For as Fabriques should bee *regular*, so Gardens should bee *irregular*, or at least cast into a very wild *Regularitie*." See Henry Wotton, *The Elements of Architecture* (1624), extracts in John Dixon Hunt and Peter Willis, eds., *The Genius of Place: The English Landscape Garden, 1620–1820* (London: Paul Elek, 1975), 48.

31. Benoit B. Mandelbrot, *The Fractal Geometry of Nature* (rev. ed., New York: W. H. Freeman, 1983), 17–18.

32. Ibid., 17.

33. This is surprising given Bauman's earlier work on hermeneutics (*Hermeneutics and the Social Sciences* [London: Hutchison, 1978]). Moreover, while the notion of "effective dimension" may have become of central importance to the new physics, especially from the early twentieth century on, its interpretive insight is not all that new, given the long tradition of hermeneutical interpretation. Cf., for instance, Hans-George Gadamer on the "principle of effective-history" (*Truth and Method* [New York: Continuum, 1975], esp. 267 and following).

34. Compare these images to some produced in the eighteenth-century "plurality of worlds" debate. See, for instance, Thomas Wright of Durham, *An Original Theory or New Hypothesis of the Universe*, intro. Michael A. Hoskin (1750; rpt. London and New York: MacDonald/American Elsevier, 1971), plates 12, 15, 16, and especially 17, 31, and 32, that Wright describes as finite views of infinity. What could also be conjectured is a kind of parallel between topology's "twisting and turning" of mathematical spaces and the "twisting and wiggling" of "rococo" in the three-dimensional space of the eighteenth-century landscape garden. On this latter aspect, see John Harris, "The Artinatural Style," in *The Rococo in England: A Symposium*, ed. Charles Hind (London: Victoria and Albert Museum, 1986), 8–20.

35. Mandelbrot, *Fractal Geometry*, 23–24.

36. Bauman, *Legislators and Interpreters*, 83.

37. While noting the responses of Marin Mercenne and Pierre Gassendi to this crisis—the formulation of a *via media* between absolute skepticism and absolute certainty—Bauman states that this sort of response enjoyed only temporary popularity, while René Descartes's position was far more important and enduring (ibid., 86–87). However, as the research of Keith Hutchison has demonstrated, the notion of a via media, of constructive/mitigated skepticism was crucial in the rise of the new natural philosophy in the seventeenth century, especially in England. See Keith Hutchison, "What Happened to Occult Qualities in the Scientific Revolution," *Isis* 73, no. 267 (1982): 233–53. See also, Richard H. Popkin, *The History of Scepticism from Erasmus to Spinoza* (Berkeley: University of California Press, 1979); Henry G. van Leeuwen, *The Problem of Certainty in English Thought, 1630–1690* (The Hague: Martinus Nijhoff, 1963); Barbara J. Shapiro, *Probability and Certainty in Seventeenth-Century England* (Princeton, N.J.: Princeton University Press, 1983).

Moreover, a decisive aspect that seems to be assumed in Bauman's argument is Foucault's one-sided account of mathematical probability in which the emergence of modern probability is equated with the *Port Royal Logic*. For a critique of this account, see Douglas Lane Patey, *Probability and Literary Form: Philosophic Theory and Literary Practice in the Augustan Age* (Cambridge: Cambridge University Press, 1984), appendix A, "The Foucault-Hacking Hypothesis," 266–73.

38. Consider Thomas Whately's recommendation of the *expressivist* moment over the *emblematic* in his *Observations on Modern Gardening* (1770; rpt. New York

and London: Garland Publishing, 1982). Referring to the use of temples, cascades, cypruses, and so on as means to invoke subjects of history, poetry, and tradition, Whately writes that such allusion is "naturally" inappropriate to the garden. Rather, "it should seem to have been suggested by the scene: a transitory image, which irresistibly occurred; not sought for, not laboured; and have the force of a *metaphor*, free from the detail of an allegory" (151, emphasis added). Later in this same section, Whately leaves us in no doubt as to the effect he is writing about: "It suffices that the scenes of nature have a power to affect our imagination and our sensibility; for such is the constitution of the human mind, that if once it is agitated, the emotion often spreads far beyond the occasion; when the passions are roused, their course is unrestrained; when the fancy is on the wing, its flight is unbounded; and quitting the inanimate objects which first gave them their spring, we may be led by thought above thought, widely differing in degree, but still corresponding in character, till we rise from familiar subjects up to the sublimest conceptions, and are rapt in the contemplation of whatever is great or beautiful, which we see in nature, feel in man, or attribute to divinity" (156). Whately's *Observations* was extremely popular, going into many editions as well as French and German translations. It was often used by foreign visitors to the famous landscape gardens of England, including Thomas Jefferson on his garden tour in 1786 (see the preface to the reprint edition).

39. For a contemporary example of this, see the critical legal studies of Roberto Unger (e.g., *False Necessity* [Cambridge: Cambridge University Press, 1987]). Cf. Andrew Fraser, "Reconstituting Enlightened Despotism," *Telos* no. 78 (1988–89): 169–82; Peter Murphy, "To Create Anew the Universe: Political Romanticism and the Promethean Vision of Roberto Unger," *Thesis Eleven* 28 (1991): 113–26.

40. Jacques Le Goff, "The Wilderness in the Medieval West," in *The Medieval Imagination* (Chicago: University of Chicago Press, 1988), 47–59.

41. Ibid., 52.

42. Ibid., 56.

43. See Tim Luke, "The Dreams of Deep Ecology," *Telos* no. 76 (1988): 65–92.

44. Le Goff, "Warriors and Conquering Bourgeois: The Images of the City in the Twelfth-Century French Literature," in *Medieval Imagination,* 168.

45. Compare, for instance, Georges Duby, *The Age of the Cathedrals: Art and Society, 980–1420,* trans. Eleanor Levieux and Barbara Thompson (Chicago: University of Chicago Press, 1981); Emmanuel Le Roy Ladurie, *Montaillou: Cathars and Catholics in a French Village, 1294–1324* (Harmondsworth: Penguin, 1980); Le Dantec and Le Dantec, *Reading the French Garden,* 13–20.

46. This is basically "a cogitivistic reduction of culture." Here culture is conceived of "as a programming instance which does for society—*mutatis mutandis*—what the genetic code does for the organism." See Johann Arnason, "Culture and Imaginary Significations," *Thesis Eleven* 22 (1989): 36.

47. Hunt and Willis, "Introduction," in *Genius of Place,* 32.

48. Ibid.

49. Horace Walpole, *History of the Modern Taste*, 264.

50. Cf. Ferenc Fehér, "The Cult of the Supreme Being and the Limits of the Secularization of the Political," in *The French Revolution and the Birth of Modernity*, ed. Fehér (Berkeley: University of California Press, 1990), 174–97. See also, Fehér, "Redemptive and Democratic Paradigms in Radical Politics," *Telos* no. 63 (1985): 147–56.

51. Hannah Arendt, *On Revolution* (Harmondsworth: Penguin, 1973).

PAUL R. HARRISON

Border Closures

The United Provinces fought an ultimately successful war of independence from Spain between 1568 and 1648 that included the creation of a Dutch Republic in 1581. The significance of these events for the constitution of political modernity has been underestimated compared to the attention paid to the American war of independence in the 1770s. The Dutch were participants in a process that effectively destroyed the attempts of Spain to establish a territorially based empire. Spain's desire for empire was driven by the archaic imaginary of medieval Christendom combined with the means of modern statecraft and, increasingly, by the proto-totalitarian logic of the counterreformation that sought to extirpate all social division. Spain's failure was an essential ingredient for the emergence of the modern European state system. Such a system provided an arrangement of checks and balances and an essential ingredient of what one historian has called "unity in diversity," which enabled European economic dynamism to develop in the context of a complex set of mutual constraints and beneficial competition that could not have been present in an imperial system.

Baruch Spinoza's life began after the demise of Iberian hegemony and coincided with the rise of the United Provinces to hegemonic status in the world economy. Spinoza was present, therefore, at the birth of the modern nation-state, while we are living through, perhaps, the moment of its death. Of course, it is probably still far too soon to utter the funeral rites, yet the signs of its increasing obsolescence are all too prominent. Earlier we only looked toward the system of international relations to provide us with the means to ensure that the diversity of our interests was constrained by a recognition of our mutual interest in the stability that only peaceful relations among states can bring.

Currently, we are witnessing the collapse of a world economy made in America and the emergence of something historically new. One scenario is that this new world economy will contain two centers—Brussels and Tokyo/New York—or, more probably, three centers—Brussels, Tokyo, and New York, where Brussels stands for European integration perhaps as far east as the Urals, Tokyo for Asian-Pacific integration, and New York for the integration of the Americas. The other scenario is the emergence of new types of horizontal relations that do not pass necessarily through any form of regional integration whatsoever. This scenario would see the emergence of what Fernand Braudel calls the "economy of the world" or what, following Sismondi, he refers to as the "market of the universe." The project of an economy of the world without either a world economy or hegemonic centers has both appealing and disturbing consequences. Its appeal lies in the potential globalization of all forms of economic, technological, social, and cultural relations. This is the imaginary project of the world as a multiplicity of communication channels, which would permit a tumult of information that would do more than just transgress state boundaries. This imaginary scenario is, perhaps, one in which the proximity of the economic internationalism and voodoo economics of the New Right to the autopoetics and intellectual junk bonds of postmodernism is sufficiently clear to warn us of its dangers. The question is what room is there for politics and, in particular, democratic politics. Are we to live in a bureaucratically integrated multipolar world or the depolarized, deterritorialized world of the postmodern New Right?

We are also witnessing what Spinoza himself saw: the aftermath of the breakdown of an imperial system of domination. In our case, the Soviet system has crumbled, for him it was the Spanish. Although the differences between the two systems are enormous, some tentative parallels are also clear: the destruction of internal economic development through the expulsion of economically active groups, the development of a religious or quasi-religious system of ideas that defines for all what must and must not be believed, the prosecution of the drive to destroy all social division within and beyond the boundaries of the nation-state. The outlets for this drive, which soon found their limits within Europe, were also projected outside of Europe: for Spain, it was the Americas; for the USSR, it was the third world in general. The destruction wreaked by this indissoluble, if changeable, connection between politics, profit, and theology or quasi-theology was already counterpoised by Spinoza to the peaceable commercial practices of the

Dutch. Of course, the Iberian interlude brought Christianity and fire-arms to Japan. The Dutch brought trade, and in order to secure it the Dutch East India Company was prepared, as Spinoza approvingly notes, to prohibit Christian religious practice among its employees.[1] In this chapter, I will concentrate on this uncoupling of theology from social life, both economic and more particularly political life.

• • •

At the heart of Spinoza's political philosophy is the attempt to free politics from religion and to think through the constituents of the form of human government most conducive to human liberty, given the passions of mankind. The attempt to free politics from religion passes through the question of interpretation, whereas that of government passes through social contract theory. This is not peculiar to Spinoza. Thomas Hobbes's work also attempts to work out new relationships both between the individual and the state and between religion and politics. The invention of modern politics passes through a radical de-sacralization of the institution of society that rediscovers a different type of relationship between one individual and another, which as a con-sequence effectively places back on the agenda the question of democ-racy. This occurs through the splitting of the religious into both a shell of superstition and a kernel of universal faith, as well as into inner belief and outward observance. The privatization of inner conviction and the institution of a minimalist belief system effectively detaches religious passions from the public realm, and the question of the institution of society can, therefore, be posed in a radically new fashion.

In order to achieve this position, both Hobbes and Spinoza had to raise the question of interpretation, because what was at stake was a reading of the Bible and, more particularly, a reading of the miracles and prophecies in it. They wanted to rescue the Bible from the popu-lar imagination. Thus, Spinoza's interpretation was guided by the op-position between the imagination, the miraculous, and the popular, on the one hand, and reason, on the other. Imagination is a kind of ple-beian cognition, and the interpretation of the Bible's narrative tales prepares the way for some theological legislation. This takes the form of an outline of certain nonrational elements of dogma that must be publicly recognized in order to assure the obedience of subjects in a state free of religious discord.

This simultaneously interpretive and legislative move in Spinoza's political theory was undoubtedly precipitated by what historians have called the general crisis of the seventeenth century. I will not rehearse the multiple dimensions of this crisis other than mention the importance of the religious conflict and the subsequent intellectual reaction. According to Stephen Toulmin, this reaction took the form of an attempt to decontextualize intellectual questions in order to render them immune to the religious quarrel that would have otherwise prohibited their solution.[2] Hence, the modernist intellectual strategy of decontextualization is contrasted by Toulmin to the postmodern strategy of recontextualization. There is something to this argument, but there is also something curiously simplistic about taking at face value the programmatic statements of philosophers, particularly when they presuppose almost entirely that René Descartes is the modernist philosopher par excellence. If we examine Spinoza's *Ethics* (and Spinoza is a seventeenth-century philosopher who is curiously neglected by Toulmin), then we can find some confirmation of Toulmin's point in the geometric method that Spinoza chose to demonstrate his philosophy and in his intellectualization of faith that prohibits all recourse to the traditional rewards promised to those who keep the faith. This is a decontextualizing gambit that certainly promised a solution that transcended the warring parties.

What is played out in the *Ethics,* however, is a more complex game of contextualization and decontextualization than Toulmin would admit. It is a similar case with Spinoza's *Theologico-Political Treatise.* This work appears to lead quite straightforwardly, and in conformity with Toulmin's argument, from a critique of the rhetorical excesses of the popular imagination to the bases of a dogmatic religion. Yet Spinoza is quite clear that his is a work of interpretation on a series of interpretations that he will qualify, perhaps all too conventionally, as imaginative. Furthermore, he is also quite clear that his act of interpretation is both an historical act and quite contextually specific. The interpretation of the Bible is to pave the way for the consideration of the type of sovereign power needed to radically neutralize the religious question.

Hence, the first task of the *Treatise* is to free politics from a type of religion, while its second task is to consider the institution of a civil state. In the context of a civil state, the way Spinoza uses social contract theory also seems to displace the classical question about the best form of government onto what is considered to be the more fundamental question concerning the rights that the individual retains after the institution of society is complete, because they are the rights for which they surrendered their power by entering into an agreement in order to secure them more rationally. The confrontation with religion that early modern political thinking undertakes goes hand in hand with the conceptualization of a presocial individual without any tie or *religio.* The state of nature exists, according to Spinoza, "prior to religion."[3] It is an image of humans where their passion and power are coextensive and where, according to Spinoza, their imagination leads to action that escapes conscious control. The assumption that humans are not already social animals places thinkers like Spinoza before the question of the very possibility of the institution of society itself. The dictum that society does not exist is one possible variation that could emerge from this type of questioning. Yet, the real purpose of this type of questioning is to allow early modern political thought to question the prevailing institution of society. The social bond is to be refashioned beginning with, and entirely through, the passions and power of that presocial atom that is an individual in the state of nature.

Spinoza begins his *Treatise* by stating in his preface that law must be prohibited from entering "the domain of speculative thought" and that "revelation and philosophy stand on totally different footings."[4] Theology must henceforth respect the autonomy of philosophy as an intellectual activity and, just as importantly, theology must desist from employing the law in order to control opinion and thought. Spinoza defines human law as "a plan of living which serves only to render life and the state secure," whereas the divine law "only regards the highest good, in other words, the true knowledge of God and love."[5] The realpolitik of human law that emerges here conceptualizes human law as a kind of emergency brake on human passions, that is, as an activity that aims to neutralize the conflict between one human's power and another that exists in the state of nature. The definition of democracy that emerges out of this conception of human law is one that sees it as "a society which wields all its power as a whole."[6] In other words, the theory of democracy that emerges in Spinoza's work emphasizes, albeit with very important additions and qualifications, the centrality of instituting a securely established sovereign power. The preeminent importance that Spinoza accords to nation building for the attainment of security reflects that long-term process of the domestication of physical force that Max Weber and Norbert Elias, among others, have pointed to in various works. Hence, the intellectualization of culture, the separation of politics from religion, and the identification of politics with rendering a state secure (three hallmarks of modernity) are already delineated by Spinoza in this work. The intellectualist approach to culture emerges most strongly in Spinoza's interpretation of the Bible. The separation of politics from religion appears in a quite interesting form in his interpretation of Hebrew theocracy. Finally, some additions and qualifications must be made with regard to Spinoza's theory of democratic politics.

At the end of his *Ethics*, Aristotle devotes his attention to the horizontal ties of friendship (*philia*), while at the beginning of the *Politics* he talks of the successive formation of associations up until the formation of the city-state that has as its goal not merely the securing of life but the securing of the good life. The continuity between ethics and politics is broken in modern politics as is ultimately the continuity between theology and politics, but the separation of theology from politics does not preclude the use of theological models in examining the form of modern politics. The vertical relationship that exists between God and humankind is used as a vehicle to think through the relationship that exists between the state and its citizens. We find that, for example, Hobbes devotes the second half of the *Leviathan* to a study of the Bible in order to discover the foundations of a Christian commonwealth and that Spinoza devotes the major part of his *Theologico-Political Treatise* to a study of the miraculous and of the political history of the Hebrews.[7] Hence, both the question of interpretation (and its relationship to reason) and the question of the imagination (and its relationship to reason) are raised in a primarily theological context.

In Hobbes's *Leviathan* the topic of the imagination is introduced directly after that of sense and long before that of reason. Imagination is defined, in effect, as decaying sense, and as such it is related to memory, dreams, apparitions, visions, ghosts, prophecies, prognostications, and the like. Reason, on the other hand, is defined as reckoning and, hence, the rendering of an account is evaluated strictly in terms of accountancy. The problem for such an accountant's conception of reason is to render an account of the religious and those types of revelation such as the miraculous and the prophetic that are thought to belong mainly to the imagination. As these miracles and prophecies are a large part of the Holy Scriptures, Hobbes is left with the problem of reconciling these events to his reason. His solution is to interpret the Bible in such a way as to construe those things that are beyond reason as above it but yet not contrary to it. He proposes to do this by "captivating," as he puts it, his understanding and reason.

Spinoza's interpretive strategy is not so much one of forbearing contradiction as of exposing it. He wants to read the Bible historically so as to remove the speculative shell and thus arrive at the moral kernel. This makes his reading rational as well because the moral kernel is that which reason rescues from the shell of superstition. Here again, as with Hobbes, the superstitious and the imagination tend to be identified. Yet, what also must be emphasized is the way in which interpretation is made compatible with reason and the way in which a simultaneously interpretive and legislative mode of thought work together. Interpretation sets to work on biblical narratives. Spinoza's "universal rule" for interpreting scripture is "to accept nothing as an authoritative Scriptural statement which we do not perceive very clearly when we examine it in the light of its history."[8] This means, first, that a scriptural statement must be subject to linguistic analysis. Second, the metaphorical nature and meaning of a figure of speech can only be decided from within the resources of the text(s) within which it is lodged and not by direct recourse to our natural reason. Moreover, the history and subsequent reception of the text must also be reconstructed.

What makes Spinoza's theory of reading necessary is the fact that "no one except Christ received the revelations of God without the aid of imagination, whether in words or vision."[9] This means that prophecy or revelation is mediated knowledge, that is, knowledge that, except in the case of Christ, necessarily passes through the mediation of signs which, as extrinsic reasons, assure us of the objective reality of the imagination. In addition, such knowledge is impossible without imagination, and the more vivid the imagination, the more valid the knowledge. Prophets are those who possess an imagination that enables them to believe themselves breathed into by the spirit or *ruagh* of God. Hobbes refers to this by the English word inspiration and defines it as "the blowing into man [of] some thin and subtle aire, or wind, in such a manner a man filleth a bladder with his breath; or if Spirits be not corporeall, but have their existence in the fancy, it is nothing but the blowing in of a Phantasme."[10] For both Hobbes and Spinoza, the classical doctrine of the imagination is captured within an interpretive strategy that relegates it not just to inferior modes of knowledge but to religiously determined modes. Of course, there is really no need to trek back through those immense black European forests filled with spirits and spiritualism that gave birth to Nazism, back to those prophetic and poetical texts with their inexhaustible thinking about fire and the flame which, as that which is heterogeneous to origin, both shape the way we think about spirit and are able to escape the circularity of Western metaphysics themselves in order to escape this religious capturing of spirit and imagination.[11] In short, there is more to Western thought than its Platonizing tendencies and, hence, an escape route into either pagan or prophetic thought is not needed.

Interpretation becomes, therefore, a reading strategy that controls the excesses of imagination that appear in the prophecies and miracles that attune the Bible to the popular imagination but which a disenchanted reading uncovers through a process of historical interpretation. The upshot of such a reading is an attempt to design a universal faith that will command obedience out of the speculative quarrels that emerge from the differing readings of the Bible. Thus, the freeing of theology and philosophy from faith takes the form of the development of a kind of minimalist theology that frees dogma from the religious imagination of the multitude.

Spinoza's *Treatise* is dominated by the opposition between interpretive and prophetic knowledge and by the opposition between superstition, grounded in imagination, and the claims of reason that are denied by religious fiat. The place accorded to imagination in Spinoza's "Treatise on the Emendation of the Intellect" and in the *Ethics* is, however, somewhat different. On the one hand, Spinoza's ontology and ethics remain both very traditional and conform to the stance taken in his *Theologico-Political Treatise*. At one point, he notes: "Someone, perhaps, will think that fiction is limited by fiction, but not by intellection."[12] In reply to this very modern or postmodern issue, Spinoza gives a traditional response. His answer is that there are, in effect, eternal truths of reason that the intellect can clearly and distinctly perceive and that the path toward the separation of fictions from eternal truth lies through the emendation of the intellect. The province of the imagination becomes that of singular and corporeal things. Thus, the imagination only flourishes when acted upon by singular things, such as this or that piece of theater, but is unaffected by the class of all possible theatrical pieces. Similarly, the imagination only flourishes when it is affected by bodies. The imagination and the fictions that emerge therefrom are due to the imagination's dependence on fortuitous sensations that arise from external causes. Hence, miracles, prophecies, and the like, which depend on external signs, are products of the imagination.

On the other hand, Spinoza's ultimate relativization of the imagination only occurs after he has accorded it an extraordinarily important place. This occurs in two different respects. First, Spinoza argues that, for example, when the intellect perceives things eternally it perceives things as infinite in terms of number and duration and, hence, it has no need of the imagination. However, Spinoza also asserts that when the intellect "imagines things, it perceives them under a certain number, determinate duration and quantity."[13] The imagination may merely rave, as Spinoza writes elsewhere, when it deals with substance and eternity, but when he deals once again with measure, time, and number he argues that they are nothing but modes of imagination. This emphasis on the schematizing capacity of the imagination means that Spinoza paves the way for the emergence of the modern concern with the imagination that occurs with the inauguration of the analytic of finitude.

The second respect in which the imagination acquires extraordinary importance is with respect to the human body. The purportedly postmodern view that the impact of power relations on the body cannot be resisted through an appeal to the universal but only through the "counterstroke" of other powers that are embodied in other forces is distinctly premodern or, more accurately, early modern. For Spinoza, an affect can only be restrained by another stronger affect that is opposite to the first. At this point of his doctrine there is no room for the knowledge of good and evil except insofar as they are considered as affects.[14]

What is an affect? Affects or affections are, for Spinoza, "affections of the body by which the body's power of acting is increased or diminished."[15] The affects of our body are determined, according to Spinoza, by the imaginations of the mind. As a consequence, "the Mind, as far as it can, strives to imagine those things that increase or aid the Body's power of acting."[16] The imagination is, therefore, that part of the unconscious force or striving that determines how the body will represent to itself the various possibilities that it may have at any time to both preserve itself and increase its own power. Our imagination both directs our power and augments our joy. This emphasis on the representational capacity of the imagination with respect to the body and its striving paves the way for the modern concern with the imagination that occurs within modern conceptions of the psyche.

• • •

The notion of the affects and their relation with the imagination determine how Spinoza treats the main question of the *Theologico-Political Treatise*, namely, the institution of a civil society. The notion of the affects functions to remove politics from moral considerations by conceiving of humans as beings for whom virtue and power, or right and power, are initially understood as one and the same. Here, once again, the supposedly postmodern and pragmatic view of humans or the self as a "centerless and contingent web" is already present in early modern philosophy from Francis Bacon to Baruch Spinoza. Hence, the question of the institution of civil society does not concern the moralization of this self, rather it is a question of the use of affect against affect, power against power, threat against threat. The institution of politics is, first of all, the institution of a civil state. The form of a civil state is subsidiary to the role it plays in making "a common rule of life" possible through threat. The institution of a civil state in conformity with reason results in the formation of a community in which power is not so much curbed as transferred. Individuals are no longer "conditioned by the force and desire of individuals, but by the power and will of the whole body."[17] Only after the institution of a state will it become possible to separate right from power, that is, after the investment of power in the sovereign. Spinoza's contractarian view of the institution of the state results in his definition of democracy, in the first place not so much as a type of government but as an inaugural gesture of full and equal surrender of humankind's natural rights and powers to a sovereign state.

Nowhere is the early modern fascination with the notion of a compact, contract, or covenant more deeply held than in Spinoza's work. The strange and modern aspect of his *Theologico-Political Treatise* is that his focus on the idea of a covenant leads him to break out of the classical doctrine of politics with its tripartite division of politics into monarchies, aristocracies, and democracies. This division is employed in Spinoza's more conventional *Political Treatise*. What concerns Spinoza in the *Theologico-Political Treatise* is the form of government he calls theocracy, because the original model of the idea of the contract or covenant that fascinates Spinoza as a contract theorist is found in the history of the Hebrews as it is described in the Old Testament. Spinoza describes the emergence of the Hebrew state as an act of free and equal transference of everyone's natural rights—which he qualifies as being "as in a democracy"—to God, rather than to another person. This religious covenant forms the model through which the social contract itself will be thought, although the two are otherwise quite distinct.

Although the relation between the individual and the institution of politics is modeled after that between the individual and God, Spinoza puts the accent not so much on God as a transcendent source as on the power of the "we" or the community of God's "equal and beloved children" that is formed out of the contract. The upshot of his interpretation is not the justification of theocratic rule but the identification of the importance of splitting the public form of faith from theological and philosophical ideas, as well as the proposal that the state should concern itself with the theological and leave the philosophical alone. What he is arguing against here is both the intrusion of partisan religious superstition into the affairs of state and the ability of the spiritual powers—whether they be Protestants or counterreformationists—to usurp (or try to usurp) the temporal powers. Hence, Spinoza's definition of security as the primary purpose of human law seems to be satisfiable only if the spiritual power is subordinated to the secular power. This is what his political history of the Hebrews provides him with: an image of a state as a secure state because the religion is, in effect, a civil religion or a religion of belonging.

This solution anticipates, in many ways, Jean-Jacques Rousseau although Rousseau's models are Roman. It is a solution that says, in other words, the worship of God does not interfere with the security of the state, where dogma is defined as minimally as possible and in a way that emphasizes the power of the community. The result is a state made secure by, as Rousseau puts it, "ardent patriotism." The state is to acquire a kind of weak sacral power immanent to it as an association of free and equal citizens. In this way, the insecurity of modern European states, which results from the complete splitting of spiritual from temporal power, and the multiplication of religious dogma that this produces, can be overcome.

In Spinoza's theory, therefore, the creation of a community of citizens is not simply an act of establishing such a community as sovereign but an act that comes about through the full and equal surrender of natural rights to a state that creates a community of citizens whose principal virtue is obedience. The act of participation and the process of coming to an agreement is one that precedes the establishment of a community of citizens and, in Spinoza's politics, both the security of the state and the patriotism of its citizens arise out of such a surrender. What is modern about such a conception is that it accords security priority over democracy and, indeed, mainly views democracy in terms of an inaugurating act that institutes a civil state via a covenant.

The significance and peculiarity of Spinoza's version of contract theory goes further. First, Spinoza depicts the Hebrew state before and after what he calls Moses' "sovereign kingship." Spinoza sketches a picture of a primitive democracy before Moses where "all had an equal right to consult the deity, to accept and interpret His laws, so that they all had an exactly equal share in the government."[18] He then describes a theocratic form of government after Moses that functions in the context of a separation of powers that sees powers counterbalanced by other powers in a way that anticipates the interpretation of the English model of government in Locke and Montesquieu. This comes about because Moses, according to Spinoza, "invested no one with the power of consulting God" and, as a consequence, "no one wielded all the power of a sovereign."[19] Government then became the administration of a legacy of religious law. Governing power, as Spinoza notes, was shared between those who interpreted the law (a kind of judiciary) and those who constituted the executive (a kind of warrior elite). The warrior elite rather than the judiciary provided the state with strong executive government.

Despite the fact that there is little organized popular participation, Spinoza argues that the government rested on popular support. The main benefits of such a system lie, according to Spinoza, in the security it provided for life and property. Moreover, citizens were protected from despotism because of the absence of hereditary kingship, from tyrannical government because of the separation of powers, and from the usurpation of their rights because those rights formed a part of religious law whose continued observance by the governing powers established, for Spinoza, the popular nature of such a form of government. The significance of the model is in its example of a strong and powerful community that has a strong yet balanced form of government resting on popular support without being dependent on popular participation. It is with this model that Spinoza tries to think through solutions to the political problems of the United Provinces and of European states in general.

The second peculiarity of Spinoza's doctrine, and the one that he contends distinguishes his contract theory from Hobbes, is his argument in favor of the right to freedom of speech. If up until now I have stressed security, it is both because it has priority in relation to the institution of a civil state and because the argument in favor of liberty is, in fact, predicated on the priority of security to liberty. The modernity of Spinoza's politics lies, first, in the fact that his conception of a democratic institution of a civil society presupposes the institution of majority rule on the basis that the individual should not cede his power to a form of government over which he would have no further influence. Second, it lies in the fact that not all rights or powers are transferred by individuals to the sovereign power and that, as a consequence, individuals still have rights against the community thus instituted. Third, it rests on Spinoza's argument that it is the fact and not the motive of obedience that makes humans subjects of a state. Hence, the sovereign power does not have the minds of her subjects at her disposition. Spinoza explicitly excludes, therefore, the idea that individuals can either willingly or by compulsion transfer their "natural right of free reason and judgement."[20]

The idea of the continued existence of natural rights means, in effect, that the total surrender of all natural rights would endanger the purpose of entering into a covenant, which is of course to provide the security of living in a human community. Government is rational government insofar as it continues to pursue that aim. If a government should act tyrannically toward a subject, it would, in effect, be abrogating an individual's right to live in security free from fear. Hence, government should also have liberty as an aim, for its task is to enable individuals, as Spinoza writes, "to develop their minds and bodies in security, and to employ their reason unshackled."[21] This means that the state has no right to intervene on speculative matters that are the province of individual judgment. Moreover, on matters of human law, individuals may exercise their power of judgment to criticize a law that they must nevertheless continue to obey. The idea of civil disobedience emerges, therefore, as a right or power of control over, or monitoring of, the activities of government in the light of the purposes of the institution of civil society itself.

Thus far my interpretation has emphasized the modernity of Spinoza's politics. However, it is possible to interpret his work in an antimodernist or postmodernist frame.[22] First, this is true because his philosophy in general is a philosophy of immanence rather than of transcendence. This means that thought and extension are modes of one substance, rather than two differing substances. This one substance called God or nature is immanent in the world, and everything in the world expresses it. The result is an ontology in which some of the inherited dualisms, such as that between mind and body, or free will and necessity, are relativized insofar as they are already viewed as modes or attributes of the one substance. Thus, in his political philosophy the argument for the rationality of the transition from the state of nature to the civil state is one in which the notion of reason cannot play any part that is contrary to nature. It is not reason that curbs natural power, but natural power itself.

Moreover, the opposition between individual and community can be relativized insofar as the principles that underlie the transition from the state of nature to the civil state do not involve the limitation of the individual's natural power by already established principles of right, but by the mere transference of the individual's power into the hands of a collective body embodying the collective power. Hence, it is not collective right that curbs the natural rights of the individual but the collective power that is now in the hands of the community. This community will, on the basis of its power, determine what is right. This is a framework in which relations of force or power are pitted against other relations of power, and the possibility of mediation (and the rationality of mediating criteria) is ruled out of court as a "stepping out of immanence" or, quite simply, "teleological."

Such an interpretation brings either the danger of the overestimation of power and/or the danger of merging the idea of power and community in a way that constitutes a model that we could call communitarian vitalism. Spinoza's well-known horror of the multitude, which is particularly clear in the way he both constructs his reading of the Bible and sets limits to popular participation, argues against such an interpretation. Moreover, the conclusion of Spinoza's reading of the

Hebrews' political history is that the repetition of such a model in modernity is no longer possible where the social contract is a secular rather than religious model, where the advent of Christianity means that the word is inscribed in humans' hearts and not in stone and, most importantly, where the necessity of states to live peaceably among themselves is paramount.

Yet, what is also clear is that in thinking through the form that modern politics should take, the Hebrew rather than the Greek model holds the important lessons. Hence, Spinoza wants a state in which the sovereign power is the sovereign interpreter of religion so that the state may have a strong but minimalist national-religious imaginary that is not fractured by rival religious imaginaries. Although it is also a state with popular sovereignty, it is one in which the existence of a strong and powerful executive with the ability to enforce its decrees seems more important than the existence of organized popular assemblies with the right of permanently exercising popular sovereignty. It is a state in which an individual retains a natural right "to think as he pleases and say what he likes," but Spinoza does not say, or did not live to say, how and under what institutional mechanisms such a right could be exercised. Moreover, it is a state in which commerce will flourish due to the state's ability to insulate commercial activity from religious considerations and influence.

Spinoza's design for a rational civil state shows the influence of his time, where the needs to uncouple the religious imagination from politics and to create a secure state with a strong national imaginary, while leaving room for liberty, were all important. This context dictated his choice of interpretive models and the supremacy of the twin values of security and liberty. Spinoza's politics are not the only politics in which the contract model is deployed. The contract model itself is but one of several models that were deployed in modern political philosophy. Thus, its specific influence on the shape of modern politics is less easy to determine than the effects of the model of the social contract. What is, in many ways, singular about Spinoza's version is the way in which the political history of the Hebrews becomes a focus for the rethinking of modern politics. In Spinoza's work the nature of modern democracy sounds less Greek than those who are accustomed to thinking with their ears would like to admit.

• • •

The usage of the Hebrews' political history leads to what is, in many respects, the most remarkable aspect of Spinoza's contract theory: its attempt to push beyond the concept of state and toward that of nation. The notion that the modern state can no longer tolerate religious differences due to the inevitable conflict arising out of sectarian disputes means that the tolerance of individual differences, which Spinoza supports, is born out of the neutralization of fundamental communal differences. The modern nation-state effects a fundamental closure of its borders against, above all else in Spinoza's time, religious infiltration. It initiates a homogenizing effect on the basis of which heterogeneity will be allowed to prevail. Of course, the border closure that the nation-state of the nineteenth and twentieth centuries effected was not one founded mainly on religious criteria. The criteria employed were mainly linguistic, ethnic, and even racial.

The current reemergence of the nation in the Soviet Union and Eastern Europe is a process in which mainly ethnic criteria are being mobilized. The Armenians of Nagorno-Karabakh, for example, live on one side of a border between two ethnically different republics of the former Soviet Union, which only became the wrong side of the border when those constituent parts of a greater Empire started to form their own autonomous political institutions. The modern nation-state still finds it difficult to say "we" when there are still plenty of "them" around.

Of course, from the time of the American and French Revolutions there has been an alternative model of nation-state formation that has relied both on more formalistic and voluntaristic criteria of citizenship. However, the creation of an American Republic did not have to deal with problems of ethnic heterogeneity, if we exclude the indigenous populations that were simply not taken into account. The celebrated diversity of America in this regard largely postdates its national foundation. The work of fashioning a homogeneous France out of its constituent elements was already substantially accomplished by the French monarchy. This inheritance provides one of the elements of continuity that allowed the political experimentalism of the revolution. Hence, the idea of the nation as "a daily plebiscite" (Renan) presupposes the historical work of countless prenational generations. There is no doubt that, whatever its causes, the possession of closed borders enables far more universalistically defined borders—criteria for citizenship and the like—than would otherwise be the case for a state beginning its life with contested borders.

Spinoza's politics point toward such a voluntaristic model. There is no doubt that the attempt to protect the state from religious disputes through the elevation of the principle of the security of the state over the religious differences that wracked seventeenth-century Europe represented a decisive step in what is conventionally called the process of secularization. However, it is nowhere clearer than in Spino-

za's texts that what the state gains in the process is a quasi-sacred nimbus that both legitimates and is made possible by the state, namely, the
nation as a focus of loyalty beyond such things as religious differences. Within this context, democracy becomes possible. Therefore, the
lesson of Spinoza is not so much that the importance of a secular state
in a nation is threatened by religious absolutism but that the obsolescence of this quasi-sacred nimbus now called the nation (that attach-
es itself to the state) constitutes the continuation of the religious into
the present.[23] In a world of emerging nations, the choice of a religiously
and politically homogeneous people as a model for thinking through
solutions to the problems of modern states certainly made sense.[24] In
the increasingly postnational Western world, the task is more to think
past the border closures produced by the modern nation-state.

Notes

1. Baruch Spinoza, *A Theologico-Political Treatise and a Political Treatise* (1670,
1677; rpt. New York: Dover, 1951), 76.
2. Stephen Toulmin, *Cosmopolis: The Hidden Agenda of Modernity* (New York:
Free Press, 1990).
3. Spinoza, *Theologico-Political Treatise*, 210.
4. Ibid., 5, 9.
5. Ibid., 59.
6. Ibid., 205.
7. Thomas Hobbes, *Leviathan* (1651; rpt. Harmondsworth: Penguin, 1968).
8. Spinoza, *Theologico-Political Treatise*, 101.
9. Ibid., 19.
10. Hobbes, *Leviathan*, 440.
11. Jacques Derrida, *De l'esprit, Heidegger et la question* (Paris: Galilée, 1987).
12. Spinoza, "Treatise on the Emendation of the Intellect," in *The Collected
Works of Spinoza*, ed. E. Curley (Princeton, N.J.: Princeton University Press,
1985), 1:27.
13. Ibid., 44.
14. Spinoza, "Ethics," in *Collected Works*, 1:550, 553.
15. Ibid., 442.
16. Ibid., 502.
17. Spinoza, *Theologico-Political Treatise*, 202–3.
18. Ibid., 220.
19. Ibid., 223, 225.
20. Ibid., 257.
21. Ibid., 259.
22. See Toni Negri, "L'antimodernité de Spinoza," *Les Tempes Modernes* 539
(Juin 1991): 43–61; Negri, *The Savage Anomaly: The Power of Spinoza's Metaphysics
and Politics* (Minneapolis: University of Minnesota Press, 1991).

23. See Y. Yovel, *Spinoza and Other Heretics: The Marrano of Reason* (Princeton, N.J.: Princeton University Press, 1989), 172–205.

24. Julia Kristeva's argument that Judaism has a quasi-voluntarist definition of belonging, because election involves trial and because foreigners were accepted, is unconvincing both because the idea of a trial does not eliminate the particularism inherent in the doctrine of election and because the identification of the foreigner with the converted, which she herself points to, is scarcely compatible with the acceptance of the "foreignness" of the foreigner. See Julia Kristeva, *Étrangers à nous-mêmes* (Paris: 1988), 95–113.

BARRY HINDESS

Power and Rationality: The Western Concept of Political Community

Political theory has never ceased to be obsessed with the person of the sovereign. Such theories still continue today to busy themselves with the problem of sovereignty. What we need, however, is a political philosophy that isn't erected around the problem of sovereignty, nor therefore around the problems of law and prohibition. We need to cut off the King's head: in political theory that has still to be done.

—Michel Foucault, *Power/Knowledge*

Some of the most interesting connections between reason and imagination in Western political thought can be found in the conceptualization of power and of the political community. Political theory has its obsessions, as Foucault's remarks suggest, and many of these are indeed concerned with relations between sovereigns and subjects. While the person of the sovereign may sometimes be at issue in these obsessions, their more substantial object lies elsewhere.

In the societies of the modern West, the idea of sovereign power has been elaborated with respect to two distinct but related fields of concern: dealing with relations between a political community and its sovereign, on the one hand, and with relations between distinct sovereign powers, on the other. The first is of the most interest to this chapter. Relations between sovereigns and subjects have been analyzed primarily in terms of the more general idea of a political community of autonomous individuals who can be governed by means that normally depend on their rational consent. The notion of rational consent is widely employed, in a more or less descriptive sense or as a norma-tive point of reference, in discussions concerning political power—both in academic political analysis and more generally in political life. Ra-tional consent is also, of course, regarded as something of a fiction. Much of the conceptualization of power in Western societies depends on the invocation of an imaginary community that can be governed by the use of reason. To the extent that the understanding of political power turns on the relationships between some such fiction and the conditions that can be found in any particular society, it will continue to be a matter of interpretation and therefore of dispute.

After a short discussion of the quantitative understanding of pow-er, the first part of this chapter examines the idea of sovereign power and related understandings of power that have been elaborated in terms of the conceptualization of imaginary communities of autono-mous, rational individuals. The second part begins by noting that the conceptualization of a political community in these terms is radically incomplete. Imaginary communities of autonomous, rational individ-uals are invariably subject to other determinations—of culture, ethnic-ity, or language. The chapter concludes with some reflections on the relations between rationalistic and other determinations of the politi-cal community in Western political thought.

• • •

Two conceptions of power have dominated Western political thought in the modern period. One is the idea of power as a quantitative and cumulative phenomenon, a kind of generalized capacity to act. The other is the idea of a power that operates by means that presume on the rational consent of those over whom it is exercised. Thomas Hobbes presents a version of the first in *Leviathan:* "The power of a man is his present means to obtain some future apparent Good."[1] Power in this sense is simply the capacity to pursue at least some of one's objectives, and its possession is a condition of human agency. Power refers to a heterogeneous collection of attributes and possessions that need have nothing in common except that they might be useful in the pursuit of some human purpose.

In fact, neither Hobbes nor subsequent students of power have re-stricted themselves to what can be said about power in this broad sense. Hobbes often writes as if power in the sense of his definition could also be understood as a quantitative and cumulative phenomenon, some-what analogous to physical force—so that, in the event of conflict, those with more power will invariably prevail over those with less. This suggests a sense of the effectiveness of power, indeed, a sense of determinism, that is certainly not required by Hobbes's definition. It also suggests a homogeneity, as if beneath the diverse resources that could be employed in pursuit of human purposes there lurks a generalized capacity or essence of effectiveness endowed on the possessors of those resources. In this interpretation, then, power itself is not a resource. Rather, as Anthony Giddens insists: "Resources are the media through which power is exercised."[2]

This Hobbesian understanding of power has an obvious attraction to social scientists of a positivistic bent, since it appears to promise that questions of the distribution of power could be settled by empirical investigation. In fact, that promise is illusory for two rather different reasons. First, empirical investigation of the distribution of power has frequently been used to further other political agendas. I will return to that issue shortly. Second, the quantitative conception of power is profoundly flawed. There are certainly cases in which the conditions of action so favor one side in a dispute that the outcome can hardly be in doubt, but it would be wrong to treat such cases as if they were paradigmatic for the analysis of conflict in general. If the world were so simple, there would be few problems left for social analysis—and no independent inquirers around to study them. The idea that outcomes of conflict can be determined simply by totaling the resources available to each side and subtracting one from the other ignores both the heterogeneity of those resources and the fact that their deployment will often depend on conditions outside the agent's direct control. More seriously, it ignores one of the most basic and pervasive features of social life, namely, that conflicts over divergent objectives really are conflicts: they are not the acting out of a preordained script. Consider, for example, the conflict between the United States and North Vietnam in the 1960s and 1970s. Any purely quantitative analysis of the resources available to each side would have left little doubt as to the inevitable outcome.

Many academic commentators have nevertheless insisted that this is the essential meaning of power. In *Power: A Radical View*, for example, Steven Lukes maintains that while the concept of power is "essentially contested" by different investigators holding different social values, these alternative views of power may all be reduced to one underlying conception of power in the quantitative sense.[3] There is no doubt that some such notion of power is widely employed both by academics and more generally in contemporary Western societies, but it would be a serious mistake to suggest that this one concept underlies all significant contemporary usages. There is, in fact, a second major conception of power in modern Western thought. Lukes himself notes that Hannah Arendt and Talcott Parsons do not employ his underlying concept, but he dismisses as idiosyncratic their alternative treatments of power as a function of consent.

In Parsons's view, power is "the generalised capacity to secure the performance of binding obligations by units in a system of collective action when the obligations are legitimised with reference to their bearing on collective goals and where in the case of recalcitrance there is a presumption of enforcement by negative situational sanctions."[4] Parsons is not renowned for the felicity of his prose, but his definition presents the fundamental idea of a power that operates by means that presume the consent of those over whom it is exercised. It suggests that force and sanctions of various kinds come into play only when the appeal to obligations is either ineffective or unavailable.

This second conception of power is one that has played a central part in Western political thought in the modern period. Sovereign power, for example, is now usually understood in terms of the implicit consent of its subjects and of the rights and obligations entailed by that consent.[5] Hobbes introduces sovereign power as if it were a power in the sense of the quantitative understanding of his initial definition. It is a power that is greater than the power of any subject or group of subjects, since it combines the powers of all of them. However, his account of how that power is constituted, in numerous presumed acts of authorization, suggests that sovereign power is a *right* to make use of the powers of its subjects. It does not follow, as Hobbes would have us believe, that the sovereign will therefore have an effective *capacity* to utilize those powers. There is an elision here between the ideas of power as a capacity and of power as a right, which is endemic to classical political theory. For all its problems, the assumption that the sovereign is or should be the single most important power in a society, and that it works primarily by means of decisions that its subjects normally accept as binding, has dominated the discussion of power in the modern period.

This elision brings us to a second reason for the failure of the quantitative analysis of power to deliver on its empirical promise, namely, that its use has normally been animated by broader concerns relating to questions of sovereign power and its legitimacy. Despite appearances, what is at stake in debates about the distribution of power in contemporary Western societies is not the simple empirical question of who does or does not have power in the quantitative sense. All parties to the American community power debates of the 1960s and 1970s took for granted that the central issue concerned the capacity to make binding decisions for the community and, in particular, whether that capacity was in the hands of those with a right to hold power (the people and their elected representatives) or had been usurped by an (undemocratic) elite. Binding decisions are those that citizens are obliged to follow, so this is a matter of a power that depends on the presumption of rational consent. It is one thing to agree, as did all parties to these debates, that the system of political power in America does not conform to the traditional model of a democratic republic and quite another to agree on how that fact should be evaluated. Does it indicate that the model should be adapted to account for modern conditions, or that power has been usurped by an unrepresentative elite— or some combination of these? Empirical questions are certainly involved here, but the decision is hardly a straightforward empirical one.

The *idea* of a power that operates by means of rational consent has played a central part in Western political thought in the modern period. It suggests a model of the proper relations between ruler and ruled, which in turn presupposes a very particular model of the legal and moral capacities of the ruled themselves. The extent to which social conditions have ever in fact conformed to the requirements of these models is another matter. Any attempt to apply the models in the analysis of social conditions will require decisions on a number of highly contentious questions: In particular, do relations between ruler and ruled in fact conform to the model? And to what powers are the ruled subjected if these relations do not conform? Locke's concept of tyranny, for example, refers to an exercise of power to which the ruler has no right, while his concept of usurpation refers to conditions in which laws are made by those with no right to make them.

As for the ruled, there are several rather different sets of issues. First, some of the ruled may be regarded as lacking the legal and moral capacities required of those who are to be governed primarily by means that presume on their rational consent—women (until recently in most Western societies), minors, inhabitants of subject territories, corporations, and other legal persons that are not human individuals. What rights, if any, do such persons have, and what powers, if any, do governments have over them that they do not also have over their citizens? Locke's treatment of paternal (or parental) power offers a model for dealing with some but by no means all of these cases. His anodyne account of parent-child relations in the *Second Treatise*,[6] together with the norm of the rational citizen, serves to justify a paternal power over those who are regarded as not at present able to conform to that norm. It is a power that represents itself on the one hand as benign in intent and on the other hand as not accountable to those over whom it is exercised. The obvious temptations of paternalism and the equally obvious dangers that it poses have been a perennial source of dispute.

Second, the sovereign power that works through the obligations of its citizens must be supplemented by powers of other kinds if it is to perform its duties effectively, including specialized state agencies and systems of inducements and sanctions to keep the citizens in line. Once again, there is considerable scope for debate regarding the legitimacy or otherwise of some of these other powers. Locke's *Second Treatise* poses the question of a government's legitimacy in terms of an ideal model of a political community governed by civil law, that is, by a system of laws laid down and maintained by a power that is itself sustained by the rational consent of the governed.

Book 2 of his *Essay Concerning Human Understanding* notes that two other kinds of law also play an important part in the government of human behavior: the divine law and "the Law of Opinion or Reputation."[7] Locke argues that our moral understandings are formed as a result of the rewards and sanctions occasioned by our conformity or nonconformity to law. He suggests that the third law, the law of opinion, has governed the greater part of human behavior throughout history. It works through people expressing their approval and disapproval "of the actions of those whom they live amongst, and converse with."[8] This is a law that relies on no central authority, for either its enunciation or its enforcement. It is generated and sustained by the social interaction that occurs in the daily life of what later writers would call "civil society."

What has this account of law and morality to do with the discussion of contemporary Western understandings of power? First, it is important for a reason that relates to the reception of Lockean political ideas in North America and especially in those societies of continental Europe governed by absolutist regimes. Together with the idea of a government based on rational consent, the idea of a law—and especially of a morality—that arises out of the life of society itself, and not from the actions of government, offers a powerful moral foundation for a radical critique of political power that could be directed against these regimes. Since this essentially moral critique of political power has little foundation in practical experience of the activities of government, there is a danger that many of its prescriptions may turn out to be somewhat utopian. For all its moral force, then, as Reinhart Koselleck argues, this mode of critique has little to offer by way of practical guidance for dealing with the problems of government that might follow the overthrow of the established political power.[9] Nevertheless, it has provided a significant motivation for political action in modern European history—most spectacularly, of course, in the French and subsequent revolutions.

The Lockean account of morality is also important because it suggests the idea of a decentralized power that molds the thoughts and desires of its victims. This is Lukes's third dimension of power, a concept that relates to the Gramscian notion of hegemony and to the analysis of power in contemporary critical theory. Locke's account of the law of opinion and reputation involves a model of human persons as governed in their thought and behavior by acquired habits. Such habits may be developed through specialized training and, less formally, through repeated experiences of the pleasures and pains that regularly follow from behaving or failing to behave in particular ways. Others' responses to our actions are important sources of such experiences. In addition to its direct effects on behavior then, the law of opinion and reputation can also work to promote or modify the internal standards by which individuals regulate their behavior and judgment. This is one of the virtues of participation that has been particularly stressed in democratic and republican political theory: democratic participation exposes individuals to the regulation of their behavior by others—in such a way as to promote the qualities needed for them to be able to meet their obligations as citizens. (This is a major point of Carole Pateman's critique of the pluralist construction of "classical" democratic theory.[10]) Thus, civil society may be regarded as molding the personalities of its inhabitants. I return to another implication of this idea in a moment.

Therefore, we have two models of the citizen: (1) a free moral agent naturally endowed with a developed faculty of reason and (2) an individual formed by training and social conditions—to say nothing of models of the person that might be employed when it comes to dealing with those who are thought to lack the qualities required of citizens. Locke's account of the legitimacy of political power in *Two Treatises of Government* makes use of the first, but his treatment of morality in *An Essay Concerning Human Understanding* is clearly based on the second. Both models have played and continue to play an important part in Western political thought. On the one hand, the model of the rational citizen provides a norm against which we can measure the present organization of society, the behavior of its citizens, and government regulation of their lives. It provides a readily available basis for many popular styles of normative political critique. On the other hand, the idea of the person as malleable implies that in the absence of appropriate social conditions people will not develop the qualities expected of them as citizens. This suggests that a republic should take care to educate, train, and regulate its subjects so as to ensure that they do have the required qualities.

The capacity of civil society to mold personalities should not necessarily be regarded as benign, or even as merely anodyne, in its effects. Critical theory combines the idea that civil society molds the personalities of its inhabitants with a Marxist view of civil society as an arena of class conflict: class power structures civil society and thereby influences the thoughts and desires of individuals. In this way civil society may be regarded as the site of an insidious power whose exercise is not normally recognized, even by those who are its victims. In the hands of critical theory, the idea of the citizen as a free rational individual and the closely related idea of the civil society that would be required to foster and sustain individuals of that kind set a standard against which actual conditions can be compared, thereby providing a measure of the impact of power. The imaginary ideal of life in the absence of power then enters into the description of existing social conditions.

Lukes presents the issue in terms of a third dimension of power that prevents people from recognizing their real interests. His normative ideal is a situation in which people recognize their real interests by "exercising choice under conditions of relative autonomy and in particular, independently of A's power [i.e., the power that stops them from recognizing their real interests]—e.g., through democratic participation."[11] Notice that relative autonomy is not identified as a condition in which the effects of power are absent. On the contrary, it is a condition structured by power based on rational consent—and, of course, by the ubiquitous effects of Locke's law of opinion and reputation. Lukes decides to treat the choices he imagines would be made under the influence of such powers as if they were a measure of real interests. In marked contrast to Lukes's focus on autonomous individuals, the central concern of Jürgen Habermas's *Theory of Communicative Action* is with the rationality of a lifeworld that is shared by individuals and collectivities, especially with language and intersubjective relations.[12] Nevertheless, Habermas's analysis is also based on the ideal of a realm of social existence that is not structured by the illegitimate effects of power—that is, on the utopian vision of an idealized civil society. The inhabitants of that society would, of course, be precisely the autonomous rational persons required by the Lockean account of political power. In their different ways, then, Lukes and Habermas acknowledge the reality of heteronomy, the fact that the attributes and capacities of persons are crucially dependent on social conditions, while retaining the Lockean ideal of the autonomous rational person at the center of their political critique of the present organization of society.

• • •

I have argued that the use of the model of a sovereign power that operates primarily through rational consent as the starting point for the analysis of social conditions invariably brings other considerations into play. It raises both descriptive and evaluative issues, and it involves the employment of some combination of at least two models of the person as subject to the exercise of power. Decisions on these matters bring the model of sovereign power together with one or more alternative conceptions of power: as a supplementary aid to the normal workings of sovereign power, as a tyrannical extension or usurpation of its constitutive right, as properly taking the place of a power based on consent in conditions where, because of the legal or mental incapacity of the persons concerned, the presumption of consent does not apply, as a means of conforming the attributes and capacities of citizens to the requirements of a power that pretends to act through their consent, as a dispersed form of social regulation that is independent of direct central control, and, in the hands of critical theory, as an illegitimate and insidious means of affecting the very thoughts and desires of its victims, thereby preventing them and their society from attaining the condition in which social life may be properly governed by right and obligation.

The diverse relationships between the idea of sovereign power and these alternatives suggest a sense in which Foucault's complaint that "political theory has never ceased to be obsessed with the person of the sovereign" might be misdirected.[13] The most important features of Foucault's critique of classical political theory concern his understandings of government and of the person as subject to the exercise of power. First, he argues that government (in the sense of *the* government) uses targeted, individualizing powers in addition to the generalized power of sovereignty, and second, that the government of others is not restricted to *the* government and its agents. With regard to the person as subject to power, he insists that the attributes and personal qualities of subjects should not be regarded as if they were formed independently of the effects of power. In fact, these points have often been noted. If there is a problem with existing ways of thinking about power, it is not simply that they are obsessed with the person of the sovereign and the conceptual baggage that goes with that idea—although some of them may be. Rather, the problem is that the modern understanding of relations between sovereign and subjects is elaborated in terms of what Foucault calls the city-citizen game, that is, it refers to a world of autonomous individuals who may be governed by means that presume on their rational consent.

To say that governments employ individualizing techniques of power, and that the qualities of subjects are not independent of their effects, is also, of course, to say that that world is a fiction. But it would be misleading to suggest that Western political thought had failed to acknowledge its fictional character—far from it. Rather, the problem is that political thought nevertheless continues to use that world and its inhabitants—both as a surrogate for the present and as a normative model to identify what does not exist but should be created. Versions of the city-citizen game surface in the language and institutional framework of democratic government, in the formulation of norms for social policy intervention against which the condition of deviant or disadvantaged minorities can be measured, and in diverse moral critiques of political power. Remarkably similar fictions are invoked both by those who would use them to legitimize current practices and by radical critics of those practices.

Many of the most influential Western understandings of political power turn on the invocation of an imaginary community of autonomous, rational individuals. In effect, this is a self-governing community of citizens: even Hobbes's Leviathan may be regarded as a means by which members of such a community choose to govern themselves. In this respect, the consideration of political power is a major focus of relations between reason and imagination in Western thought. It would be a mistake, however, to leave the matter at this point, since identification of the imaginary community as a community of citizens is incomplete in at least three important respects. First, the idea of a self-governing community of citizens directs attention to the political activities of the body of citizens, but it is clear that these activities cannot exhaust the life of the community. The political influence of citizens will not always derive from their standing as citizens acting more or less on a par with other citizens—and some citizens will be considerably more equal than others. The political inequality of citizens is, of course, a striking feature of all modern democracies, but these are also societies in which the citizens are far from being the only significant political actors. The most obvious examples of noncitizen political actors in the modern world, and in many ways the most important ones, are governmental and nongovernmental organizations (I have discussed this issue at length elsewhere[14]).

The second and third respects in which the representation of the community as a community of citizens must be regarded as seriously incomplete relate to the question of community membership. Consider, for example, one of the earliest recorded invocations of the city-citizen game: Thucydides' rendering of the funeral oration delivered by

Pericles in the winter of 431–430 B.C. Contemporary versions of the city-citizen game have drawn on other classical sources, including some that are more recent. They offer a variety of accounts of republican government, many of which emphasize the fundamental Roman ingredient of the rule of law, and they have tended to play down the military and essentially masculine qualities taken for granted in earlier understandings of citizenship. These various accounts are by no means equivalent, and there are important issues at stake in some of their differences. Nevertheless, consideration of Pericles's oration will serve to introduce persistent features of this Western invocation of imaginary communities of citizens.

Pericles describes Athens as a democratic community in which significant differences in wealth coexist with a fundamental equality of status. Its citizens collectively govern and defend it. These citizens are also soldiers—and they are Athenians who are the sons of Athenians. Pericles' oration honors those who have fallen in battle, by celebrating the community to which they belong. It is a eulogy of Athenian *democracy*—although its democratic content is in marked contrast to the distinctly aristocratic tone of his address.[15] Many commentators have noted that the city portrayed in Pericles' oration does not entirely coincide with the Athens in which he lived. In addition to its citizens, the community of Athens included Athenian women and children as well as significant populations of slaves and resident aliens. The imperial and cosmopolitan metropolis of postwar Athens was even more remote from Pericles' fictional community. Athenians of the classical period inhabited a cosmopolitan, multicultural city, but they could look back on a comparatively recent past in which—except for women, children, and slaves—the community of governors could be regarded as more or less coinciding with the community of the governed.

Similar points apply to the Rome that is so often invoked in republican political thought. By the time of the late Republic, Roman citizens were members of a larger and considerably more diverse community—and they had to look somewhat further back to find an image of cultural homogeneity. Nevertheless, political thinkers in these multicultural communities appeared to have little difficulty in employing the fiction of a community united by a common culture as a vehicle for elaborating many of their political concerns and objectives—and even at times for analyzing the political life of the societies in which they lived.

These points suggest two respects in which the representation of Pericles' Athens (or of the Roman Republic) as a community of citizens must be regarded as seriously incomplete. On the one hand, the attributes and capacities that individuals must have if they are to perform their duties as citizens in the public life of the community are not themselves sufficient to identify those individuals as members of the Athenian community: they must also be Athenians. Other Greek men residing in Athens might also be regarded as possessing the necessary qualities of courage, rationality, and so on, but they would not thereby be admitted as citizens. The community of citizens, then, must also be identified *as a community* in other ways—in this case as a community united by culture and descent. On the other hand, the self-governing community of citizens in fact governs a community that is larger than itself—sometimes by a considerable margin. The community of the governors rarely coincides with the community of the governed.

The Athenian funeral oration has no exact equivalent in the modern world, and it would clearly be a mistake to look for realism in this or other such ritual pronouncements. Nevertheless, the gaps that I have noted in Pericles' representation of community membership can also be found more generally in Western political thought. The image of a culturally homogeneous political community has often been thought to identify a feasible political project. In parts of northwest Europe (and also in Japan, which has a very different classical heritage), this image has sometimes seemed to provide a plausible description. It has always been considerably less plausible in other parts of Europe or, since the beginning of European settlement, in the Americas—where the idea of the melting pot provides an interesting variation—or in Australasia.[16] Nevertheless, the idea of a culturally homogeneous political community, consisting of autonomous, rational individuals, has continued to dominate those forms of political thought in which the people are regarded as taking an active part in governing themselves.

The assumption of a common culture is absolutely central to Locke's account of the workings of the Law of Opinion and Reputation, as well as to subsequent accounts of the beneficial workings of what later became known as civil society. Where the assumption of a common culture is not required—notably, of course, in absolutist political thought and in some forms of conservative political theory—it is because the people are not regarded as capable of governing themselves. Hobbes's case for Leviathan is an obvious example. It does not require the assumption of a common culture because what he advocates is essentially a society in which no political life independent of government is allowed to exist.

I argued in the first part of this chapter that the model of a community of autonomous, rational individuals has dominated the discussion of political power in the societies of the modern West. Scholars generally acknowledge that the model is something of a fiction and, in particular, that individuals are in fact the heteronomous creatures of social conditions. The tensions between the ideal of autonomy and the recognition of heteronomy frequently translate into projects to create or maintain these fictional communities and to fashion people to inhabit them. Such projects are an integral part of the life of all modern societies—and there is an important sense in which heteronomy must be presumed as a condition of their possibility.

I have noted two further respects in which that model must be regarded as a fiction, both related to community membership. First, any attempt to employ the model in relation to existing societies must identify community membership in two distinct and possibly opposed respects. On the one hand, citizenship is conceived of as a matter of the minimal satisfaction of the conditions required for autonomy: freedom, rationality, and moral sensitivity. However, satisfaction of these conditions does not in itself identify a person as a member of one community rather than another. On the other hand, then, since the world is divided into numerous distinct communities, citizenship must also be subject to highly particularistic determinations—most commonly of culture or ethnicity.

Since we are dealing here with fictional communities, the relationships that may be imagined to hold between these two sets of determinations are many and various. The capacities required for a person to live as an autonomous member of a community of citizens may be regarded, for example, as a human universal—that is, at least in principle, as independent of a cultural or ethnic background. Supporters of this view tend to treat the relationship between the universalistic (rationalistic) determinations of citizenship and the highly particularistic determinations based on culture or ethnicity as if they were merely contingent—that is, as if ethnocentricity, national chauvinism, and racism could be regarded as signs of a lack of cultivation on the part of individuals and of an incomplete modernization on the part of societies. Unfortunately, there is nothing in the fact that these capacities can be defined in universalistic terms to ensure that they will in fact be regarded as human universals. Influential traditions in Western political thought have also regarded these characteristics as the exclusive possession of certain cultural or ethnic communities, or as existing only in one of a number of discrete forms, each of which belongs to a particular ethnic or cultural community.

The second respect in which the model of a community of citizens must be regarded as something of a fiction is that it does not normally coincide with the community of the governed. In modern Western societies slavery has been abolished, women are generally eligible for citizenship, and there are few remaining colonial possessions. The gap between the community of citizens and the community of the governed is now filled largely by children and resident foreigners. Many of the latter have a cultural background and a continuing cultural identity significantly different from that of the host community.

In both respects, then, the cultural and ethnic pluralism of Western societies poses serious problems for the more rationalistic variants of Western political thought. To the extent that our conceptualization of political power takes the assumption of cultural uniformity for granted, it provides a poor foundation for the understanding of politics in a culturally diverse and ethnically diverse political community. To the extent that projects to create, maintain, or reform political communities and to mold the characters of their inhabitants assume the existence of an homogenous community, or take the creation of such a community as their objective, they will produce unexpected results.

Yet there is more at stake than the need to bring a somewhat greater degree of realism into political discussion. The adoption of an ideal model of cultural homogeneity has allowed political thinkers to treat cultural and ethnic diversity as an unfortunate but contingent reality to be remedied, as the case may be, by education coupled with more or less benign repression, by federalism or national self-determination, or by the denial of political rights to those who are regarded as outsiders—that is, by imposing uniformity on the one hand, or by allowing or enforcing some kind of political exclusiveness on the other. Neither solution is satisfactory: the first is difficult to reconcile with universalistic standards of liberty and the rule of law normally presupposed by the model of a community of citizens, while even benign versions of the second assume that the mixing of diverse populations can be readily avoided or reversed.

The emergence of a governmental multiculturalism in many Western societies can be seen as an acknowledgment that cultural and ethnic diversity is an inescapable feature of the modern world—or at least as a recognition that such diversity could be avoided only at a cost that would be unacceptable. At another level, attempts to build political support around one or more ethnic constituencies in the United States—and to a lesser extent in other Western democracies—can be regarded as a pragmatic adaptation to that perceived reality. These developments are often measured against normative standards based on an ideal model of the political life of a community of autonomous, rational individuals—and in those terms, of course, they are all too easily found wanting.[17] I have suggested, rather, that the problem lies in a political discourse that depends on an ideal model of that kind, and in particular on the assumption, of cultural homogeneity that continues to play such an important part in our understanding of what we like to call democratic politics.

Notes

An earlier version of this essay appeared in *Alternatives: Social Transformation and Humane Governance* 17, no. 2 (1992). Copyright © 1992 by Alternatives. Used with permission of Lynne Rienner Publishers, Inc.

1. Thomas Hobbes, *Leviathan* (1651; rpt., Harmondsworth: Penguin, 1968), 150.

2. Anthony Giddens, *Central Problems in Social Theory* (London: Macmillan, 1979), 91.

3. Steven Lukes, *Power: A Radical View* (London: Macmillan, 1974).

4. Talcott Parsons, *Politics and Social Structure* (New York: Free Press, 1969), 361.

5. Frances H. Hinsley, *Sovereignty* (Cambridge: Cambridge University Press, 1986), esp. chap. 4.

6. John Locke, *Two Treatises of Government* (1690; rpt., Cambridge: Cambridge University Press, 1988).

7. Locke, *An Essay Concerning Human Understanding* (1690; rpt., Oxford: Clarendon, 1957).

8. Ibid., chap. 28, par. 10.

9. Reinhart Koselleck, *Critique and Crisis* (Oxford: Berg, 1988).

10. Carole Pateman, *Participation and Democratic Theory* (Cambridge: Cambridge University Press, 1970).

11. Lukes, *Power,* 33.

12. Jürgen Habermas, *The Theory of Communicative Action,* 2 vols. (Boston: Beacon Press, 1984, 1987).

13. Michel Foucault, *Power/Knowledge* (Brighton: Harvester, 1980), 121.

14. Barry Hindess, "Imaginary Presuppositions of Democracy," *Economy and Society* 20, no. 2 (1991): 173–95.

15. See the discussion of this point in Nicole Loraux, *The Invention of Athens: The Funeral Oration in the Classical City* (Cambridge, Mass.: Harvard University Press, 1986), chap. 4.

16. William H. McNeill, *Polyethnicity and National Unity in World History* (Toronto: University of Toronto Press, 1980).

17. Alain Finkielkraut, *The Undoing of Thought* (London: Claridge Press, 1988) is an interesting polemic on this issue.

PETER MURPHY

Classicism, Modernism, and Pluralism

At the very heart of the Western project lies the image of a world in which civility, rather than necessity or utility, is preeminent. To be civil means to relate to the world intrinsically, not instrumentally. It is, as Hannah Arendt put it, to have a love of the world. Those who have a love of the world, an *amor mundi*, judge and appraise what is in the world in terms of value or worth, not interest. For such people, a thing's value is independent of its usefulness or necessity. To judge something as useful or necessary is to express an interest in that thing. By contrast, to judge something as valuable is to appreciate it for its own sake. Anything can be appraised in terms of either its interest or its value. I can, alternatively, ask the question: Is it a useful (or necessary) means to an end, or is it an end in itself? In raising and pursuing the former question, I reason instrumentally; in raising and pursuing the latter question, I reason practically. Practical reason answers the question: what carries *unconditional* or *categorical* value? The unconditional or the categorical may be described as the protovalue of the West.[1] This protovalue defines, or gives meaning to, the Western project. It is the source to which it returns, as well as from which it departs, its principle (*principia*) in each of its phases of development and renewal. It is that which provides the *horizon of meaning* and *criterion of rationality* for its varied, and various, episodes and enterprises.

• • •

As befits its originary status, this protovalue can only be "defined" in the *negative* as the antithesis of utilitarian and necessitarian determination, and because it is only defined in the negative, it is open to multiple positive *interpretations*. The first interpretation, as opposed to definition, of this protovalue was given by Aristotle. In his interpretation, Aristotle spoke for the world of the classical (Mediterranean) city-state. Aristotle interpreted the protovalue of the Western project as being constituted by *actions that are done for their own sake* (actions that are ends in themselves). He called such actions *praxis,* identifying at least four kinds: virtuous action, civic participation, cultivated leisure (*schole*), and friendship. Each of these actions was civilized—in other words, appropriate for the city. In whatever form, each also constituted a kind of *freedom*—the freedom of the *participant.* Participants engage in something not because they have to—because their behavior is necessary or useful to some ulterior end—but because their action is an end in itself. Such action, where it is oriented by the virtues, is constitutive of the *good.*

To speak of the good, and especially in Aristotle's manner, meaning "excellence in action" (*arete*), has a vaguely conservative ring to most modern ears. Undoubtedly one of the reasons for this is that the classical "philosophy of praxis" was interwoven with a conception of the world that was hierarchical. Aristotle sought to rank the different forms of praxis he identified. He wanted to answer the question: Which was the *supreme* end, the highest good? His notion of praxis was also inextricably tied to the idea of a class society in which some but not all persons would live their lives engaging in forms of praxis. The rest would serve as the condition of the possibility of such praxis. Accordingly, those who were "lacking" or "deficient" in the virtues made possible the virtuous actions of others. They were the *means* to others participating in actions that were ends in themselves. In modern times, this became unacceptable. Symbolizing the change in attitude is Immanuel Kant's formulation of the categorical imperative. Kant no longer speaks of actions as ends in themselves but of *persons* as ends in themselves. The change in terminology represents an epochal shift.

The idea of freedom has been reformulated. It is no longer the freedom of the active participant in the life of the city but rather the freedom of the individual. Freedom is no longer represented by the good but by the right. The idea of rights or modern freedom is tied first and foremost to *persons,* not to *actions.* The reconceptualization of freedom as the freedom of persons was closely tied to the question of *universality* or *equality.* The Achilles' heel of the classical conception of freedom was its interlacing with social hierarchy. The modern idea of the freedom of the individual promised the end of the instrumentalization of persons. It promised, in Kant's great formulation, that no person would be treated as a means to another's end—as someone else's slave, servant, or lackey—but always as an end in themselves. Modern freedom implied universality, because modern freedom was set against the hierarchies of the ancien régime. Modern rights were universal or equal rights, attributed to all persons. The converse of this, of course, is that universality implied a particular concept of freedom. Modern universalism imagined a world in which *everyone* made choices and decisions about their lives. Against the benchmark of this imaginary humankind, the social authorities of class and community could be judged and found wanting.

To be no one's servant, to make our own choices, is a mighty thing. We must not forget that. But we should not at the same time ignore the tendency in the modern world for freedom and civilization to be torn asunder. Emancipation does not of necessity involve, or require, participation in the *civitas* and its treasures. Classical freedom meant participation in the affairs of the city; modern freedom means the freedom of the subject, *the freedom of the will*.[2] The willing subject is one who *deliberates between* aversions and desires and, in the final moment of deliberation, chooses a course of action. The will is the desire or preference upon which the person acts.

The willing subject—the modern subject—is free in a twofold sense. First, the process of deliberation frees the subject from the automatism of desires and appetites (i.e., from the compulsive, impulsive, or obsessive aspect of the appetite). Second, the will frees the subject from the grip of routine and precedent. The person who wills—who is willful—does not follow a socially prescribed routine or manner of behaving. The freedom represented by the will is the freedom to act on the basis of our own reflections and considerations—weighing the costs and benefits, pleasures and pains of a possible or contingent course of action and then finally deciding to enact it or not. The freedom of the will is the freedom to *begin* new courses of action—courses of action that are not socially predetermined or prescribed. The freedom of the will interrupts the naturalistic reproduction of society. The lovers who defy their families and elope, the laborer who defies his class and goes to night school, and the sister who defies her brothers and leaves home for the big city are all exercising their freedom of will. In doing so, they cancel out the past. They negate the grip of those communal determinations handed down from the past.[3]

The modern subject possesses the power of self-determination, the power of moving oneself to action, rather than being heteronomously (i.e., socially) determined. (This freedom from social determination, of course, is only relative, never absolute.) The modern subject's freedom from the grip of communal or class determinations (i.e., social authorities) is exhibited in the *freedom of each subject to choose* his or her own occupation, place of residence, partner, and so forth. The subject can base such choices on various components, such as the individual's own desire, feelings of pleasure and displeasure, conception of happiness or welfare, or anticipation of achieving some desired effect. But, in such cases, as Kant pointed out, the subject looks to grounds that are valid only for his own will. What about the wills of others? The modern world may have brought about the gradual dissolution of communal and class determinations, and their implications—the use of human beings by collectivities and hierarchies for heteronomous ends, but Kant recognized that the liberalization of society (represented in the withering of communal and class determinations) did not mean that individuals would stop being used by others. It might be that those others could no longer speak on behalf of tradition, community, or hierarchy, but liberal societies were susceptible, Kant recognized, to their own forms of instrumentalism.

In this setting, an autonomous subject could well decide a course of action that either denied other persons the power to choose or denied them anything meaningful (such as time, property, work) upon which they might exercise their choice. In liberal societies, autonomous subjects may determine themselves but in doing so may well act in a way that would deny other persons their self-determination.[4] Kant was interested in the relationship between autonomous subjectivities, how the freedom of one subject could be reconciled with the freedom of another subject. This question poses the problem, not of the good, but of the right. Right, as Kant observed, concerns the relationship between the will of one subject and the will of another subject. To live in a state of right means that we, as *human* beings, are entitled not to be denied or deprived by other persons or human agencies of our capacity for self-determination—the capacity to choose and decide for ourselves. The essence of the Kantian conception of freedom is that subjects ought to treat other subjects as ends rather than as means. In other words, the noncontingent ground of anyone's choice is respect for all human beings' capacities to choose and decide. As Kant puts it: autonomous subjects, persons who are able to choose and decide for themselves, do not just have an instrumental value for us; rather, they are ends in themselves. They are not to be used merely as a means to our ends; rather, they are intrinsically valuable. They are unconditional or categorical ends.

• • •

When he took the antiutilitarian notion of the end in itself and applied it to persons rather than actions, Kant also in effect reinterpreted the idea of freedom. But such a reinterpretation has not been unique in modern times. The paradigm of pluralism—associated with figures as diverse as Montesquieu and James Madison, Max Weber (the Weber of the essays) and Karl Jaspers, Hannah Arendt, and Jean-François Lyotard—has offered another reinterpretation of freedom that in some sense complements, but also somewhat rivals, Kant's universalistic and modernistic conception. Whether as a complement or rival, the pluralistic paradigm highlights the limitations of the Kantian project, in particular its conceptualization of freedom in terms of the self-determination of the subject. The Kantian or modernist paradigm fails to address the question of what, having secured human autonomy, it is that we do with this autonomy—apart from exercise it in the abstract. The fear of the modernist always is that, if we speak about the *content* of the will, we end up in effect determining the will (from the outside) and thereby violating the modernist postulate of self-determination. In other words, the modernist's freedom, the freedom of the self-determining subject, is the freedom of contingency. What I freely choose, I could have chosen differently. The fact that I choose *this* and not *that* is a matter of my desire, my conception of my welfare, and so on, which is, ultimately, a matter of contingency. My choice might have been different yesterday; it might be different tomorrow.

Kant, of course, accepts some limits on this contingency, such as other people, or rather their freedom of choice. What the pluralist, by contrast, sees as the problem of self-determination is not the one that Kant identified (i.e., the problem of intersubjectivity); rather, it is the problem of the *circularity* and thus *emptiness*, the spiritual vacuum, of the self-determining subject. For Kant the objective ground for the self-determination of the will is universal or consistent respect for the self-determining subject.[5] To choose rationally rather than sensually, I choose what enhances, or at least does not deny, my own and others' autonomy. Autonomy is the object of autonomy. But this is a vicious circle of self-referentiality. What the pluralist argues is that, on the contrary, self-determination is not the only objective end of the rational being. Self-determination is complemented by, and exercised in relation to, a number of *value ideas*. Value ideas give a content to an otherwise empty self-determination; they reconnect the ideas of freedom and civilization that modern society tends to separate.

Choice, opportunity, autonomy, self-regulation, and so on are often invoked as if they could answer each and every question about the form or shape of a human life. But they cannot. In the end, human beings have to grapple with questions about the value of the kind of activities they engage in. The pluralist makes a virtue of this; the pluralist does not deny that we are choosing beings, but says that we are also *cultural beings*,[6] and as such we are beings who can enter into certain spheres, or certain kinds, of activities that are "meaningful," that have some significance, worth, or value. The pluralist further assumes that in a civil society there are different value spheres, each oriented toward distinctive value ideas or "valid values."[7] This has always been true. Civilization is closely related to the founding and existence of cities, and at the very heart of the city lies the "axial crossroads" that symbolically unite the city's different quarters and the specialized or differentiated activities and forms of life represented by these quarters.[8] The lines of demarcation between significant human activities, of course, change over time, as do participants in those activities.

In the contemporary world, the universe of value is differentiated into four primary spheres of value: morals, work, citizenship, and learning. In the sphere of morals, people form relationships of solidarity, community, or personal friendship. In the work sphere, people design ends, project aims, posit goals, and act in deliberate, selective, methodical ways to attain goals. In civic action (citizenship), people participate either in making collective decisions or in monitoring the enactment of such decisions; they look to civic well-being. In learning, people enrich and deepen their comprehension of the language, customs, and objects of their own immediate world, as well as encounter and come to understand, even appreciate, other worlds.

In addition to these four primary value spheres, we can also distinguish a secondary sphere or *topos* of value: the public sphere. This realm (the realm of the political) properly speaking is not really a sphere at all. Rather it is the topos where all spheres intersect. It is like art or philosophy, a realm or world where *all that has been set apart is brought together.* It is secondary not in the sense of being less important but rather in a logical sense. The public topos is the place where the conflicts between ultimate values, and the partisans of those values, are mediated. In the public domain, the representatives of different value spheres encounter each other.

Individuals have recourse to ultimate values in order to judge the validity of their life conduct and to orient their individual choices and decisions. These values give coherence to, and provide the formative context for, the will of subjects. Where the choices and decisions of modern subjects fit a value context, or frame, those choices and decisions acquire a significance and meaning they would otherwise lack. As Weber put it, the dignity of the "personality" lies in the fact that for it there exist values around which it organizes its life.[9] The continuous realization of such values represents for each subject a vocation—a point of continuous reference and orientation for the subject. Without such an organizing principle, the consequence for the modern, self-determining subject is a chaotic, disorganized life. The complicating factor, of course, is that the world offers more than one ultimate value orientation.

In the contemporary world, human beings can look toward the vocations of work, understanding, intimacy, and citizenship. The values of an enterprising and worldly occupation, of learned curiosity, of love and of civic involvement have been split over time and have expanded into the distinctive cultures of inner-worldly asceticism, paideistic-humanism, communitarianism, and republican activism. So doesn't this mean that values themselves, in the end, are matters of choice? And doesn't that mean that values, far from orienting the self-determining subject, are simply contingencies, to be chosen by each subject on the basis of desire, taste, or respect for autonomy? Not necessarily. The difference is that the so-called "choice" of value-orientation is, in certain respects, tantamount to the forfeiture of the will. For the choice of our vocation is something that commits us to a lifetime of working through, of returning again and again, to our starting point. Our choice—if it can be called such—may be tested, sometimes sorely tested, and in some cases even undone. But by contrast with the choices and decisions we normally make—which do not have the capacity to inform and shape a whole life—this choice actually *displaces our sense of contingency,* the sense we have that whatever we have chosen we could have chosen differently.

The sense of contingency, of course, is central to the nature of the modern subject. The orientation to a value sphere displaces, at least partially, this sense of contingency with a sense of continuity. For this reason I would, therefore, want to speak less about the contingent nature and more simply about the differentiated nature of value spheres that contemporaries face. I want to suggest that the differentiated, or *polyvalent,* nature of a civil, and indeed civilized, society—its regime of value pluralism, if you like—in certain respects limits, in other respects complements (with an otherwise missing substance) modernist notions of contingency and contingent choice, in other words, of freedom.

But what of that other key dimension of modernism—its universalistic outlook? We might well assume that the heterogeneous and heterological nature of the pluralist regime is also at odds with the universalistic beliefs of the modernist. I would be cautious, however, in jumping too readily to such a conclusion. The relationship between modernism and pluralism, universalism and heterogeneity is not one of either/or. True, modernists' attempts at various historical junctures to present rational-ascetic, communitarian, even republican forms of life as generalizable or universally applicable have been quite contrary to the logic of polyvalence and, what is more, politically and socially oppressive.[10] This begs the question: Is universalism, and more particularly here, modernistic kinds of universalism, conceivable without dogmatism? I would suggest that a nondogmatic universalism is only possible where actors adhere to a strictly self-limiting or modest form of universalism—of the kind reflected in the "minima moralia" of Kant.

Kant still has something to teach us. His minima moralia is a *universal* morality. As such, it applies to everyone. Its categorical imperative is never treat any person as means but always as an end in themselves. Everyone is bound by this maxim and entitled to what it guarantees: human autonomy. This is a *modern* morality in the sense that it does not tell me what to do; its maxims are merely prohibitive. To tell me what to do would violate the modern conception of freedom—the freedom of individual. Modern, or Kantian, morality merely tells me what not to do or, more specifically, it tells me not to interfere with the autonomy—the freedom of will—of others. By contrast, the kind of morality of which the pluralist speaks is the morality of the good person, or that of the friend. Unlike the minima moralia of the modernist, neither the life of the good person nor the life in which friendship assumes center stage can be universal.[11] All that can be universal is "elementary human decency"—respect for others' autonomy. But what persons *do* with that autonomy, what *forms* of life they invest their energies in, is not the same for everybody. The life of the good person—the person who is absorbed in being helpful toward others, responsive to their needs, attentive to their problems, the person for whom alleviating the suffering of others is not a burden, chore, or duty but goes to the very core of their existence and endows them with a lightness of being—is the life of a person who has found a vocation and through that vocation has found a kind of emancipation.

In a pluralized world, there are other ways of achieving this—through work, citizenship, and humanistic-paideistic culture. That is to say, we have other ways of employing our autonomy. We can do so by orienting to any of a number of ethics—of the inner worldly ascetic, of republican citizenship, of humanistic cultivation. Each of these ethics forms the soul in different ways. Each complements and provides alternatives to the ethic of moral solidarity—the ethic of the good or helpful person. Each regulates complex and demanding activities.

In a pluralized world, the actor enters one or another of these ethical cultures. In each, we find one attribute of value (e.g., the inquiring mind) that is emphasized so as to overshadow others (e.g., intensity of relationships or empathetic closeness). The value sphere of morals emphasizes the faculty for closeness of contact with other human beings, either through forms of intimacy or solidarity. The value sphere of work emphasizes the faculties we have for methodicality in action, for constancy and determination in carrying out plans of action, and for imagining and projecting the aims and goals of that action, in other words, our capacity for teleological design. The value sphere of citizenship emphasizes the faculty for participation or active contribution to the civic good. The value sphere of humanistic culture emphasizes both the faculty of inquiry—the curiosity that prompts us to find out about the world around us—and the faculty of understanding (for making sense of what is alien, especially other worlds, and thus for expanding our horizons).

In the public domain, by contrast, it is trans-spheric capacities that are valued. Trans-spheric capacities—indeed, more generally, the capacities to unite what has been set apart—are called upon in public life, art, and philosophy. Just as great artists are endowed with a sense of beauty, and great philosophy surmounts and surpasses all of the contrary tendencies in the thought of its age, so greatness in public life requires a powerful sense of objectivity, in other words, of consistency or justice (fairness). Of course, *all* persons, whenever they transcend everyday life and enter the universe of value demonstrate *some* facility for intimacy, solidarity, teleological positing, constancy, participation, contribution, curiosity, understanding, and objectivity. These are called upon, in some respect, in *any* value sphere and in *any* trans-spheric activity. However, those who move most easily or fluidly within or between particular spheres will, necessarily, have at least *one* capacity (e.g., intensity of relationships or objectivity) developed to a high level. Such a person has a *vocation*—for moving in one sphere as opposed to another or for bridging between spheres. This person has a special sensitivity, a heightened capacity, to observe either norms of morality (norms of solidarity), participation (like courage, prudence, or generosity), perseverance (constancy, inner discipline, and determination) and spiritedness (control of anger, knowledge of oneself, eagerness), tolerance (openness), or justice (fairness and consistency). I am not arguing here that only some people can be methodical, tolerant, courageous, moral, or just. Everybody can be. But in the case of the person who has a vocation for justice, morality, civic courage, or whatever, it is their *life task*. They live and breathe it.

Take the case of justice. We all can be expected to behave justly. But unless our vocation is political—and this may happen to be in the guise of a judge, administrator, representative, or adviser—we will simply not be called upon continuously to weigh questions of justice. All of us will encounter in the course of our lives situations where we must make a decision: How can I do justice in this situation? For somebody whose vocation is political, this is a daily question. For most other people, it is a much more occasional question. Even for those whose vocation is a civic one, who are dedicated citizens and active in contributing to civic life, justice is not the central issue; rather the issue is their generosity in being prepared to commit time and resources to civic enrichment or their courage in facing threats and foes in the civic domain. And that makes the difference. The person who has a political vocation must excel in just action and judgment—which is to excel in objectivity and impartiality.

Along with the idea of a vocation comes the idea of the *sanctity* of a vocation. When political, civic, rational-ascetic, paideistic-humanistic, and moral forms of action are developed to a high degree of distinctiveness (with their own norms, language games, etc.), alongside this develops a particular *sense of autonomy:* a sense that no value sphere should be degraded to the status of an instrument of any other sphere. Methodical-rational concerns should not dominate cultural and educational, civic-building, or moral ones, and vice versa. *Each sphere obeys its own norms.*

The political actor must be keenly sensitive to that. As an example, a strong sense develops that a political actor should not be expected to give priority to moral norms. This does not, however, make the political actor an immoralist, nor does it mean that the political actor has license to engage in murderous or cruel actions. Rather, the political actor's first concern is to weigh carefully—impartially, objectively, justly—the competing demands of the different value spheres. The political actor cannot be a moralist. If this was so, the political actor could not render just judgment on the claims of the moralist. On the other hand, the political actor is not of necessity an immoralist either. He or she merely *brackets* morality (in the sense of solidarity). Morality is one of the competing demands that the political actor must balance in trying to arrive at a common good. But the moral person, the good person, can afford no such impartiality. The moral person says, "Look, people are starving, in misery; people have been humiliated, tortured—I will use all of my energies and resources to help them." The moral person acts morally.

He or she tries to restore or rebuild a shattered human bond. The political person, on the other hand, acts politically, to *balance* concern for close human ties with other values. For the moral person, the highest value is intensity in relationships; for the political one, objectivity ranks highest. The temptation to politicize morals, or moralize politics, is great. But the principle of autonomy of the value spheres resists this. It resists the instrumentalization of one sphere by another. The person who does not instrumentalize one sphere, from the standpoint of another sphere, of course, acts civilly.

Civility implies respect for the norms of each sphere of action and leads to an equilibrium between the spheres of action in society. A civil society is one where there is an equipoise between competing spheres of value. The search for equilibrium is a very old motif of Western civilization. It dates back to the Ionian enlightenment and via the Pythagorean tradition was a general influence on the crucible of Western civilization in the Mediterranean, and shaped in different ways both Rome and Greece.[12] The notion of equilibrium is thus central to Western classicism. Indeed, that which is "classical" (be it a state, artwork, or whatever), that which is "a classic," can be identified by the equilibrium—the elegant, harmonic intersection or arrangement—of its parts.

The categorical imperative of a pluralized world is to treat each value sphere as an end in itself. For the pluralist, finding a just equilibrium of countervailing forces is, at the most, a means to realize this categorical imperative. (Other means may be conceivable.) For the classicist, by contrast, the injunction to find a just equilibrium has a categorical status. Such an equilibrium, it must be stressed, does not represent a bland or smothering social harmony. Rather, it is the realization of a (just) *relationship of opposites*. In this conception, an equilibrium is a relationship between two distinct things that allows each to retain its own essential nature. It is the "just union of contraries," as Simone Weil put it.[13] When such a just union exists, communities of actors in different spheres accept the limits of their particular sphere; they desist from forcing their value priorities on others. When a just union prevails, the community of actors of each sphere has the power to repel the pressures of those who overstep the limits, should self-limitation fail (as it invariably will, from time to time). Limits are important. Without respect for limits, spiritedness becomes wild enthusiasm, economical behaviors become merely acquisitiveness, learning becomes nothing more than the endless accumulation of books and artifacts in museums and libraries, community is inflated into an oceanic and claustrophobic togetherness, and civic activism descends into intrusive policing of citizen's lives in the name of "republican virtue." The over-stepping of limits is so easy, and only, in the end, where the ambitions and driving force of one sphere is matched by the counterweight of other spheres can the integrity, the independent nature, of each sphere be maintained.

• • •

The world of politics stands in a special relationship to the spheres of society. Politics is concerned with relations between the different value spheres. It is concerned with doing justice to the different values in the world. Doing justice means finding the right balance between different spheres. But how, in matters of value, is this possible? In contemporary Western societies the expressing of opinions has become a pervasive experience. It is an experience that arises out of the multidimensional character of those societies. To live in such societies is to live in a "multicultural" world. Each culture represents a worldview, and when different worldviews clash, those who hold a particular worldview find an unbridgeable, or seemingly unbridgeable, disjunction between the particularity of their view and the world-dimension of their view. Usually, this disjunction is resolved in favor of *particularity* or *difference:* "It is just *my* view, my *opinion*." Individuals reinterpret their culture as their personal taste and construct themselves as belonging to taste cultures. What else can they do? *No worldview is held by the world.*

There is no universal view of things. To suggest otherwise would be to deny the deep divide between bourgeois, humanistic, and other forms of life. When the rational-ascetic, the paideistic-humanist, the communitarian, and so forth confront each other, what can they offer to each other but their respective opinions? What can they offer each other but expressions of personal (or group) taste: this pleases me, that displeases me; I love this, I loath that? For many purposes, of course, it is enough to express an opinion. Nothing more is needed. But, in many circumstances, it is not enough. It is not enough, for example, for the humanist to express an opinion against the destruction of old buildings and for the economic rationalist to express an opinion favoring the reconstruction of the city along Cartesian lines, *if they have to live in the same city.*

Why is it not enough? The answer to this question depends upon individuals' *paradigmatic* assumptions. If we are convinced modernists, it is not enough because to be modern means to be able to project and choose between alternatives; moreover, convinced modernists assume that societies and their decision makers will be able to choose between different unconditional values or categorical ends in much the same way that individuals choose between alternatives. But this is impossible, as various thinkers skeptical of modern reason, from David Hume to Jean-François Lyotard, have realized. It is impossible because individuals choose, as Aristotle knew, the conditional means to their unconditional ends.[14] They choose different paths to explore the categorical. The rationality of their choice is measured by whether the means chosen are consistent with the ends. But what happens when society internalizes more than one unconditional end? Or, when it no longer allocates different unconditional ends, hermetically, to different social estates?

The response of the nonskeptical modernist is that society has to *choose between* different unconditional ends. But how can this be, the skeptic asks, if we can only rationally choose means, not ends? It is reference to ends that makes the rational choice of means possible. By contrast, there is nothing to ground, so to speak, the choice of the categorical. Indeed, such a choice is a contradiction in terms. It might be objected, of course, that when individuals choose a vocation they make a choice between the different unconditional ends offered by the modern world. They may do so but only in a figurative sense. Their choice is largely a leap into the dark. It is, as Weber stressed, not rational but a matter of faith. Or, if you prefer a less religious metaphor, it is a *wager* that may or may not pay off. If individuals cannot *rationally* choose between different unconditional ends or values, then neither can society. Yet a *modernist* society constantly frames everything in terms of such choices. So when it is proposed to redevelop the inner cities and then, also, to refurbish the inner cities, the modernist logic of either/or, of means-ends rationality, demands the adoption of one or the other proposal—*either* Cartesian development *or* an inner-city renaissance. Either by enlightened fiat or by rational argument, a choice will, indeed *must*, be made.

The skeptical interpreters of the modern condition argue that such a choice cannot be made in any way that makes sense. In addition, when such a choice is made—when we choose between the unconditional—it can only be made *on the basis of injustice.* Such a choice will mean, inevitably, injustice to one party or another. Lyotard grasps this well with his concept of the *differend.*[15] These sorts of cases end up as a differend, where the settling or regulation of the conflict between two parties—in this case, the protagonists of development and those of renaissance—inevitably takes place in the idiom of *one* of the parties. Any wrong liable to be suffered by the other party can never be signified in that idiom; nor can the nature of the complaint of that other party ever be properly registered or understood.

In a theoretical manner, Lyotard grasps a very common experience of those living in modern societies. Yet what he does not tell us, in light of this, is what kind of decisions (rulings) legislators, planners, or citizens can make about the city (or anything else for that matter). If decisions crucially affecting a number of unconditional ends cannot be based on choices—because those choices would be choices between what cannot be chosen between—how else can we, to use Lyotard's expression, "regulate the conflict" between alternative unconditional values or categorical ends?[16] The skeptical (or post-) modernist, like Lyotard, typically cannot answer this question because the issues at stake are generated by and are internal to the modernist logic of choice. They are, in fact, questions from within the paradigm and assumptions of modernism, albeit posed from its skeptical margins. These are questions posed by skeptical thinkers who, like all skeptical thinkers, are sensitive to the pluralism of ultimate ends (principles) in the world, yet who cannot avoid the pressure of the modern imperative to choose.

Significantly, these are not new questions. Hume was grappling with them. So were the analytic philosophers of the twentieth century. The analytic philosophers drew from the experience of modernity the conclusion that cultural attitudes, judgments of value, and so on were incommensurable expressions of taste (mere opinions) that could not be argued—choices devoid of reason.[17] The political and juridical implications of this are significant. To say that something is a matter of taste effectively excludes it from being legitimately ruled upon by a tribunal or council. Why? Because tribunals hear arguments from both sides, while councils argue the merits of both sides for themselves. But to say something is a question of taste places it beyond rational argument and indeed beyond dispute. To say that I favor or disfavor some plan of action on grounds of taste is to say that the project simply pleases or displeases me. And, as Hannah Arendt put it, "the it-pleases-or-displeases-me is almost identical with an it-agrees-or-disagrees-with-me. The point of the matter is: I am directly affected. For this very reason, there can be no dispute about right and wrong here. . . . There can be no dispute about matters of taste. No argument can persuade me to like oysters if I do not like them."[18]

Hannah Arendt's merit as a thinker was her unwillingness to submit to the prerational and apolitical consequences of this position. After all, in a case where we have two propositions before us—to redevelop or to rejuvenate the city—we still have to decide a course of action. The skeptical interpreter of the modern condition says, "You cannot rationally choose." To choose invariably means to do an injustice to one or another of the cultural values underpinning the proposals. So, how do we decide? Perhaps we are better not to employ a modernist logic of choice in order to decide? Again, Arendt's merit as a thinker is demonstrated by her willingness to explore this possibility.

While Arendt in many respects forswore the modernist paradigm, she did so not by occupying the halfway house of the skeptical or postmodernist. The skeptical modernist, faced with incommensurable cultural values or categorical ends, resorts to (prerational) taste to decide between them. Just as the person confronting a plate of oysters in a restaurant will respond either with liking or loathing, so our personal taste, the skeptical modernist assumes, dictates the values we choose and the value spheres we inhabit. Arendt did not want so much to contest that proposition as to suggest that there was another way of relating to the variety of categorical ends or values that did not presuppose a logic of choice. In simple terms, Arendt's suggestion was that we can relate to the diversity of categorical ends in contemporary Western societies not only as *choosers* but also as *spectators*. The spectator is not interested in choosing one particular opinion in preference to another but is interested in the interrelationship or interplay between the particular opinions. The spectator is interested in the whole, rather than the parts. To this end, the spectator employs both the faculty of the imagination and the faculty of the understanding. Yet in the public sphere—the sphere of the spectator and critic—neither imagination nor understanding are dominant. What has priority is the faculty of judgment, and both the imagination and the understanding are enlisted in its cause of objectivity. Both imagination and understanding are transformed under the sign of the faculty of judgment (or objectivity).

What the imagination provides is a *reflective distance* from each particular opinion, value, or cultural tradition. Where they are imagined, particulars do not directly affect the spectator. They are not immediately present; each spectator only has contact with them through the mediation of her imagination. In the imagination, the spectator *re*presents them. This transforms the way the spectator *feels* about the particulars. As Arendt notes, what pleases in representation is different from what pleases in sense perception or taste. For the spectator, it is the represented object that arouses pleasure or displeasure, not the direct perception of the object; significantly, the pleasure that a person can experience from representations of an object is akin to that of disinterested delight. In other words, the relationship of the spectator to the particular-become-object is a disinterested one. Distanced from each particular, the spectator does not react in terms of his or her taste, liking, or loathing, and this, in turn, creates conditions for impartiality. But so, also, does the spectator's employment of the faculty of understanding.

The understanding is a *synthesizing* faculty. It permits a fusion of horizons, the relating of particular opinions so as to create a meaningful whole. We understand that which is not chaotic, that which has syntax, structure, and form, and, in the moments of greatest understanding, that which has beauty. In the case of the spectator, what is imagined is concurrently synthesized. The spectator can "see" with the inner eye. At one remove from the world, the visible events that the spectator witnesses are represented by the synthesizing imagination as part of a whole (totality). In other words, what the spectator's external senses perceive is converted into an object for the inner sense. The spectator is in a position to "see" by the "eye of the mind" and, in so doing, to "see" *the whole that gives meaning to each particular.*

The first spectators were singers. The ancient Greek poets sang of the totality of their world; acts of suffering and heroics, grief and joy, cunning and cruelty were all imaginatively and (according to the power of the poet's imagination) dispassionately represented in the singer's story line. The poet's words provided a reconstruction of a complete but strife-torn world. In contrast, the melodic "archetypes" or rhythmic "patterns," the *nomoi,* of the singer's songs provided an intimation of a harmonious order of the cosmos. Even while recounting the most dreadful episodes, the music of the singer gave the audience an experience of an order of beauty that human beings could enjoy simply by listening to the singer's song and by contemplating the beauty of the singer's performance. The tears of existence dissolved in the form of the singer's song and in the way it created a union of melody and rhythm, pitch and movement, sight and sound, voice and instrument. This beautiful spectacle had no point outside of itself. It was pure *energeia* and as such an exemplar of a perfect freedom.

The second spectators were the audience of the singer. The audience watched, listened, clapped, and danced to the music and then "judged" the excellence of the singer: the quality of the singer's voice, the instrumental skill, movements, theatrical presence, and the correspondence between meter and rhyme, word and melody. Audiences loved to see the excellence of the singer-poets tested in competition. In ancient Greece, music competitions were as commonplace as athletic competitions, and often one and the same. Out of this spirit of *agon,* of competition, developed a public life. It may well have been the space (the dancing floor, *choros*) shared by singers and audience that was the first public space where the meaning of society was articulated in public for the first time. In the Ionian and greater Greek world of the eighth, seventh, and sixth centuries B.C., the choros between singer and audience emerged along with the development of city life. The choros was not the possession of a particular household, tribe, status, or community. It was in the "middle" of each of these, a place where social divisions or strife were put aside for the sake of both the excellence of the performer and the shared admiration for the great performance. If the singer was outstandingly skilled and the performance a wondrous marshaling of melodic, rhythmic, and other elements, the audience would experience a contemplative delight or pleasure—even an ecstasy, a losing of the self—in a beautiful order of things: an "order without ordinance," a "lawfulness without law." The Greeks called their tunes nomoi, or laws. These laws did not dictate, hector, compel, or punish, and if it was outstanding, an audience could behold in the singer's performance a harmonious ordering of imagination, mind, and body that was an intimation of a perfect freedom.

Moderns can easily recognize themselves in this. Moderns are no less captivated by the power of the great musical performance and no less disappointed by the failure of the singer to create a beautiful order of things. In pleasure and disenchantment alike, modern audiences render "judgment." Kant thought that such judgments were the epitome of moderns' sense of art. Arendt followed him in this. No less than with the Greeks, the search for "lawfulness without law" underlies the deepest aspirations of moderns. The singer-storyteller is as much a symbol of these aspirations as in Homeric times. Judgments pay homage to the longing to live in a realm of freedom where creation, work, and feeling, indeed all of the human powers, surging and defiant, are brought together in an order that exacts from them neither submission to each other nor to the demands of wealth, status, or any other social-institutional power. When he spoke in the *Critique of Judgment* of conformity to "law without a law," Kant touched (perhaps unconsciously) upon an idea that emerged out of the Ionian world of Homer, Heraclitus, and Pythagoras: the idea that contrary forces or polar movements could be ordered "musically." Kant displayed little interest, though, in the artist's contribution to this ordering, preferring to dwell on the appreciative judgments that audiences or spectators make. What Kant in effect suggested in light of this was that we only know what "order without ordinance" is when we behold it, but we cannot explain its genesis nor should we try. Kant's refusal to attempt to elucidate how "lawfulness without law" is produced is an evasion—and a misleading one, if it implies that the beautiful order of things appears only ever as a contingent event that we cannot explain.

In the Kantian view the spectator can only tell us that an "order without ordinance" exists but not how it came into being. But how is even *this* possible? The spectator has no role in the "making" of an order of beauty, but the spectator does have the capacity to appreciate such an order. This is, in part, because the spectator views events from afar, as if watching actors on a stage. In the theater of human affairs, the advantage of the spectator, as Arendt remarks, is that this person sees the play as a whole, while each actor knows only his or her part.[19] The actor is partial by definition, while the spectator is, potentially, impartial. Thus, the spectator is in a position to *judge* events, deeds, and projects, because she can see, in a disinterested way, the play as a whole. Through the combined faculties of the imagination and understanding, the spectator is liberated from private conditions and can attain the *impartiality* that is, for Arendt, the specific virtue of judgment. The spectator displays both distance from particulars and a capacity to comprehend them as a totality.

To judge means to express an impartial assessment. Both the imaginative distance and comprehensive understanding of the great singer-storyteller are to be found also in the appreciative spectator, and these faculties collude to help the spectator to adopt a general, or cosmopolitan, standpoint from which to judge. This means that the appreciative spectator does not judge one particular from the standpoint of another particular. Rather the spectator assumes a third standpoint, related to the two particulars, yet distinct from both.[20] This enlarged perspective or mentality considers each of the other elements or standpoints, yet without surrendering the capacity to critically assess the particulars in question. Indeed, all particulars are held up for criticism, even those we most sympathize with. This is the discipline of objectivity:[21] of the judge who searches for the limits of all things, finding what they are or are not fitted for, rebuking their excessive pretensions, and praising their proportionality.

Judgment is by analogy a political faculty. Judgment anticipates an "order without ordinance." To live well in a highly pluralized world, with its inevitable polarization, requires an intelligible ordering of divergent currents but one that is neither authoritarian, administrative, nor juridical. The person who makes a judgment tacitly invokes, or appeals to, the idea of "lawfulness without law." Such judgment requires an enlarged mentality that, in turn, makes possible the rendering of a just or impartial assessment about matters of common concern. In relation to any question, there will be a variety of value standpoints and commitments. The moralist, the inner worldly ascetic, the dutiful citizen, and the lover of culture will confront each other. To think politically requires each personality to take account of the others' values. This does not mean we simply ditch our own view and think as the other person thinks—that is not an enlarged mentality, simply the mentality of sheep—conformism.

An enlarged mentality means that, in the context of the public world, we can look at an issue or question from our own view as well as from the other's perspective. In the public realm, we attempt to form a third view, a judgment, that will do justice to the first two original views by treating them impartially and objectively. Treating different value perspectives impartially and objectively is not the same as saying that we have discovered the truth of the matter. People enter the public world with preexisting value commitments and as the bearers and antagonists of moral values or civic values, of paideistic-humanistic or rational-ascetic values, and so on. Depending on their standpoint, they give priority to goodness, civic participation, learned curiosity, mettle and methodicality, and so forth. Politics, in this respect, is a drama of competing values: there is no transcendental perspective, no "higher truth" that will bring down the curtain on the drama. Each person—each of us—has a value standpoint. We cannot do otherwise in a pluralized world. It is our fate in such a world to be caught in the Olympian struggle of the gods. There is no transcendent perspective or position we can take that will *still* the struggle. But we can search for a "musical ordering" of these polarized values—for nomoi that provide consonance without obliterating contraries. Justice demands that we conciliate—accommodate—other, different value perspectives. Justice demands that we treat them fairly and impartially, evenhandedly. Justice, we can say with Aristotle, is the sum of all of the virtues.

Notes

1. I borrow the term "protovalue" from Cornelius Castoriadis. See his "Value, Equality, Justice, Politics," in *Crossroads in the Labyrinth*, by C. Castoriadis (Cambridge, Mass.: MIT Press, 1984).

2. On the concept of the freedom of the will, see Hannah Arendt, *The Life of the Mind* (New York: Harcourt Brace Jovanovich, 1978), esp. vol. 2. On the modern subject, see the discussion by Roberto Unger in *Knowledge and Politics* (New York: Free Press, 1975), chaps. 1 and 2.

3. And they do so for the sake of individual purposes that they imagine and project into the future—*their* future. Modern subjects imagine possibilities for themselves. Life *could* be like this or *could* be like that. Modern subjects dream of shining futures, not of golden ages in the past. They dream of what *could be*. Most of these dreams are not acted upon. They remain the stuff of desire, not of the will. Even when they are acted upon, they are most often not realized. Disappointment is the norm for modern subjects. But even when (mod-

ern) reality is at its most harsh, it is rare that there is "one thing and one thing only" that a person can do in a situation. Moderns at least have choices—sometimes invidious or unappealing choices but choices nonetheless. Modern subjectivity means that life is no longer *pre*scribed by social authorities—by parents, priests, or princes—so that there is only one course of action (the honorable course) open to a person—a course that has been laid down "before hand," a course for which there is a *pre*cedent.

4. Kant's thematization of autonomous subjectivity, of course, was not limited to moral issues. It was as much concerned with questions of law and state as with morals. In this respect, Kant differs from both strict liberal (libertarian) and romantic (anarchist) ideologists whose image of autonomous subjectivity is antithetical to any notion of law and state. Kant reconciles law and state with autonomous subjectivity because of the role such determinations can play in reconciling the freedom of one subject with that of another. Law and state in traditional society assumed the heteronomy of the subject; this is not so in the modern state, Kant suggested, where law and state can be conceived as doing no more than preventing one autonomous subjectivity from annihilating the autonomy of another subject. Law and state, in this modern conception, function to uphold the rights of subjects, and the rights of subjects—their rights to determine themselves in respect of their bodies, property, speech, and so on—are claims upon others to respect their autonomy. One subject's denial of another subject's autonomy means the denial of rights, and the denial of rights justifies the intervention of the law or state to rectify or prevent such denial.

But of course, as the Kantian tradition clearly understood, it is not only individuals but also institutions, indeed the very law itself, that can deny autonomy and be complicit in the domination of some wills over others. Social institutions, state institutions, and the law can deprive one group of the very civil rights enjoyed by another group—rights to dress, live, marry, establish a business, seek a job, enroll in a school, and so on. In the Kantian state (the *Rechtsstaat*) the law provides "equal protection" for all groups and individuals. Some of the greatest struggles of the modern epoch have been precisely the struggles to entrench the equal or nondiscriminatory protection of the law, to entrench a system of law that cancels all laws and institutions that permit some people autonomy yet deny it to others. This struggle for civil rights has been a struggle for equal rights that has been complemented on yet a higher level of political rights. Paradoxically, the very law and the very state that function to either extend or constrain self-determination become, in turn, objects of self-determination, of will and initiative. Just as moderns learn to choose business or marriage partners, so also they learn to choose political representatives and propositions in referendums, to reform the laws and institutions, to decide whether to continue with them or rescind and replace them. Moderns gradually learn to think and then speak for themselves rather than on behalf of their god, community, or class. In doing so, they assert and affirm that in the end they are not the instruments of external forces, not subject to the alienations of god, community, and class, not, in a word, heteronomously determined.

5. For Kant, the matter of consistency is a matter of the form of the will (i.e., of the *consistent* form of the will). In making choices, autonomous subjects should consider what would happen if their will, or more particularly the maxims of action they choose for themselves, took the form of a universal law of nature. Consider a primitive version of this self-reflective exercise: if a subject chose deceit or murder as a subjective principle of action, what would happen if everyone murdered or deceived? What would happen if others behaved toward the subject as the subject chose to behave toward them? In raising these sorts of issues, Kant was not just regurgitating the Golden Rule (do unto others as you would have them do unto you). Kant was not just interested in the form, in this case the universality, of action, but in the form (or universality) of the will. The difference is crucial. Kant's point is that autonomous subjects can will (choose) actions that in effect destroy or undermine others' autonomous subjectivity or power of self-determination. By choosing to humiliate another I can take away their confidence to choose; by expropriating another, I can take away their material capacity to choose, and so on. Kant's insistence that *rational* willing or choosing beings look to the *form* of their will simply emphasized, and brought home, the contradictory nature of such exercises of the will. What if others behaved toward me as I have chosen to behave toward them? Would not my will, in the form of universal law, destroy itself? Would not the determinations of my autonomous subjectivity, if directed toward me, destroy that very autonomous subjectivity? Am I not being inconsistent?

Kant recognized the problem of bad will and posed the question: what would a *good* will be? A good will, he suggested, would be exhibited in the case where the grounds the subject looked to when determining an action were valid for the will of any rational being. It wasn't enough that self-determining subjects looked to their own pleasures, desires, or purposes. Rather, they should look to the very idea of themselves as rational, as choosing or self-determining beings. For the willing subject, self-determination is not, and cannot be, a contingent or subjective end but an objective one. We cannot be willing subjects and choose not to choose. Autonomy is a ground valid for the will of all autonomous beings.

6. For an insightful account of the origins and character of the culturalist paradigm, see the work of Johann Arnason. Of particular interest (and in English) are "Rationalisation and Modernity: Towards a Culturalist Reading of Max Weber," *Sociology Papers* (La Trobe University) 9; "Culture and Imaginary Significations," *Thesis Eleven* 22 (1989); and "Civilization, Culture and Power: Reflections On Norbert Elias' Genealogy of the West," *Thesis Eleven* 24 (1989).

7. On this, see my "Civility and Radicalism," in *The Social Philosophy of Agnes Heller*, ed. John Burnheim (Amsterdam: Rodopi, 1994) and "Postmodern Perspectives and Justice," *Thesis Eleven* 30 (1991).

8. For one account of the axial crossroads, see Lewis Mumford, *The City in History* (London: Secker and Warburg, 1961), 207.

9. Max Weber, "'Objectivity' in Social Science and Social Policy," in *The Methodology of the Social Sciences* (New York: Free Press, 1949), 55.

10. More dangerous still, of course, has been the impact of anti-Enlightenment or antimodernist universalism, which managed to fuse the world-historical horizons opened by the Enlightenment with the exclusivist mentality of the pre-Enlightenment lifeworld (promoting and soliciting particularistic integrations), treating classes, nations, and ethnic identifications as universals, thereby justifying the dismissal, subordination, or elimination of anyone or anything that did not belong to these self-proclaimed world-historical integrations. Such oppressive universalisms seem never far from the surface in modern life. We see today how easy it is for even modern movements, propagating universal rights, to degenerate into proselytizing, with dogmatists seeking to elevate categories of race and gender to the status of a new universal class.

11. For a contrary argument, see Agnes Heller, *A Philosophy of Morals* (London: Basil Blackwell, 1990).

12. See my discussion of this in "Romantic Modernism and the Greek Polis," *Thesis Eleven* 34 (1993).

13. See Simone Weil's "Spiritual Biography," in *The Simone Weil Reader,* ed. George A. Panichas (New York: David McKay, 1977), 22. See also her comments on the subject of equilibrium and its relation to the idea of justice in "Analysis of Oppression," "The *Iliad,* Poem of Might," and "Equality," essays in the Panichas volume. Weil's views on this topic are also discussed competently by Peter Winch in *Simone Weil: The Just Balance* (Cambridge: Cambridge University Press, 1989) and by David McLellan in *Simone Weil: Utopian Pessimist* (London: Macmillan, 1989). Weil often pointed to the significance of the Pythagoreans in contributing to the development of the notion of justice as a kind of recriprocity of opposites.

14. Aristotle, *Ethics,* bk. 3, esp. 1111b5–1113a34.

15. Jean-François Lyotard, *The Differend* (Manchester: Manchester University Press, 1988).

16. For an attempted solution of these problems from within the framework of a universalistic modernism, see my "Moralities, Rule Choice and the Universal Legislator," *Social Research* 50, no. 4 (1983).

17. See, e.g., Charles Stevenson, *Facts and Values* (New Haven, Conn.: Yale University Press, 1963).

18. Hannah Arendt, *Lectures on Kant's Political Philosophy* (Chicago: University of Chicago Press, 1982), 66.

19. Ibid., 68. See also Arendt's comments in *Life of the Mind,* 1:11.

20. Arendt, *Lectures on Kant's Political Philosophy,* 76.

21. On the importance of objectivity, impersonality, and so forth for Arendt, see Richard Sennett's discussion of her work in *The Conscience of the Eye* (New York: Alfred A. Knopf, 1990).

GILLIAN ROBINSON

To Think What We Are Doing: Reconsidering Citizenship and Philosophy

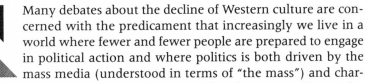Many debates about the decline of Western culture are concerned with the predicament that increasingly we live in a world where fewer and fewer people are prepared to engage in political action and where politics is both driven by the mass media (understood in terms of "the mass") and characterized by the sterility of conformity. In this chapter, I will consider one approach to the malaise of Western political culture and thought, which is provided by Hannah Arendt's invocation of the public realm of antiquity as the location of the greatest human endeavor and achievement.[1]

For Arendt, modernity represents, in some sense, an inverted mirror image of antiquity that is constituted by negative characterizations that portray the "human condition" as an incomparable loss of human experience. The ancient public realm, on the other hand, was the arena that inspired the political qualities of citizenship—dignity, honor, courage, and excellence—and was simultaneously the place of freedom and plurality. Since it was always the place that preserved each individual's distinctiveness and uniqueness, it was also where the potentiality of the human condition could be fulfilled. Moreover, the preeminent political values of thinking, as they were conceived in pre-Socratic philosophy and incorporated into Arendt's work, belong to and are united in the public realm, and it is this that provides for the true expression of the human condition.

Part of Arendt's contention is that the concerns of both the political actor (freedom and action) and the philosopher (contemplation and immortality) have been viewed as qualitatively different since the time of ancient Greece. According to Arendt, Plato first distinguished the world of contemplation from the world of action, granting contemplation an "enormous superiority" over activity of any kind, including political activity.[2] She also claims that Aristotle's articulation of the different ways of life was similarly guided by the ideal of contemplation. Aristotle distinguished three ways of life in which individuals might choose in freedom, ruling out all activities associated with the primary goal of basic survival—those conditions of necessity that rule the life of *animal laborans*, as well as the conditions of the working life of *homo faber*, the craftsman, and the acquisitive life of the merchant.[3]

The three ways of life distinguished by freedom are first, the way of life concerned with the beautiful, that is, with things that are not necessary or merely useful—in other words, a way of life that enjoys the bodily pleasures in which the beautiful is consumed; second, the way of life devoted to the polis where excellence produces beautiful deeds;[4] and third, the way of life of the philosopher, devoted to inquiry into the eternal and its contemplation, "whose everlasting beauty can neither be brought about through the producing interference of man nor changed through his consumption of them."[5] Moreover, incorporated into the idea of ancient freedom as release from the necessities of life and compulsion by others, the Greek philosophers added the understanding that freedom also meant the cessation of political activity. In other words, they suggested the philosopher had to be freed from the worries and cares of the political life for the life of contemplation. This ancient conviction of the primacy of contemplation over political activity was based on the belief that no work of human hands could "equal in beauty and truth the physical *kosmos*, which swings in itself in changeless eternity without any interference or assistance from outside."[6] The Greeks believed that the eternity of the world only revealed itself to "mortal eyes" when all movement and activities had come to rest. Arendt contends, however, that the philosopher's relation to the world of contemplation, and to eternity, bears some relation to the condition of mortality because to experience the eternal is to leave the world of humankind behind.

The philosopher's experience of the eternal, which to Plato was *arrheton* (unspeakable) and to Aristotle *aneu logou* (without word), and which was later conceptualized in the paradoxical *nunc stans* (the standing now), can occur only outside both the realm of human affairs and the plurality of men. This is evident in the Cave parable in Plato's *Republic*, where the philosopher, having liberated himself from the fetters that bound him to his fellow man, leaves the cave in perfect "singularity," neither accompanied nor followed by others. Arendt suggests here that, if to die is the same as "to cease to be among men," the experience of the eternal is a kind of death, and the only thing that separates it from real death is that it is not final because no living creature can endure it for any length of time.[7]

As Leah Bradshaw suggests, the valorization of the contemplative world over the world of action means that the philosopher's preoccupation with the divine,[8] and particularly the divine mystery of life which is death, has worked against the concerns of history, politics, action, and community,[9] all of which are connected to humankind's earthly immortality and stand in sharp contrast to Arendt's ontological category of natality as the crucial factor in action and politics. The Greek philosophers nevertheless recognized the importance of the *vita activa* because this was the space where freedom was located. In particular, they recognized that freedom was the result of political activity and that it constituted the antithesis of the necessity characteristic of household organization. To the Greeks, freedom was an essential condition of what they called *eudaimonia* (felicity). Yet because of their understanding of the action of mortals as boundless and unpredictable, the Greeks always remained suspicious of action. This suspicion caused the valuing of the *vita contemplativa* over the *vita activa*. Arendt considers modern philosophy as antithetical to politics because it stresses the life and thought of the singular and solitary individual, the ground for which can be found in early philosophic thought. The early philosophers believed that all the calamities of action arose from the human condition of plurality. Their attempt to hide, to take shelter, from events results in the Platonic belief that "one man, isolated from all others" can remain "master of his doings from beginning to end."[10]

Plato's idea of a philosopher-king ruling the chaos of the earthly world, whose wisdom could save the perplexity of the many, is a variety of one-man rule; it is Plato's solution to the problem of plurality. Plato's (and Aristotle's) work assumes that a political community consists of those who rule and those who are ruled, which led to another solution. Arendt argues that in the *Statesman*[11] Plato opened a gulf between the two modes of action, beginning and achieving. Arendt maintains that the vicissitudes of action arising out of the human condition of plurality have historically given birth to new forms of political action. Attempts to escape the predicament and moral irresponsibility of action usually give rise to the political solution of monarchy, one-man rule. Forms of one-man rule share in common the removal of the citizen from the public realm in an attempt to create stability and permanence away from the unpredictability and conflict of the public realm. This so-called escape from the frailty of human affairs is the hallmark of the concept of rule and is tantamount to the abolition of the public realm itself. Nonetheless, these sui generis concepts of rule indicate a continuing suspicion of action.

The most fundamental version of escape from the world is to be found, Arendt argues, in this work of Plato. In the *Statesman* Plato differentiates the two modes of action. Politically, this means that "the beginner" who initiated the action has become the ruler and rules over those who execute his action. Thus, knowing what to do and actually doing it become vastly different.[12] In both traditional and modern life, she contends, this separation of "knowing" and "doing" has become the basis of all theories of domination. Although Arendt wishes to defend Plato's thought, particularly in regard to the substitution of action by rulership and the concomitant reevaluation of making and fabrication entailed by "execution," it is nevertheless apparent to her that the consequence of basing the state upon the organization of the household is that the political situation from which action issues, and through which action is undertaken in the state, carries with it the prepolitical attributes of the household. Such action can then only be oppressive and discriminatory, and hence a denial of freedom.

Arendt notes that Plato's contention, that the rules of behavior should be derived from the master-slave relationship, actually implies that action should not play any part in human affairs. The corollary of this was not that each citizen was denied a role in public affairs, but that all citizens should act as "one." In effect, this entailed the end of plurality by denying a place for discussion and dissension. It is fundamental to the human condition itself that action, pluralized and differentiated by being seen and heard, is always simultaneously an attribute of the individual; thus, anything that stands in the way of the actualization of this potential inhibits the development of authentic citizenship and problematizes the conditions of democracy.

In Arendt's interpretation[13] the problem for Plato was to make sure that the beginner remained master of what he had begun, while others executed his orders. To this end, Plato proposed a revolutionary transformation of the polis based on the administrative maxims of the well-ordered household. This new concept of rule was to be the chief mechanism for the ordering and judging of human affairs, thereby removing them from the chaos of action. Henceforth, the Platonic identification of knowledge with command and rulership, and of action with obedience and execution, became authoritative for the whole Western tradition of political thought. Arendt's contention is that the separation between knowing and doing is an everyday experience of fabrication and, since Plato, the public realm and its activities have been interpreted in terms of an image of a fabricated object. Just as the artisan creates an object for a particular use, Plato believed that the ideal political actor is the insightful ruler who molds the polis for a particular end.

Arendt argues strongly that the image of the political realm as a fabricated object lies in the doctrine of ideas and thus at the center of Platonic philosophy.[14] For Plato, the ideas are variations of the beautiful when they are not concerned with political philosophy. In the *Republic*, however, the ideas are transformed into standards, measurements, and rules of behavior that are pertinent to the Greek sense of the word "good," in the sense of "good for" or of "fitness." This transformation of the meaning and intent of the ideas, that is, Plato's declaration that the highest idea was the good and no longer the beautiful, was for one purpose only, Arendt maintains. It was essentially for the political purpose of eliminating the character of frailty from human affairs.[15] In the political context of the *Republic*, the idea of the good is an absolute standard of political and moral judgment. The introduction of absolute standards into the world of humankind provided a transcendent measure to judge the activities of humankind. The technical advantage of this was that it removed the personal and pluralized element from rulership in its participatory sense, and it provided the institution of rulership with a quasi-divine quality in the person of the ruler that sharply distinguished her or him from those s/he ruled.[16]

This radical separation of philosophy and politics, or thought and action, in the public political sphere always concerned Arendt. Therefore, for her antiquity represented the ideal period of time where thinking had remained active in the world of appearance, while the modern age, on the other hand, represented the complete separation of thought and action and the demise of morally adequate action. In the modern age, thinking became a principal enemy of politics, she argues, because it stressed the life and thought of the individual.[17] As a consequence of this, politics has henceforth been associated with the less meaningful attributes of the world of humankind, such as work, fabrication, and labor. She argues further that an authentic understanding of politics was also corroded by the Christian belief that freedom was an internal condition of the undisturbed private life. As Bhikhu Parekh shows, the Christian contempt for the world is clearly seen in the separation between the Christian notion of goodness (that is, the purity and value of the act that remains only when the act is hidden) and worldly appearance, and in the interpretation of political activity, or earthly recognition, as degrading and corrupting.[18] Arendt suggests that this corrosion of politics was not a necessary development of the relationship between thought and action; rather it was the case that these historical events associated with the rise of Christianity brought to light an underlying—and in that sense internal—problematical relationship between thought and action.[19]

Arendt argues that Socrates's death is the turning point in the tradition of political thought because it makes Plato despair of polis life and makes him doubt some of Socrates' fundamental wisdom. Although this turning point is also visible in Arendt's work, it does not create an unreconciled or unresolved problem for her, as has been suggested elsewhere.[20] Rather, it is possible to integrate Arendt's political philosophy of action with her purely philosophical understanding of thinking under the normative guidance of Socratic philosophy.

Arendt's first attempts to incorporate thinking within the vita activa occur in her discussion in *The Human Condition* of art objects produced by homo faber. Here she introduces the relation of thought to creativity, and this is one of the early indications of the significance of thought to the construction of the world. It is possible through Arendt's understanding of Socratic philosophy to redraw the relationship of the philosopher to the political actor in a way that overcomes the separation of the worlds of contemplation and action. Thus the links between thinking and reflectivity, as they actively relate to action and to morally adequate action, recontextualize the fully developed human person in the public political world. Arendt's argument is that the duality inherent in the Socratic two-in-one dialogue both prepares us for a role in the world and is also the manner in which we are inserted into the world's plurality. Thus, the movement in her work between the solitary nature of philosophy and the ancient Greek understanding of thinking as an activity constitutive of action enlarges our understanding of what it means to act.

In Arendt's interpretation, after Socrates's death Plato, in particular, doubted the validity of persuasion. In ancient Greece, persuasion was a specifically political form of speech (in contradistinction to violence and other acts of prepolitical behavior) through which the Greeks, in contrast to the barbarians, were able to conduct their affairs without compulsion. After Socrates was unable to persuade either the citizens or the judges that his behavior was in the best interests of the city, Plato draws the conclusion that the lives of the polis and philosopher are antithetical poles of human existence.[21] The conflict between the philosopher and the polis leads to Plato's demand that a philosopher should rule the city. He argued against the prejudice of the polis that the philosopher was incapable of knowing what was good for himself or by extension what was good for the polis.[22] The ancient Greeks maintained that the philosopher's concern was with truth, not with the world of human affairs and the love of the beautiful, and concluded that philosophy "drove its adherents out of the polis and made them unfit for it." Plato did not deny that the philosopher was concerned with "eternal, nonchanging, nonhuman matters," but he did not agree that a political life was unsuited to the philosopher.[23] He claimed rulership[24] for the philosopher on the grounds that only the philosopher could behold the idea of the good, and he asserted that the philosopher's concern with the eternal did not prevent her or him from being beneficial or useful to the polis.

Arendt argues that these issues are very clearly seen in Plato's allegory of the Cave, which she insists must be read as a politically contextualized work. The allegory of the cave is the biography of the philosopher. There are three stages in the life of the philosopher. Each of these stages represents the *periagoge,* the "turning-about," of the whole human being, so indicating the formation of the philosopher.[25] The first turning-about is metaphorically the story of the scientist who turns about to find how things are in themselves, regardless of the opinions (the *doxa*) of the multitude. Because the image on the screen represents the opinions of each individual from her or his position, to see[26] things as they really are each person must change their position. Every opinion depends on, and corresponds to, an individual's position in the world. The second turning-about occurs when the future philosopher leaves the cave through a stairway to the clear sky. "Here appear the ideas, the eternal essences of perishable things and of mortal men illuminated by the sun, the idea of ideas, which enables the beholder to see and the ideas to shine forth."[27]

The philospher's third turning-about is the return to the world: the philosopher must return because s/he is mortal. The philosopher, however, no longer feels at home in this earthly environment and is in danger of having lost the common sense needed for an orientation in a world of commonness. The thoughts of the philosopher henceforth contradict the common sense of the world, and s/he is often in conflict with it. This interpretation of the relationship between the philosopher and the polis provided another ground upon which Plato could base his claim for a philosopher-king to rule the polis: the philosopher had to assume rulership, even though uninterested in it, in order to prevent the chaos of rule by opinion. Moreover, the individual of common sense has an innate trust in her or his own capabilities and sense, whereas the philosopher is always searching for causes and predictable outcomes.[28] Consequently, the philosopher is suspicious of the unpredictable nature of the revelatory capacity of speech and action in the public realm.

The allegory of the Cave supports Arendt's contention that politics, the realm of human affairs, is viewed from the perspective of the philosopher. For her, the most politically significant things about human activity are missing from the behavior of the cave dwellers. They do not talk and act; rather, they look at the screen upon which they see their *doxei*.[29] The cave dwellers share only one characteristic with the philosopher: they are all potential philosophers.[30] Thus politics appears to philosophy, Arendt argues.[31] The purpose of the philosopher is, for Plato, to find in the realm of philosophy those standards appropriate for the public world of humankind,[32] who, while remaining cave dwellers, have nevertheless formed opinions about the same matters as philosophers.

Plato henceforth denies the validity of persuasion through his condemnation of opinion. Platonic truth is absolute truth, the very opposite of opinion. Absolute standards became the measure against which all human action could be judged and through which human thought could achieve reliability.[33] Thus Plato, through the purely philosophical doctrine of the ideas, introduced transcending standards into the realm of human affairs. This belief rose out of the Socratic experience that only rulership could guarantee the philosopher the earthly immortality that the polis was supposed to ensure for all its citizens. These tensions became evident because, on the one hand, thought and action were always threatened by their own instability and by human forgetfulness in the realm of public affairs and, on the other hand, the thoughts of the philosopher were exposed to willful oblivion. This occurred when the philosopher submitted her or his truth—a reflection of the eternal—to the polis. Immediately, it became one opinion among many, and this constituted a threat to the immortality of the philosopher.[34] The philosopher's reflection lost its distinguishing quality and became no more than mere temporality, threatening the existence of the realm of contemplation when it was added to the opinions of the public realm.

Arendt maintains[35] it is through the consideration of Socrates' trial that Plato arrived at his conception of truth ("his tyranny of truth") as the opposite of opinion and his notion of a philosophical form of speech, *dialegesthai*, as the opposite of the Socratic understanding of persuasion and rhetoric. For Socrates, opinion was the formulation in speech of *dokei moi*, the "it-appears-to-me."[36] In other words, dokei moi comprehended and encapsulated the world as it opened itself to reception by the individual. It was, therefore, neither subjective and arbitrary, on the one hand, nor absolute and valid for all, on the other. The assumption underlying dokei moi is that the world opens differently for every person according to their position in the world. Dokei moi is thus part of the plurality of the public sphere. This Socratic influence can be clearly seen in the Arendtian public sphere. First, although the world opens differently to every individual, its commonness resides in the fact that the same world opens to everyone, notwithstanding the differences between individuals and their positions. This confirms, Arendt writes, that "both you and I are human."[37] Second, doxa means not only opinion but also splendor and fame. It is thus directly related to the political realm: to assert one's opinion belonged to being able to present oneself and thus to be seen and heard by others. The attributes of splendor and fame are also constitutive of the heroic and dramatic nature of the public realm. Socrates thus asserts the value of human plurality and the interconnectedness of thought and action.

Socrates always remained in the agora waiting to help others find the truth in their opinions. He called this *maieutic,* the art of midwifery. Arendt argues that this process is the same one Plato later calls dialegesthai. The method of maieutic has a twofold significance. Each person has her own opinion, her own opening to the world. Because we can never know what kind of dokei moi, the "it-appears-to-me," the other possesses, Socrates always began with questions. Socrates wanted to bring out the inherent truth of the opinion that everyone potentially possesses. For Arendt, the method of doing this is "talking things through, [where] this dialectic brings forth truth *not* by destroying *doxa* or opinion, but on the contrary reveals *doxa* in its own truthfulness."[38] For Socrates, the process of maieutic was a political process characterized by inconclusiveness and open-endedness.

Arendt was always ambivalent about the juxtaposition of truth and opinion, as well as the disclosing of truth through opinion. On the one hand, she warns us that the search for truth, and truth itself, can destroy doxa because it can destroy the specific political reality of the citizenry—in other words, truth can destroy opinion, leaving no opinion at all. On the other hand, an inconclusive end to a dialogue may not be an indication of an abyss between truth and opinion. Rather the point is that the distinction between opinion and truth may lead to a state of productive tension, inasmuch as doxa is essential to the search for truth. After Socrates, the philosopher could only protect her- or himself from the suspicion of the world by an indifference and contempt for the world of the city. In all post-Platonic philosophy, Arendt argues, two things are obvious: philosophy no longer has a special task in the world of politics, and the philosopher has less responsibility for it than any other citizen.[39]

Plato also makes a distinction between doxa and *thaumadzein*, which is simultaneously the wonder at that which is as it is and pathos, something that must be endured. Thaumadzein is quite distinct from opinion. Wonder is the beginning of philosophy. The pathos resulting from enduring wonder is expressed by Arendt as "now I know what it means not to know; *now* I know that I do not know."[40] The ultimate questions arise from the experience of not knowing. In asking these questions humankind establishes itself as a questioning species.[41] This is one of the basic aspects of the human condition. The difference between the philosopher and the multitude is that the multitude refuses to endure the pathos of wonder, *not* that it knows nothing of it. Having opinions about things we know only in speechless wonder is what Arendt terms *doxadzein*. In this situation it is possible for opinion to become the opposite of truth because doxadzein is the opposite of thaumadzein.

This expresses the twofold conflict of the philosopher with the polis. The precondition of the political realm is speech. Speech confirms humankind as a political animal, a *zoon politikon*. Speechless wonder, however, puts the philosopher outside the realm of human affairs. Furthermore, the philosophical reception occurs to the philosopher in her or his singularity. In this situation the philosopher is removed from equality as well as from distinctiveness with all others. The philosopher is thus alienated from humankind.[42] Moreover, the pathos of wonder experienced by the philosopher is part of the general human condition that most choose not to endure. This causes an increasingly intolerable situation for the philosopher in the realm of public affairs. The philosopher's own experience of speechless wonder produces unanswerable questions. The philosopher has therefore no clearly defined opinion to add to the other opinions that help construct the common sense of the world. If the philosopher starts to speak into the world of common sense, the result is common sense being turned upside down. The philosopher, in the course of her or his engagement with the public world, becomes well aware of the incompatibility between fundamental philosophical and political experiences.

This explains, for Arendt, why Plato opted for solitude but not Socratic solitude. Socrates' insight is the relationship between politics and the philosophical experience. The philosophical experience of solitude is the two-in-one dialogue that enables the philosopher to live with others, which begins with living with oneself. Conscience in its most general sense is based on the fact that I can be in agreement with myself;

this means that I do not only appear to others but also to myself. This is of the greatest relevance for politics because individuals attain their full humanity in the public political realm not only as they *are*, but as they *appear*. Even while engaged in the dialogue of the two-in-one we are never separated from the world of plurality that is, in its most generalized sense, humanity. This enables the philosopher to form opinions. The philosopher's opinion, because he can endure pathos, never becomes dogmatic as does the doxadzein of mere opinion holders. Plato, on the other hand, wanted to prolong the fleeting moment of wonder and turn it into a way of life, the *bios theoretikos*, thus separating philosophy and politics, thought and action, for eternity.

Therefore, Arendt interprets the classical tradition as beginning with Plato's political philosophy in which the utopian reorganization of polis life is directed by the insight of the philosopher—an insight, Margaret Canovan argues, that has no other aim than to make possible the philosopher's way of life.[43] Yet, it is more than this for Arendt. Plato's "turning away from politics and then returning in order to impose his standards on human affairs"[44] is also constitutive of the modern tradition of political philosophy as she reads it. As George Kateb points out, the standards with which Plato returns to politics are antithetical to it. According to Arendt's interpretation of Plato's hostility to politics as irresponsible and immoral action, the Platonic return to politics restricts free action; in Kateb's analysis, it means "to impose strict order inhospitable to freedom." Moreover, Plato makes clear that he did not believe he had found *another* principle to order human action but rather a *higher* principle. For him, this higher principle was the moral virtue attained in the contemplation of the good.[45] Plato's demands for "a surcease from political activity"[46] construe action not only as the worldly activity of the interests and aims of individuals pursued in society but also, therefore, as the disturbance (the "unquiet") and uncertainty that is characteristic of and internal to human affairs. The originary classical philosophical suspicion of politics thus arises from two fundamental beliefs in Platonic thought: (1) the view that the public space lacks the necessary moral boundaries to counter the turbulence and open-endedness of action in the public space, which, as Kateb argues, Plato and Aristotle believed impeded the attainment of a properly human life,[47] and (2) the valorization of contemplation over action as the most exemplary form of human activity.[48]

For Plato and Aristotle, the capacity through which humankind is distinguished from all other forms of life is not action; rather, it is self-rule and its corresponding organization.[49] Yet, the classical philosophers were also aware that self-rule could easily become the imperfect rule of the political tyrant.[50] This understanding of politics led Plato and Aristotle not so much to doubt that freedom is located in the public realm but rather to conceive of human affairs and the outcome of action as being directed by an invisible hand behind the scenes.[51] Hence, the early philosophers were not only aware of the boundlessness of action and its lack of moderation, but they were also concerned with its inherent unpredictability. Their identification of politics as "unquiet" emerges from their belief in the inability to foretell all the logical consequences of a particular act.[52] The only solution for the early Greeks appeared to be the renunciation of action. This is why, Arendt argues, the Socratic school turned to the functions of legislation and foundation, even though these were understood as prepolitical forms. In this shift away from authentic politics, legislating and the execution of decisions were considered political activities because their results were tangible products and the processes had a clearly recognizable end. For the Socratic school, this form of political activity introduced stability and reliability to the world of human affairs.[53] Nevertheless, Arendt argues that these activities were not truly acting but making (fabrication) and thus were not constitutive of an authentic political way of life. In contradistinction to the classical philosophers, Arendt believes that "action alone is the exclusive prerogative of man" and that it is humankind's capacity for action that makes politics possible and constitutes a public political realm of freedom. Moreover, action constitutes a human community because it relies upon the presence of others as a constitutive fact.[54]

It is this understanding of philosophy that explains Arendt's problematic relationship to the work of Martin Heidegger.[55] Although her first sustained critique of his work was in *The Life of the Mind*, in an earlier, unpublished address to the American Political Science Association in 1954, Arendt had interpreted Heidegger's work as an example of the abandonment of the philosopher's position as the "wise man" of the polis—one who knew the "eternal standards for the perishable affairs of the City of men"[56]—for the retreat to the solitary world of contemplation.[57] This is an interpretation she never really revises. In Heidegger's work, "the old hostility of the philosopher to the *polis* is only too apparent," Arendt states in her address. Heidegger's abandonment of the position of philosopher in the public realm, and hence the claim to wisdom, has important consequences for that realm, Arendt argues. First, it opens the whole public realm to a reexamination in light of the elementary human experiences within that realm itself. She suggests that such an analysis encourages the discarding of concepts and judgments that do not emerge from the public sphere but that "have roots in altogether different kinds of human experience."[58] Second, this examination is guided by a social and political contextualization, for Arendt "the concept of historicity" that never reaches its center: "man as an acting being."[59]

Heidegger himself undertakes such a reexamination in *Sein und Zeit* (Being and Time) by analyzing human existence from the perspective of a phenomenology of everyday life. The quest for the Platonic understanding of truth as solitary activity, of which Heidegger is representative for Arendt, makes the philosopher hostile to action and freedom.[60] Heidegger believed that willing (action) and thinking were conflictual, and his eventual repudiation of willing left him firmly within the Platonic philosophical tradition. In Arendt's interpretation, Heidegger clearly rejected any understanding of politics and the possibilities that action presented.

Arendt also saw in Heidegger the possibility of the tyrant. Heidegger inherits, she maintains, the conflict between the perception of the divine and the ties that bind us to the human condition: the existential condition of the philosopher. This was the conflict that Plato rationalized and generalized as the conflict between body and soul. The more a philosopher becomes a true philosopher the more the body must be separated from the soul. In other words, the philosopher must rule over the body as "a master rules over slaves."[61] The philosopher is thus already acquainted with tyranny. It was a recognition of the will to rule and dominate (tyranny) that Heidegger tried to come to terms with in his later work.[62] The separation of thought and action that so clearly consumes Arendt's intellectual effort is interpreted quite differently by Heidegger. For him, the faculties of thinking and willing are opposites. Rather than the harmony of the Socratic two-in-one dialogue of consciousness, Heidegger interprets consciousness as "an ongoing conflict between will and counterwill, between command and resistance."[63] Moreover, thinking and acting become one for Heidegger: "thinking is actually acting."[64] Arendt argues that in Heidegger's later work solitary thinking in itself constitutes the only relevant action.

It is axiomatic for Arendt that modern political philosophy[65] manifests the philosopher's negative attitude toward the affairs of humankind, of which she is, at the same time, a member. This attitude involves and expresses the relationship between the specifically philosophical experience of singularity and solitude, and the experience of moving among others. Arendt's concern with the problematic of the inherent conditions of duality (action) and singularity (thought) as they reflect on the human condition and its moral capacity for action in the context of a modern public sphere forms the basis of her critique of Plato and Aristotle and opens onto her discussion of the merits of Socratic philosophy and its relevance for action in modernity. Arendt argues this in a twofold sense: from the standpoint of what is philosophically appropriate for politically contextualized action and, equally as important, from the position of a heightened relevance of Socratic philosophy for morally adequate action within the context of the modern human condition. Arendt's discussion of the relationship of the philosopher to the realm of contemplation indicates that the philosopher, while nevertheless engaged with the realm of contemplation, is simultaneously aware of the realm of action and the activities that pertain to it and remains tied to it inasmuch as the philosopher is always a human being. Here, Arendt identifies the tendency in Plato to "hide" from the consequences of action in the realm of contemplation, a tendency that she registers as the radical separation of philosophy and politics, or thought and action, with which we are familiar in modernity.

By moving outside of the modern trajectory of philosophic thought attributable to the Platonic-Aristotelian tradition, Arendt recasts philosophy from the vantage point of the relevance of the Socratic two-in-one dialogue for action in modernity in the following way, and this is what constitutes the Socratic turn in her work. She proposes a way of reconciling the various ways of being in the world, the active public political life and the life of contemplation. She suggests, through her explorative unfolding of the Socratic two-in-one dialogue, that thinking has always been of central significance to the human condition and to the activities of the realm of human affairs. Through our self-understanding, which articulates us as thinking beings, the reconciliation between thought and action occurs in the move between the so-called singularity of thinking and the plurality of action, a reconciliation that becomes clearer to us when we understand that the thinking process itself is a process of duality internal to each individual and that this condition of plurality ties the thinking process to the world of appearances. This duality is located in the conversation I have with myself whenever I am engaged in the thinking process—in other words, the duality internal to the Socratic two-in-one dialogue.

The thinking process constructs an individual as a moral personality—the self as a "somebody." This in turn constitutes limitations in the political sphere because it recasts the possibility of extreme evil, as in the case of totalitarianism, against the self-understanding and projective action of the ethically constituted modern person. Here, Arendt proposes that it is through language in a twofold sense that thought itself intrudes into the realm of appearances in a manner similar to the way that the realm of appearance intrudes into the world of contemplation. First, thought manifests itself in the actualization of human action and activities that are retold and reenacted in public political spaces; second, language actualizes thought itself and so in turn is self-constitutive of the thinking and acting being. Language, we may argue, actualizes the moral predicaments in which individuals find themselves and then, in a constitutive sense, expresses the individual as an acting and autonomous individual in the world of appearances through the thinking process. This is the manner, Arendt suggests, in which we reflect on the problems that concern us as citizens and as acting beings. The duality of the thinking process (the reflection entailed in our self-consciousness) thus prepares us for the move from the singularity of contemplation to the plurality of the public political realm.

It has often been suggested that Arendt's understanding of language (as the expressivist component of the agonistic moment of individuality forged in the public sphere) is unsatisfactory.[66] This critique rests on an acknowledgment that some contemporary issues arising from the private sphere, such as the emancipation of women (or ethnic communities, students, or youth), are political issues that may not be issues of public conversation. Certainly, there are questions of justice involved where language appears to have a relevance to culture and to social life outside the more narrowly understood Arendtian public political sphere. Yet what is missing in such critiques is the acknowledgment that for Arendt there are always questions of conscience to which each individual must respond—in the Socratic sense, to discuss with her- or himself. It is in this manner that the dialogues we have with ourselves, or in other words with our conscience, are prepared for entry into the public realm that neither makes of principled moral reason a matter of conscience only nor provides a disjuncture between morality and politics.[67] Rather, the relationship we have with our conscience through language contextualizes our action as morally adequate action and positions the fully developed human person in the public political world. To argue otherwise is to neglect the role of practical reason as conscience in modernity in favor of the idea of a free and equal moral human being somehow confined to the idea of citizenship or autonomy as defined through communicative action and discourse ethics. In all the discussions we have with ourselves, the germ of plurality is always present, and this assists us in making the issues of conscience fit for the bright light of day.

I believe that a mark of what is truly human about us is that we bring the imaginative, creative, and self-reflective processes to bear in the *act* of citizenship and in the act of being a full-fledged human being. Moreover, our conscience assists in making us citizens, but in this sense our conscience becomes a contextually sensitive practical reason. I would argue that this guarantees public discourse and debate in a political democracy rather than the proceduralism of a discourse ethics grounded in communication. Communicative action, understood procedurally, does not protect those who are inarticulate (the aged, the ill, or children). Our empathetic reactions to the needs of other human beings spring from our ability to know and to have conversations with ourselves, and it is in this way that we understand the other person's point of view. This is the reciprocal meeting point in a democracy. We can argue that self-reflection and self-consciousness are a part of a much larger universe of culture and values, a culture that potentially provides for the mutuality, respect, and reciprocity among human beings that is demanded by our acknowledgment that we are moderns. Arendt had a wonderful answer that provides a guarantee for the public sphere and for the individuals who inhabit it. It was contained in the message of the Delphic Oracle to Socrates: "Know thyself." To know thyself is to be an authentic and thus autonomous human being. As Arendt once wrote, to be a human being is "to think what we are doing."

Notes

1. The concern about the crisis of Western society and culture and of active citizenship and a critical public sphere so evident in the work of Arendt has once again surfaced in the contemporary debate about the nature of a political democracy and Western political thought. Cornelius Castoriadis argues that the modern public sphere, characterized by political apathy and privatization, is a result of what he calls "the retreat from autonomy," which emphasizes the loss of creativity and autonomy from the public realm. He argues that philosophy is a central tenet of the project of (individual and social) autonomy, the end of which would mean the end of freedom. Such a catastrophe for Western culture is not only found in totalitarian or authoritarian regimes but in public realms that are distinguished by their lack of conflict and critique and by the demise of the ability to question existing institutions under the conditions of modernity. This aspect of philosophy is what Castoriadis calls politics: "the explicit putting into question of the established institution of society." He also argues, similarly to Arendt, that thinking is the concern of all citizens who want to discuss and argue and that this collective activity is politics properly conceived. Yet he maintains that the polis of ancient Greece is significant not so much for its highly individualistic emphasis and the corresponding virtues of excellence and courage that characterize the action that occurred in the public sphere of antiquity (which he views as Arendt's idiosyncratic interpretation), but because of the relation it bears to the formation of democracy and to politics as deliberate ac-

tivity, and thus to autonomy. However, for Castoriadis the project of autonomy is not necessarily circumscribed by the political institution of ancient democracy but concerns the full flowering of the potentiality of human beings. Thus, the object of the political institution of ancient democracy is the development of autonomous citizenship, beyond the formal and substantive concept of democracy incorporated in the project of autonomy. As Castoriadis explains, politics "*is* a project of autonomy"—but a project also found in the institution of society and embedded in the creation of individuals who discuss *and* act. See his essays "Power, Politics, Autonomy" and "The Greek Polis and the Creation of Democracy," in *Power, Politics, Autonomy* (New York: Oxford University Press, 1991); "The Retreat from Autonomy: Post-modernism as Generalised Conformism," *Thesis Eleven* 31 (1992).

2. Hannah Arendt, *The Human Condition* (Chicago: University of Chicago Press, 1958), 14.

3. Ibid., 12.

4. Arendt notes that by medieval times this meaning of *bios politikos* had lost its significance, and action was considered among the necessities of earthly life so that only the bios theoretikos, in medieval times the vita contemplativa, was left as the truly free way of life (ibid., 14).

5. Ibid., 13.

6. Ibid., 15.

7. Ibid., 20.

8. In her essay "What Is Authority?" in *Between Past and Future: Eight Exercises in Political Thought* (enlarged ed., Harmondsworth: Penguin, 1961), 129–30, Arendt explains that philosophy can also be called "the study of death," and the fact that philosophers seem to pursue "death and dying" is because of the concern with the invisible that is perceived by the soul "which itself is something invisible after death has rid the invisible part of man of his body, the organ of sense perception." Similarly, Arendt continues, "those who have no experience with a philosophic truth beyond the range of sense perception cannot be persuaded of the immortality of a bodiless soul." Arendt concludes that it was for such people that Plato invented the tales of the afterlife: "In Plato we find for the first time not merely a concept of final judgement about eternal life or eternal death, about rewards and punishments, but the geographical separation of hell, purgatory and paradise, as well as the horribly concrete notions of graduated bodily punishment."

9. Leah Bradshaw, *Acting and Thinking: The Political Thought of Hannah Arendt* (Toronto: University of Toronto Press, 1989), 11. See also Bhikhu Parekh for the suggestion that the philosophical tradition is contemptuous of the realm of appearances because "it finds politics shallow, superficial and incapable of offering lasting satisfaction" (*Hannah Arendt and the Search for a Political Philosophy* [Atlantic Highlands, N.J.: Humanities Press, 1981], 6).

10. Arendt, *Human Condition*, 220.

11. Ibid., 222.

12. Ibid., 221–23. This political differentiation rests on the same distinction found in the household. Here the concept of rule is based upon the patri-

archal and despotic relation of the master to all household members. In the same way in which distinction and equality are always negated in the private realm, any element of distinction and equality in the polis must henceforth be denied. Thus, all political formations after the polis of classical Greece are characterized by (1) the demise of the classical features of plurality and natality that allow contestatory wills and opinions to flourish, (2) a tendential monopolization of the potential for action by the state, and (3) the removal of the body politic from the sphere of the citizen. These new political formations deny the freedom of the citizen to participate in the public realm.

13. Parekh argues that Arendt's interpretation is based on her belief that philosophy did not appreciate the dignity or autonomy of politics and consequently reduces politics merely to ruling. He interprets Arendt's understanding of politics as ruling, as she uses it in this case, as being antithetical to her understanding of politics as integral to a vigorous and participatory political community. For Arendt, ruling occurs in communities where individuals are more interested in private activities than political life (and here Arendt's analysis of the Hobbesian "bourgeois man" is insightful) and have little interest in their common political affairs, leaving them in the care of the government. Hence the government rules "over its subjects as little more than objects" (Parekh, *Hannah Arendt*, 9–14).

The community is therefore constructed hierarchically in terms of command and obedience. Moreover, Arendt argues, the cause lies with Plato, who equated politics with ruling and ignored public political life that is *shared* between individuals. For her, political experiences are part of the dimension of the public interaction between individuals and are constitutive of the freedom to appear in the public realm and to engage in deliberation, to initiate, argue, and arrive at consensual and cooperative decisions for the good of the commonweal. If the reverse is true, that is, if the government handles the business of the state, then enacted citizenship, political equality, and freedom disappear from the public realm because they are not actualized between individuals freely engaging in political activity.

14. Arendt, *Human Condition*, 225.

15. Ibid., 225–26.

16. As Parekh points out, this becomes the central predicament of Plato's political philosophy. Plato had to convince the masses of the philosopher's right to rule according to transcendent truths. To do this Plato resorted to analogic reason. He pointed to two types of relationships in which the "competing element lies in the relationship itself" and the need for authority is beyond doubt. First, there are relations where expert knowledge is required and where experts are conceded the right to issue commands. Second, there are relations in which the parties involved belong to "two altogether different categories of being" and therefore the higher must rule. Plato argues that it is this separation (that is, the separation between knowledge, the qualification to rule, and ignorance, the qualification to carry out commands) that characterizes the philosopher's relation to the masses, and ipso facto the philosopher's right to rule. See Parekh, *Hannah Arendt*, 23.

17. Bradshaw, *Acting and Thinking*, 13.

18. Parekh, *Hannah Arendt*, 29.

19. Arendt, "Philosophy and Politics," *Social Research* 57, no. 1 (1990).

20. See, for example, Margaret Canovan, "Socrates or Heidegger? Hannah Arendt's Reflections on Philosophy and Politics," *Social Research* 57, no. 1 (1990).

21. Arendt, "Philosophy and Politics," 76.

22. Ibid. The word "good" means, in this instance, what is beneficial or useful.

23. Ibid.

24. The element of rule that developed in post-Platonic thinking does not arise out of directly political experiences; rather, it more truly belongs to the conflict between philosophy and politics. See Arendt, "What Is Authority?" 113.

25. Arendt, "Philosophy and Politics," 94.

26. Plato depicts the lives of the inhabitants of the cave as if they were only interested in seeing "first the images on the screen, then the things themselves in the dim light of the fire of the cave, until finally those who want to see the truth itself must leave the common world of the cave altogether and embark upon their new adventure all by themselves." This interpretation of Plato by Arendt again reinforces her central concern that the assumption of philosophy is that even those who inhabit the cave of human affairs are only human inasmuch as they too want to see, although "they remain deceived by shadows and images" (Arendt, "What Is Authority?" 114).

27. Arendt, "Philosophy and Politics," 95.

28. Bradshaw, *Acting and Thinking*, 17.

29. Arendt refers to the metaphor of sight in a further discussion of Plato's allegory of the cave. Here, she claims that Plato demonstrates a human passion "to see," in his portrayal of the audience as immovable and noncommunicative, only watching the screen. For her, the passion for seeing precedes the thirst for knowledge that is actualized in language. The passion for seeing was Olympian in its origins and became the basic Greek attitude to the world. The sheer beauty of the spectacle was what tempted humankind to contemplation. Hence, the highest idea of the good was represented by "what shone forth most" and human virtue became neither internal to the actor nor related to the consequences of the deed but rather how the actor appeared during the action (*The Life of the Mind* [New York: Harcourt Brace Jovanovich, 1977], 1:130).

30. Arendt, "Philosophy and Politics," 96.

31. Parekh interprets the Platonic idea of the domain of philosophy as one that is "devoted to the discovery and contemplation of transcendental, objective, absolute, demonstrable and universally valid truths" (*Hannah Arendt*, 21).

32. The attempt of Greek philosophy to find some absolute standards for the realm of human affairs is, Arendt states, an attempt "to find a concept of authority which would prevent deterioration of the *polis* and safeguard the life of the philosopher." That this attempt failed is a direct result of Greek political experience which did not have an awareness of authority (Arendt, "What Is Authority?" 118).

33. Arendt, "Philosophy and Politics," 74. See also her "What Is Authority?" where she maintains that the philosopher leaves the cave for "the pure sky of ideas" to contemplate "the true essence of Being" and not to acquire absolute standards. From this Arendt concludes that the basically authoritative element of the ideas does not necessarily follow. It is only after the philosopher has returned to the cave that the ideas become measures for judging human behavior. Arendt argues that it is the philosopher's *return* to the cave that is the most significant reason for the conflict between the philosopher and the polis. Plato tells us of the philosopher's loss of orientation in human affairs, the blindness striking the eyes, the predicament of not being able to communicate what s/he has seen, and the actual danger to her or his life which thereby arises. It is in this predicament that the philosopher resorts to what he has seen, the ideas, as standards and measures, and finally, in fear of his life, uses them as instruments of domination (110).

For the transformation of the ideas into measures, Plato relies on the same type of reification of images and ideas exhibited by homo faber, who is guided in his work by something beyond the fabrication process itself. This analogy "enables [Plato] to understand the transcendent character of the ideas in the same manner as he does the transcendent existence of the model" (ibid.).

34. Arendt, "Philosophy and Politics," 78.

35. Ibid.

36. Ibid., 80.

37. Ibid.

38. Ibid., 81.

39. Ibid., 91.

40. Ibid., 97.

41. Ibid., 98–99.

42. Ibid., 100.

43. Canovan, *The Political Thought of Hannah Arendt* (London: J. M. Dent, 1974), 12.

44. Arendt, *Human Condition*, 198.

45. George Kateb, *Hannah Arendt: Politics, Conscience, Evil* (Totowa, N.J.: Rowman and Allenheld, 1984), 19–20.

46. Arendt, *Human Condition*, 14.

47. Kateb, *Hannah Arendt*, 21.

48. Thus, Plato and Aristotle inverted the relationship between action and work in favor of work, according to Arendt, because fabrication, in a manner antithetical to action, necessitated an inner affinity with contemplation and isolation (*Human Condition*, 301).

49. Ibid., 24.

50. Arendt defines tyranny as that political condition in which the individual is isolated from others as well as the isolation of rule itself, thereby negating human plurality which is the condition of all political organization (ibid., 301).

51. Ibid., 185. In Arendt's interpretation, Aristotle's cyclical view of natural and human time prevented him from developing a theory of political free-

dom and action. His cyclical understanding of time meant that events *and* opinions revolve. Aristotle was therefore unable to conceive how radically new beginnings occur in human life. See Parekh, *Hannah Arendt*, 28–30.

52. Arendt, *Human Condition*, 191.

53. Ibid., 195.

54. Ibid., 23.

55. Elisabeth Young-Bruehl writes that Arendt was very bitter toward Heidegger after his infatuation with Nazism, and consequently she tended to see in his work only the egoistical and grandiose. See Young-Bruehl, *Hannah Arendt: For Love of the World* (New Haven, Conn.: Yale University Press, 1982), 218. Later Arendt became reconciled to Heidegger and acknowledged him as an entirely original thinker (Arendt, *Life of the Mind* [New York: Harcourt Brace Jovanovich, 1977], 2:184).

56. Young-Bruehl, *Hannah Arendt*, 303.

57. This point has a further implication for Arendt. She believes that Heidegger, finally disabused of his notions of Nazism, chose contemplation as an escape from his earthly misadventures. This was a very shortsighted choice in her opinion. Rather than reinstituting new values after the destruction of the traditional framework of so-called values, Heidegger abandons the call of the public realm and "does not look out for either the re-establishment of the old or the discovery of new 'values'" (in ibid.).

58. Ibid.

59. Arendt's understanding of the concept of historicity is more complex than this. It is a social and political contextualization at the expense of action certainly, but historicity also emphasizes history at the expense of politics and therefore stresses the "event" over the coincidence of thought and event (ibid.).

60. Canovan, "Socrates or Heidegger?" 162.

61. Arendt, "Philosophy and Politics," 93.

62. Arendt, *Life of the Mind*, 2:173.

63. Ibid., 179.

64. Ibid., 180.

65. Every political philosophy appears to perform one of two functions: either it interprets philosophical experience with categories from the world of human affairs or it claims priority for philosophical experience and judges all politics in its light. This encapsulates the problem of the relationship between philosophy and the vita activa for Arendt. The philosopher, although she perceives something more than human—in other words, the divine—always remains a human being, so that the conflict between philosophy and the affairs of humankind resides within the philosopher. In Plato this was articulated as the conflict between body and soul for the first time: the body inhabits the world of humankind and the soul inhabits the divine world of contemplation. The more a philosopher becomes a true philosopher the more s/he will separate her- or himself from the body. Thus, the philosopher will rule over the body and the body politic, as the master rules over the slave. Arendt explains that if "the philosopher attains rulership over the city, he will do no more to its inhabitants than he has already done to his body. His tyranny will be justi-

fied both in the sense of personal legitimacy, that is, by his prior obedience, as a mortal man, to the commands of his soul, as a philosopher" (*Human Condition*, 92–97).

66. See for example, Patricia Springborg, "Hannah Arendt and the Classical Republican Tradition," in *Hannah Arendt: Thinking, Judging, Freedom*, ed. G. Kaplan and C. Kessler (Sydney: Allen and Unwin, 1989); Seyla Benhabib, *Situating the Self: Gender, Community and Postmodernism in Contemporary Ethics* (Cambridge: Polity Press, 1992).

67. In particular, see Benhabib's critique in her essay "Judgement and the Moral Foundations of Politics in Hannah Arendt's Thought," in *Situating the Self*.

DICK HOWARD

The Marxian Legacy and the Problem of Democracy

8 Should the events of 1989 surprise a serious leftist? I call these massive changes "events" to play on the way the French avoided coming to grips with their own, apparently inexplicable, experience in May 1968 when a student protest started a chain of actions and reactions that led unexpectedly to the near collapse of all government power—but was followed by elections that brought a massive victory to the party of order. Further, I use the term "party of order" rather than right or conservative—let alone capitalist—to recall that also in 1968, the ruling communists brought "order" back to Prague on the heavy treads of Warsaw Pact tanks. The hydra-headed, polymorphous enemy that haunts the nights of the international party of order is not the left, socialism—or communism—but *democracy.* This is not so banal a remark as it might appear. Who, after all, opposes democracy? Well, to be honest about it, many of us in the Western left did—hedging our criticism of course by saying that what we opposed was just "formal" democracy, which we denounced as ideological. But the fate of "really existing socialism" forces us to rethink our own political values and methods. We cannot undertake this rethinking as political virgins. We have a past and live in a present; we have to proceed from the cognitive dissonances that both induce.

I draw from my own past the model of Rosa Luxemburg, whom I will use as a guiding thread to understand the place of democratic politics within a leftist movement. She was a radical critic of the antidemocratic aspects of the Bolshevik seizure of power in 1917, as she had been a critic of Lenin's reshaping of the party nearly fifteen years earlier. Her status as a democratic *revolutionary* was confirmed in her last article, written from the ruins of the Spartakus uprising in January 1919. Its title, "Order Reigns in Berlin," was not merely rhetorical, and its theme remains actual. The title alluded of course to the proclamation that followed the defeat of the Polish uprising of 1831, but Luxemburg made clear its contemporary implications: "And so run the reports of the guardians of 'order' every half-century. . . . And the rejoicing 'victors' do not notice that an 'order' which must be periodically maintained by bloody butchery is steadily approaching its historical destiny, its doom." But Luxemburg expected "the revolution" to carry out history's sentence. Assassinated the day after the article was published, she became the first icon for those who refused to identify Leninism with the Marxian legacy.[1] But the conceptual and practical relation between her revolution and a radical but still democratic politics remained to be explored by her heirs.

Seeking to inherit the Marxian legacy, many postwar Western leftists experienced cognitive dissonance in their first debates with their socially critical peers from the East. What we thought was "left" was for them support of the ideological foundations of their established order; what they took as "radical" was for us support of the ideological principles of our own order. A well-known illustration occurred when Rudi Dutscke led a delegation from the Berlin SDS to meet with student rebels in Prague in early 1968. The Western left was busy discovering Marxism; the Czechs were concerned with such so-called formal freedoms as the right to demonstrate publicly or to form associations free from the tutelage of the authorities. Despite the obvious basis for misunderstanding, a dialogue took place: enemies of an order that decried them as "anarchists," both sides were seeking to give new life to *democracy*. As their situations differed, so too did their remedies. That was to be expected: democracy is not a universal form, self-identical and unalloyed. While this shared democratic ethos showed itself in practice during that heady year of 1968, it was not formulated theoretically—at least in the West, where the romantic or moral imperative called "the revolution" overshadowed the democratic demands.

Both sides could have tried to interpret their situations by appealing to Rosa Luxemburg, another so-called anarchist. She had described revolution as "the only form of 'war' . . . in which the final victory can be prepared only by a series of 'defeats.'" Despite this suggestive image, which points to the normative learning process that is necessary for politics to be democratic, Luxemburg did not identify revolution with the democracy that haunts the party of order. She was still a Marxist for whom the "haunting" specter was of course Marx's; his theory served her as a guarantee of revolutionary practice. She appealed constantly to Marx's text; for example, her critique of Eduard Bernstein's reformism is content to have shown that "in its essence, in its bases, opportunist practice is irreconcilable with Marxism." Similarly, in the depths of a world war, her *Junius Pamphlet* insisted that "Marxist theory gave to the working class of the whole world a compass by which to fix its tactics from hour to hour in its journey toward the one unchanging goal."[2] We could, of course, point to other theoretical and practical arguments that are less slavish and more creative. But the point is that we cannot resolve cognitive dissonance by invoking democracy as either a passe-partout that trumps all other positions or as a synthesis that magically unites politics, society, and economy.

Democracy does not eliminate real difference, even among its own supporters. Another example of cognitive dissonance, from another part of the world, testifies to the need to *learn* democratic politics. A contemporary Western reader of the *New York Times* might not have been surprised by the following passage in a recent article about El Salvador: "'We used to march chanting, "Socialism, Socialism,"' said the Rev. Rogelio Ponceele, a Roman Catholic priest who has lived and worked with the largest guerrilla faction for almost a decade. 'Now we march chanting, "Democracy, Democracy!"'" But what would that reader say about the continuation of the same article, which explains that after a decade of struggle the guerrilla troops are not ready to follow their newly converted leaders? The *Times* explains this as the result of a gap between the educated leaders and the "poorly educated peasants who joined after suffering from rightist repression."[3] Rosa Luxemburg would suggest a different reading. Democracy is more than a slogan used to unite the excluded against the party of order. In her polemic against the Leninist party, she admitted that "the proletarian army is first recruited in the struggle itself" but added the normative qualification that "only in the struggle does it become aware of the objectives of the struggle." This insistence on democratic learning processes is even more explicit in her defense of the program of the Spartakus League in 1919, which concludes that "the masses must learn to use power by using power."[4] Such assertions might appear to justify criticism of Luxemburg's "spontaneism," but they pose as well the question: What must one *learn* to be a democrat who is heir to the Marxian legacy?

The party of order accused the New Lefts of the 1960s of being "anti-intellectual." Seeking to reply to this criticism brought out another aspect of cognitive dissonance. As I read Richard Hofstadter's *Anti-Intellectualism in American Life*, I was surprised to find myself repeatedly siding emotionally with the anti-intellectuals' rejection of a desiccated, formal, and increasingly atomized society that relentlessly conquers all aspects of life.[5] This instinctive response was buttressed by my encounter with E. P. Thompson's *Making of the English Working Class*, and it found a more theoretical justification in Karl Polanyi's *Great Transformation*.[6] The picture of a moral economy protecting itself from the invading efficiency of the modernizing state was appealing because it pointed to the source of a native radicalism that promoted collective values in the face of the egoistic individualism of market society. Moreover, it seemed to offer support to Rosa Luxemburg's "spontaneist" politics in the *Mass Strike* pamphlet, whose foundation was that "the masses will be the active chorus, and the leaders only the speaking parts, the interpreters of the will of the masses."[7] But when I took Luxemburg's advice and reread Marx, I realized that this image of a moral economy is premodern. Marx's *Communist Manifesto* presents a hymn of praise to what Schumpeter came to call the "creative destruction" of capitalist modernization; with that praise came a critique of dreams of precapitalist communal life that can reproduce only "the idiocy of rural life." Marx's critique of capitalism did not aim for a return to an allegedly simpler or better time before the corrosive influence of modernity had spread. But the Hegelian concept of *Aufhebung*—preserving while raising to a higher level—does not explain how he could both praise and criticize what he calls the "revolutionary bourgeoisie." The magical aufhebung only added to my sense of cognitive dissonance.

· · ·

Why continue to appeal to Marx, or to Luxemburg, after the experiences of 1989? The answer depends on how we define the new challenges facing us. These cannot be defined simply as the institution of a constitution that protects certain social or economic rights. Which rights? Who decides? The countries called democratic have different constitutions; they guarantee more or less consistently their citizens' political rights. It is better to define these regimes as *liberal*, while leaving open for the moment the more fundamental question of the nature of democracy.[8] Rights that *today* appear essential to liberal societies are often of recent vintage—for example, the right of women to vote; the same rights are not present in all liberal societies—for example, privacy protections or abortion rights. These rights are sometimes violated; the political system does not always function as the constitution promises. The lack of one or another right, or even the occasional violation of rights or constitutional provisions, does not mean that these regimes are not democratic. Nor does it imply that we should return to the Marxist critique of rights as "formal."

Luxemburg understood better the implications of the Marxian legacy when, in presenting the program of the Spartakus League, she insisted that "far more important, however, than what is written in a program is the way in which it is interpreted in action."[9] Rights are guaranteed only in an historical struggle whose central issue is none other than the rights themselves. The openness to this form of political action is what makes a society *democratic*. It implies, further, that democratic societies are historical and that their future depends on how rights are "interpreted in action."

But we cannot get away from Marx so easily. The fact that formal liberal rights require protection points to the need to give them a more certain, material foundation. But this separation of a material foundation from the rights it supposedly ensures has often had unfortunate political consequences. It suggests that rights can be "temporarily" suspended in order to build the foundation that will make it possible for all citizens to enjoy them. This is the first step down the slippery slope to what is at best an enlightened despotism. Two alternatives seem possible today: "democratic socialism" as the third way sought so long by so many, or the return to the pretotalitarian autochthonous developmental process that builds from the peculiar history of each nation.

Both options assume that totalitarianism was imposed on society from without, by external political fiat. In the first case, this political imposition is said to have been made necessary by the inability of the indigenous bourgeoisie to assume its historical role; in the second case, totalitarian politics appears to have interfered with a harmonious endogenous development. Supporters of both options would do well to recall Luxemburg's warning to the Spartakus League not to imitate "the bourgeois revolutions in which it sufficed to overthrow that official power at the centre and to replace a dozen or so persons in authority."[10] The implication is that both supposed alternatives share a common assumption about the relation of politics to society: the quest for a third way makes politics the independent variable; the appeal to history makes society the primary determinant. How can the two positions be harmoniously united?

Rosa Luxemburg identified the problem. Her attempt to solve it permits us to see both the weakness of Marxism and the strengths of Marx. Luxemburg pointed repeatedly to the need to navigate between "abandonment of the mass character or abandonment of the final goal; the fall back into sectarianism or the fall into bourgeois reformism; anarchism or opportunism."[11] She thought she could synthesize these "two reefs" in the "mass strike" where "the economic struggle is that which leads the political struggle from one nodal point to another; the political struggle is that which periodically fertilizes the soil for the economic struggle. Cause and effect here constantly change places."[12] But this appealing synthesis is still produced by the addition of private griefs and individual protests. Its political result appears in Luxemburg's alternative to Lenin. Her party "gradually becomes the haven of the different dissatisfied elements of society, becoming a party of the people opposed to a tiny minority of capitalist rulers."[13] But this is not a new politics; it is still based on immediate protest rather than on public debate and critical judgment. Luxemburg remains a Marxist here; she is treating society as determined by its economic foundation. Yet the more radical insights that make her part of the Marxian legacy were based on the assumption of a democratic society.

The starting point for the conceptualization of the politics of a democratic society can be found in the young Karl Marx. He had learned from Georg W. F. Hegel that the birth of a "civil society," which is neither reducible to the private sphere nor capable of being absorbed by the political state, is the mark of modernity. Although his later work reduced its "anatomy" to mere economic relations, Marx often showed an awareness of its complexity. Both approaches can be seen in *The Communist Manifesto*. Marx's description of what he calls the "revolutionary" achievement of the bourgeoisie can be reduced neither to economic relations nor to political imperatives. "All fixed, fast-frozen relations, with their train of ancient and venerable prejudices and opinions, are swept away," writes Marx, "all new-formed ones become antiquated before they can ossify. All that is solid melts into air, all that is holy is profaned, and man is at last compelled to face with sober senses, his real conditions of life, and his relations with his kind." New needs can now arise; new forms of communication can produce a new civilization; cities can "rescue" the peasantry from "the idiocy of rural life." Such are the grounds for reading Marx as the first modernist.[14]

The contemporary reader of these lines is struck by another aspect of Marx's account. Aside from the familiar rhetoric, his analysis could have been written by Alexis de Tocqueville. But then one wonders why Marx reduces the social revolution he has described to the simple effect of a contradiction between feudal property relations and the productive forces that must "burst them asunder." The reason is clear when Marx rapidly generalizes this economistic model to portray the coming of the proletarian revolution, along the lines suggested by Luxemburg's "party of the people." This achieves two goals: it provides a material foundation for the freedom and rights Marx wishes to defend, and its foundation on a philosophy of history as a class struggle that will be ultimately overcome implies that historical change will no longer be a threat to the future communist society. But the price paid for this theoretical certainty is too great: the assumed material guarantee makes democratic political debate unnecessary while the philosophical guarantee of unity closes off the vision of an open future about which society would need to debate. There is no place in this picture for the *critic,* and no *public space* in which judgment can take form.

A different picture emerges when Marx's modern society is read through the eyes of Tocqueville.[15] The "revolutionary bourgeoisie" is seen to produce a *democratic society.* Its elimination of "solid" certainties and its profanation of the "holy" mark the end of a society in which each has his place and role; the modern individual is born with, and must confront, "sober senses," the problem of *who* he is and *with whom* he will relate. Marx does not talk about rights in this context because his earlier critique of Hegel had taught him that they were only formal. But his contrast of bourgeois and feudal societies should have led to a different conclusion. Feudal "rights" are ascriptive; they are imposed on the person from without, by God and by the "solid" nature of things. The modern individual, on the other hand, lives in a world without foundation; if that individual has rights, their foundation can only be political; they are won and ensured only by struggle. This suggests that capitalism's constant revolutionizing of social relations is a repeated challenge to newly won rights of the individual. It implies, further, that capitalism is not simply a mode of production; the history of class struggle must be reinterpreted as a history of the politics of rights, and, *unlike* economistic history, this history of rights can never end in a grand unification. In a democratic society whose foundation is the modern individual, there can be no appeal to a material or transcendent final ground of rights; history remains open and politics remains necessary. Democracy is not formal but the lived experience of a struggle for right, which can never end.

This interpretation of democracy suggests a new framework for understanding the emergence of totalitarianism. The modern society inhabited by the radically free individual is uncomfortable; men and women are atoms, alone yet together in that infinite space so feared by Blaise Pascal. Though of course modern individuals would never admit it, they know that the *Manifesto* was correct: the rights they have today, like the place they occupy, may be "swept away" or "become antiquated before they can ossify." It is this *lived experience* that makes rights appear to be merely formal and democracy appear a luxury. The demand for "real" democracy and/or for true community arises; social division is intolerable, a threat to one's very being. The quest for roots, for something "solid" and even "holy," arises; a movement emerges, perhaps fascist, perhaps communist.[16] But these movements only apparently leap to a qualitatively new moment in political history. Totalitarianism is not beyond democracy; it is *immanent* within the logic of democracy—as was the "mass strike" that sails magically between Rosa Luxemburg's "two reefs." Both democracy and totalitarianism emerge from the experience of social division in a society of alienated individuals; democracy seeks to preserve that division by creating a public space within which a politics of rights (including economic rights) can take place, while totalitarianism wants to overcome division in a new unity. Totalitarianism thus appears to be the logical solution to the tensions of democratic society. In this sense, totalitarianism is *antipolitics*.[17]

The claim that totalitarianism is immanent to the logic of democracy implies that democracy is not a state of affairs, that it is not the static liberal ideal of the formal protection of basic rights. The society described by Marx and reinterpreted by Tocqueville is not stable. It would be better to speak of a *dynamic of democratization,* referring to a process whose origins lie in the modernization that disposes of the certitudes of the old order.[18] But totalitarianism cannot impose unity on a modern society; its "politics" only apply vertically, from the top down, constantly seeking to atomize any attempts at horizontal forms of association that might create a new public sphere. Ironically, because the totalitarian project is immanent to modern *democratic* societies, its project is condemned to failure. The rapidity with which it fell should not surprise us. Its own logic turns against it. If it were indeed achieved, its very foundation— the society of individuals who must seek constantly their own roots and their own rights—would be obliterated. Of course, self-contradictory politics can be imposed by force, but when that external pressure is withdrawn, such politics collapses into nothingness.

What remains when the totalitarian alternative is avoided still needs analysis. Two centuries ago, James Madison confronted a similar problem in his attempt to justify the new U.S. Constitution. His famous tenth *Federalist Paper* pointed out that to cure the form of social division called "faction," one could destroy "the liberty which is essential to its existence," or one could give "to every citizen the same opinions, the same passions and the same interests." The first, he continued, would be "worse than the disease," while the second is not only "impracticable" but a denial of the "first object of Government."[19] Madison's solution was to *multiply* the number of factions, so that each can check the threat from the other, preserving a democratic society within the framework of a representative *republic*. One must pay attention to the words: Madison's democracy was not based on democratic sovereignty; his insight was that a representative republican state is necessary in order to preserve a democratic society. The radical and rapid collapse of the totalitarian states after 1989 would certainly not have surprised Madison.

• • •

Madison's rejection of democratic sovereignty has a further implication. If the new democratic society resulted from the actions of the "revolutionary" bourgeoisie, Marxist economism might still make sense. But Tocqueville showed that the same emerging democratic society was the product of a modernizing *state* seeking to assert its absolute sovereignty.[20] Claude Lefort argues that Marx's neglect of this modernizing state explains his inability to understand the autonomy of democratic society.[21] The *Communist Manifesto* passes from feudalism to capitalism without considering the absolutist state, whose notion of sovereignty remains with us. Thus, when Marx analyzes the French Revolution's Declaration of the Rights of Man, he cannot understand the importance of these rights, which appear to him to be only formal. The freedom to do whatever does not harm others is said by Marx only to protect the egoistic monad, rather than to liberate the individual from hierarchical society and open up the possibility of forming new social bonds. The same holds for the distinction between the public and private spheres, which is not just a formality, as Marx thinks, but rather the guarantee of a right that makes the individual free. Nor are freedom of opinion and of its communication simply formal; they create a public sphere that ensures that knowledge will not remain the monopoly of those in power. Similarly, the right to security cannot be reduced to the protection of capitalist property; it also protects the citizen from arbitrary action and thereby affirms the autonomy that permits the individual to be a critical citizen. Marx's one-sidedness even leads him to ignore the historical implication of the presumption of innocence, which for Lefort is "an irreversible acquisition of political thought."[22]

However we analyze the relation of the absolutist state and Marx's revolutionary bourgeoisie in the various national histories, one point remains common to all. Centralization and the new concept of sovereignty destroyed the hierarchical and ordered cosmos inherited from traditional society. A new matrix emerged; the individual and a politics of rights became possible. The emerging individualist society may ally with the monarch against the aristocracy or it may join the aristocracy in attacking the monarchy. More important than these familiar economic force-fields is the new configuration that opposes society to the state. This polarity should not be identified with a Marxist history of class struggle whose goal is to achieve an eventual synthesis or eliminate one of the poles to the benefit of the other. The figure is more complicated than Marx's because the society itself is a *democratic diversity* of individuals whose unity and division are structured by the system of rights guaranteed by the state.[23] Because these rights serve to preserve diversity as well as unity, they are the object of a struggle that can never end. The state affirms its sovereignty in the protection of these individual rights *and* in the guarantee of a space in which society can seek to affirm new rights. This was Madison's definition of "the first object of Government," but it has a European ancestry in the absolute state, whose first great theorist, Jean Bodin, titled his treatise the *Six Books of the Republic!*

This framework permits a reinterpretation of the history that has produced both capitalism and totalitarianism. The modernizing state—not Marx's revolutionary bourgeoisie—applies its new conception of sovereignty; the result creates the conditions for the democratization of society. It produces a society marked by individualism, difference, and division, but this society is also in quest of community, identity, and unity. The nation-state only apparently, at a brief moment in the nineteenth century, provides that link. Its position as guarantor of rights demands that it stand *outside* of society; if it claims to be identical with society, it inevitably appears, sooner or later, to have taken sides in the divisions inherent within democratic society and must pay the price in the coin of lost legitimacy.[24] It can avoid that loss only by attempting to incarnate some necessity or value *immanent* to society. With this step, however, it is on the road to totalitarianism. Its claim to be identified with society denies the diversity typical of democratic society by appealing to a putative unity, furnished by a mystical *Volk* or by a logic of history's necessary path.

Totalitarianism is not the only way in which democratic society can seek unity. Capitalism makes the same claim to social immanence. The neutral market replaces the neutral state; economic interests are substituted for political rights. Like totalitarianism, *capitalism is an antipolitics;* it denies its own nature as political. The enemy of capitalism is not the proletariat but that *democracy* whose politics is founded on the rights of humankind. Capitalism, like totalitarianism, seeks to eliminate social division; in order to control the effects of its constant revolutionizing of social relations, it must reduce them all, ultimately, to an identical *quantitative* form. The result is the atomized individualism that is incapable of formulating any legitimate political norms because its only standard of judgment is the quantitative logic of its own abstract individualism. The capitalist overcoming of social division is antipolitical in this second sense as well; it is incapable of formulating any project that would provide society with a positive image of itself. As a result, it has no norms that it can oppose to the egregious inequalities that emerge precisely on the basis of the logic of abstract market equality.

The struggles that Marxists call "anticapitalist" can be reinterpreted within this framework of democracy. We need not deny the role of interest; Madison's analysis of factions recognized that "from the protection of different and unequal faculties of acquiring property, the possession of different degrees and kinds of property immediately results" and that "the most common and durable source of factions has been the various and unequal distribution of property." Indeed, the development of interests seemed to Madison to be the mark of "civilized nations."[25] But interest and even possession of unequal amounts of property are not identical with capitalism. Rather, the challenge posed by popular struggles is anticapitalist in the specific sense suggested here: they question the claim that the capitalist *economy* provides that immanent unity that the birth of modern, individualist, democratic society had destroyed. These movements affirm the historically open and democratic character of a society in which political struggle is legitimate. They are affirmations of rights or, as Lefort puts it, of the *right* to have *rights*. It does not follow that all popular movements should be supported, or that decision is the object of public debate and critical judgment. It does follow, however, that any movement refusing to take part in that democratic process, on the grounds that its values or goals represent the immanent truth or unity of society, is to be rejected.[26]

• • •

This discussion started from the conflict between the party of order and those New Leftists whom I called democrats. I used Rosa Luxemburg, that most rigorous and therefore most contradictory of Marxists, as a backdrop for an attempt to provide a wider framework in which the Marxian legacy—and the problem of post-totalitarian societies—could be interpreted. The hypothesis suggested by Lefort, that both capitalism and totalitarianism are attempts to provide an *immanent* closure or legitimation for a divided society that cannot appeal to transcendent norms, permits a reinterpretation of the history of popular struggles over the past two centuries. It suggests, on the one hand, that these movements can—but need not—move in a direction that lends support to the totalitarian solution. That would explain why so many—

including the peasant Salvadorians and young German leftists visiting Prague to whom I referred earlier—can find themselves allied with political choices whose ultimate results they would come to deplore. The history of fellow-traveling, which Lefort decries as the party of the *bien-pensants,* can be understood from this perspective.[27] But beyond this conceptual solution to my encounter with cognitive dissonance in the wake of the events of 1989, there is still the emotional problem that was raised by the anti-intellectual temptation of a moral economy. To deal with this, I will introduce another cognitive dissonance: the East German experience.

Why were those oppositional groups, whose courageous stance showed the nakedness of the totalitarian claims, unable to play a political role once the regime collapsed? It appears that, given the totalitarian claim, only a moral stance could challenge its legitimacy, just as it took a moral certitude to support the individual refusal to accept the total regime. To be more than an individual refusal, the opposition would have had to assume that it spoke for a collectivity that had been suppressed and would emerge once the oppression was lifted.[28] But this, it was felt by some, would be the replacement of one absolute by another, one totality by another; the opposition would be the "speaking parts" for a still silent mass. Then, when the regime fell, and society found itself on its own, the opposition could not accept the legitimacy of a politics whose foundation is the plurality of factional interest. The greatest strength of the opposition now became the source of its weakness. It could not understand the materialism that was unleashed in the wake of the fall. But on what basis could the opposition criticize such self-interested behavior? Did it not have to appeal, implicitly or explicitly, to a concept of unity, the idea of a society that would be at last, by means of the proper knowledge and behavior, reconciled with itself beyond its divisions? Would that then make it, in spite of itself, a part of the party of order? Was its implicit goal not just the replacement of the old order but the creation of a new moral order?

Although its appeal to the Helsinki Accords gave it an important democratic component, the moral orientation of the opposition in the East was strengthened by the way the Helsinki principles were interpreted. The rights they affirmed were conceived within the framework of what was defined above as *liberalism;* they were not the rights that define the public space of a democratic society in which politics is the struggle for rights whose only guarantee is the political process through which they are won and reaffirmed. Such static rights can become the stuff of moralism. They contribute to the impression that political representation and the battle of competing parties are a step down the path to perdition insofar as they destroy the harmony and order of the society seeking to affirm itself against the state. With this, the static dualism that characterized the quest for the third way, or the return to autochthonous national history, replaces the dynamics of democratic politics. The reappearance of this structure suggests that, once again, the challenge is the maintenance of the dynamics of democracy against the temptation to put an end to its interminable and painful lack of certitude. Of course, the new Eastern European societies—like those in the West—are not *as* democratic as we might like, but they are *more* democratic than many of those who have been forced to help create them would have liked. Most important, they can *become* more democratic, if that is the goal we indeed seek.

The renewed dialogue between East and West permits both sides to rediscover what it is that made their politics "left." As in 1968, the radicals East and West can find common ground only around the challenge to realize democracy. As in 1968, they are the party of disorder. But now the Eastern critique of totalitarianism and the Western critique of capitalism can work in tandem: the West can learn from the East that its democracy is not simply the static system of liberal rights, while the East can learn from the West that capitalism is simply another way of reducing the qualitative differences produced within democratic societies to the quantitative neutrality of the market. Both systems are the enemy of democracy.

In turn, democracy now has an historical and theoretical foundation that avoids the reproach of formalism and abstractness that was the basis of Marxism's appeal. Now that history no longer provides us with a vector of truth, and now that rights are constantly up for challenge, there is no single "politically correct position"; there is only politics. Paradoxically, in the West, this has led to a hardening of positions; ideology seems to count for more than criticism; individuals need to assert their identities and to validate them by being "on the right side." In the East, the same paradoxical logic takes a different form; individuals seek to put a new science in the place of ideology and end up fetishizing the notion of "necessity"; the old voluntarism is replaced by a new positivism that is equally without political foundation.

The party of disorder defends the priority of the political, in the West and East. Its basic insight is that politics defines that which counts as necessary, that which a society undertakes or modifies, as well as that which it leaves to follow its own natural course. It accepts Andre Gorz's distinction between a "logic of capital" and a "logic of capitalism," and it attempts to make sure that the former is not imposed unwittingly on the latter.[29] The party of disorder of course has its programs; it takes to the streets, platforms, and public space because it has concrete goals and arguments to defend them. It knows that society must be governed, decisions made, and resources allocated, but it also knows that these are *political* choices, not answers to Marx's "riddle of history" or necessities imposed by the abstract logic of the market. Politics is defensible only by argument, program, and practice. Because of its insistence on the public forum, where opinions clash and judgments emerge from critical debate, the party of disorder does not reject but thrives on cognitive dissonances. Perhaps that is why in the end, it remains, critically, within the Marxian legacy.

Notes

1. Luxemburg's article is translated in *Selected Political Writings of Rosa Luxemburg*, ed. Dick Howard (New York: Monthly Review Press, 1971). My understanding of the notion of a "Marxian legacy," which I prefer to Merleau-Ponty's often used concept "Western Marxism," is sketched in my own book entitled *The Marxian Legacy* (2d ed., Minneapolis: University of Minnesota Press, 1987), whose first chapter presents the contradictory character of that legacy by reexamining Luxemburg's life and thought more critically than I did in the introduction to her *Selected Writings*. I will use Luxemburg as a kind of pole for reflection in the first parts of this chapter because—as opposed to Marx, for whom an autonomous political theory is impossible in capitalism and not necessary in socialism—she stands for that aspect of the Marxian tradition that at least sensed the need for a properly political theory even if her theoretical presuppositions made its elaboration impossible.

2. Luxemburg, *Selected Writings*, 130, 325.

3. Lindsey Gruson, "Among Salvadoran Rebels: A Split over Rights Accord," *New York Times*, Aug. 11, 1990, 2.

4. Luxemburg, "Mass Strike, Party, and Trade Unions," in *Selected Writings;* and "Our Program and the Political Situation," in *Selected Writings*, 406. For additional citations and examples, see my *Marxian Legacy*. In the present context, the point to be underlined, and to which I will return, is that this process has a double implication: private anger becomes a public demand that, because it is now represented in the public forum, must respect its own differences from the other demands that are also present in that public forum. This will make it possible for the new democratic power to avoid the temptation to become simply another variant of the old party of order.

5. Richard Hofstadter, *Anti-Intellectualism in American Life* (New York: Vintage, 1963).

6. E. P. Thompson, *The Making of the English Working Class* (New York: Vintage, 1963); Karl Polanyi, *The Great Transformation* (Boston: Beacon Press, 1957).

7. Luxemburg, "Mass Strike, Party, and Trade Unions," 270.

8. This distinction is stressed in Jean Cohen's "Discourse Ethics and Civil Society," *Philosophy and Social Criticism* 14, no. 3–4 (1988): 315–37.

9. Luxemburg, "Our Program and the Political Situation," 380.

10. Ibid., 380.

11. Luxemburg, "Militia and Militarism," in *Selected Writings*, 142; and "Organizational Questions of Russian Social Democracy," in *Selected Writings*, 304.

12. Luxemburg, "Mass Strike, Party, and Trade Unions," 241.

13. Luxemburg, "Organizational Questions," 303.

14. I have argued this point in "The Politics of Modernism: From Marx to Kant," reprinted in *The Politics of Critique* (Minneapolis: University of Minnesota Press, 1988), and in other essays. See also Marshall Berman, "All That Is Solid Melts into Air," reprinted in *Twenty-five Years of Dissent*, ed. Irving Howe (New York: Methuen, 1979).

15. Alexis de Tocqueville's analysis of democracy as a social structure and his attempt to formulate a political theory that could permit its fruitful unfolding while avoiding its negative potentials bears rereading—as French thinkers such as Claude Lefort, François Furet, and Marcel Gauchet have shown. In the present context, it should be recalled that Tocqueville's task, in the wake of the revolution of 1830 in *Demcracy in America*, and in the wake of both the revolution of 1848 and Bonaparte's coup of 1851 in *The Old Regime and the Revolution*, was to understand how the social victories inaugurated by 1789 could be preserved by *political* means. Those who are faced with the results of the democratic revolutions of 1989 might read him with profit.

16. The issue of nationalism could be posed within this general framework as well. However, we would have to distinguish the form of nationalism that emerged in the nineteenth century as an answer to the social challenge posed by the revolutionary bourgeoisie, and twentieth-century nationalisms that emerged to face that erosion wreaked by the economic processes of capitalism. The reemergence of nationalism in post-totalitarian societies would represent a third variant within this framework.

17. Totalitarianism is not the kind of antipolitics that East European oppositionists such as G. Konrad sought to theorize as a new political stance within *and* against totalitarianism. *That* antipolitics is an instance of what I refer to here as a democratic politics of rights. Totalitarianism cannot in fact impose unity on society; its "politics" acts vertically to atomize any attempts by groups within civil society to constitute themselves horizontally. Capitalism produces a similar effect through the quantitative working of its market logic. This explains the demand by the Czech radicals in their encounter with the German SDS in 1968 for the right to free assembly as well as the ability of the Germans to understand the Czechs intuitively if not conceptually. The problem today, however, is that this kind of oppositional politics has come to power, and it must identify and confront social and economic necessities that are difficult to integrate into the politics of rights. I will return to this problem in my concluding section.

18. To avoid any historical misunderstanding, I should emphasize that totalitarianism tends to present itself as a possibility in situations where the democratic process is *beginning* to take hold. We could cite examples such as Russia, Weimar Germany, Republican Spain, perhaps even Sun Yat Sen's China.

On the other hand, even within societies where democracy has become a *learned* mode of political behavior, radical movements calling themselves "left" must constantly face the fact that they find themselves denouncing "formal" freedoms, ideological manipulations, and the quotidian of electoral politics' quest for a mythical "center." Established democracies, like France and Italy, or even the United States during the Great Depression, can give birth to movements whose tendency is totalitarian. We must distinguish, for example, between "social rights" and "social citizenship" and suggest that the latter is not enough. The slope is slippery because democratic society is not a state of affairs but a constantly repeated challenge that can never be put to rest by the discovery or production of the ultimate foundation. God is, indeed, dead.

19. Alexander Hamilton, James Madison, and John Jay, *The Federalist*, ed. Jacob E. Cooke (Middletown, Conn.: Wesleyan University Press, 1961), 61. On the uniqueness of the American experience and its relevance to debates in the 1990s, see Dick Howard, *The Birth of American Political Thought*, trans. David Curtis (London: Macmillan, 1990).

20. Tocqueville's demonstration of this point is found, of course, in *The Old Regime and the Revolution* rather than in his *Democracy in America*. The relation of the concepts of democracy in these two volumes would merit a separate study; in the present context, reference to the work of Claude Lefort will have to suffice (see n. 22).

21. My debt to Lefort for the previous sketch of the relation of democratic society and totalitarianism should also be acknowledged. For details and references, see also Howard, *Marxian Legacy*, chap. 7, and the afterword to the second edition.

22. Claude Lefort, *L'invention démocratique: Les Limites de la domination totalitaire* (Paris: Fayard, 1981), 61.

23. We had encountered this polarity of society and the state in the political quest for a third way, or the attempt to return to a form of autochthonous historical development. Here we find its theoretical roots. It is important to underline the apparent paradox in which the birth of the autonomous and sovereign individual coincides with and is logically correlative with the emergence of the sovereign national state. If we are to seek postmodern forms of the national state, new kinds of confederations and the like, we need to bear in mind this relation to the autonomous individual and weigh the cost to individual autonomy of our new institutional choices.

24. This of course is even more poignant with regard to the treatment of minority populations, as recent history has shown.

25. Hamilton, Madison, and Jay, *Federalist*, 58, 59.

26. This is why *The Federalist* insists on the republican form and argues constantly against the excesses of democracy. When he analyzed the danger of a "faction," Madison defined it as "a majority or a minority," and it is clear that he worried more about the former than the latter. For a further argument, see my essay "The Political Origins of Democracy," whose first section is titled "Politics after 'the' Revolution" and whose concern is to articulate a "post-revolutionary politics" by developing the relation between republican politics and

democratic society. The essay is found in Dick Howard, *Defining the Political* (Minneapolis: University of Minnesota Press, 1989), chap. 15.

27. Lefort takes the term from Alexander Solzhenitsyn's *Gulag Archipelago,* where it is applied to the still-orthodox denizens of the camps and extends also to those Western intellectuals whose mania for orderly systems to avoid grey zones fits well with a moral desire to think well of themselves. See Lefort, *Un homme en trop* (Paris: Éditions du Seuil, 1976) and Dick Howard, *Marxian Legacy* (2d ed., Minneapolis: University of Minnesota Press, 1988) for the interpretive context. A somewhat different aspect of the same phenomenon takes the form of a slippage from the justified refusal to "blame the victim" to the unjustified (and often masochistically self-righteous) desire to put oneself in the service of the victim, as if the suffering somehow gave to the victim also the wisdom to know how to escape.

28. This assertion, based on East German experience, cannot be generalized to all East European oppositionists. Konrad's antipolitics thought of itself as a morality of participation; the very name of the Polish opposition, Solidarity, points in the same direction. In both cases the goal was the creation of a *civil society.* The difficulty, however, is that both strategies were conceived *within* the framework of the (weakened or "Helsinki-ized") totalitarian state. It is not clear how they can develop in the new, post-totalitarian context. Another aspect of the problem is that the assumption that there is a suppressed collectivity that would emerge once the lid of oppression is lifted makes use of an image borrowed from the arsenal of Marxism's theory of proletarian revolution. That theory, however, was seen to be *antipolitical.*

29. Andre Gorz, *Und Jetzt Wohin?* (Berlin: Rotbuch Verlag, 1991), 150.

JOHN ELY

Libertarian Confederalism and Green Politics: A Perspective on European Unification

Green politics in the present European context requires re-thinking in federalist terms. American left Greens, liberal politicians, communitarians, sociologists of the transnational corporation, advocates of Atlanticism, and Eurocrats, among others, are predicting the dissolution of the nation-state as we know it. Normally, we would regard these as predictions of a New Age guru, but such assertions are increasingly taken seriously. Those making such predictions look, among other places, to the new European Union and the Maastricht Treaty of 1992 for their arguments.

The connection to green politics is evident in, for example, the green opportunism of the German Sozialdemokratische Partei (SPD) and figures such as Johanno Strasser or Volker Hauff, who write books with titles like *Think Globally, Act Locally*—slogans pilfered from the ecology movement but directed at a specific attitude toward European unity, namely the idea of hollowing out the nation-state from both below and above. Even figures from liberal backgrounds emphasize this argument in more postmodernist terms as the need for multiple or plural identities, in such statements as "I feel as if I am a Baden-Württemberger, a German, and a European."[1] On the one hand, this viewpoint is highly cosmopolitan: it advocates, to use Frieder-Otto Wolf's formulation, an "alternative world society" to capitalist modernity.[2] On the other hand, the argument is explicitly libertarian at the point at which it focuses more on hollowing from below, or building up, local communities and direct democracy, using such terms as decentralization or grassroots control.

In terms of contemporary German green politics on the question of

Maastricht and a united Europe, Daniel Cohn-Bendit (the "multicultural" supervisor for the red-green government in the city of Frankfurt am Main) offers a characteristic view. Cohn-Bendit, famous of course for his libertarian leadership and interpretation of the spring 1968 events in Paris, argues that Europeans need to give precedence to the idea of "federation which can be multiply limbed, which springs over old national borders but also works against the idea of Europe as a centralised super-nation-state." Using somewhat utopian language, Cohn-Bendit argues that a Europe of "regions" would be best conceived as one that intensifies contacts on the one hand and, on the other, increasingly recreates the "cities and communes as social subjects."[3]

Despite the fact that Cohn-Bendit's support of inner party oligarchy weakens the integrity of his statement,[4] the idea reaches back to the central libertarian concept of the city-state, the locus of republican thought since Aristotle, and the place of revolution, as Hannah Arendt understood it. A twentieth-century ecological anarchism views the city-state as the main institution in which to organize a libertarian and ecological division of labor. As Murray Bookchin argues under the name "libertarian municipalism,"[5] political freedom as a participatory share in the polity and communist equality—the central goals of anarchist thought since Peter Kropotkin—must have some institutional foundation. The development of industrialism has demonstrated, whether in the contradictions inherent in syndicalism or in Marxism, that the union or the workplace is an insufficient, and ultimately authoritarian and catastrophic, focus for this institutional foundation, because it ends up turning human subjectivity into that of work per se.[6] Bookchin privileges the city, as has the mainstream republican tradition since Aristotle, including Niccolò Machiavelli and Jean-Jacques Rousseau. This is true of the modern libertarians, such as Kropotkin, Ebenezer Howard, Lewis Mumford, Paul Goodman, and Cornelius Castoriadis, who examine cities and their ecological and economic embeddedness in nature. In Bookchin's libertarian view, the city as the basic form of sovereignty and government is based on the idea of ethos and ethics instead of structure and "norms," on participation and face-to-faceness, friendship and appropriate scale, balance and simplicity of economic means.

Federalism in terms of European unity and the Swiss or civic republican concept of politics are both components of present Green discourse on contemporary political issues.[7] We can see many contradictions between the Greens' communitarian emphasis on decentralization and their support for a liberal, internal European market. Simultaneously, we must lament the deficit of federalist thought in the tradition of leftist thinking—whether socialist or civic republican. To be sure, libertarian or democratic conceptions of European unity are not a significant part of the present discussion over Europe outside of the slogans of civic republicanism that we hear from realists such as Udo Knapp, Winifried Kretschmann, or Daniel Cohn-Bendit.[8] Nonetheless, criticism leveled by Jürgen Habermas and his followers at the communitarians and neo-Aristotelians who privilege one particular "form of life" over another makes a point insofar as we can observe that none of the major republican thinkers—Aristotle, Machiavelli, Rousseau, Arendt, Weil—wrote on the topic of federalism. The issues of universality, differentiation, and complexity on the one hand and direct democracy, on the other, remain unanswered and unexplored. Rousseau announces a work on "political institutions" at the end of *Social Contract*. It was to deal with the issue of federations and alliances, and his failure to produce this work is, in this respect, exemplary of the tradition of civic republicanism as a whole.

This deficiency is most evident in terms of the Greens' attitude toward European unification. In the federalism discussions in general, the difference between a Hamiltonian concept of federalism and a Swiss concept is not always clear in the minds of the interlocutors. In the discussion about European unification, ambiguity over whether the European Union will be a confederation or a federal state is equally evident.[9] Despite Green rhetoric about federalism, about power to the communes and municipalities, European unification is undoubtedly taking a more Hamiltonian form. Present policies are directed at the project of building a new kind of nation-state, despite talk of a constitutional alternative for a *confederal* relation of smaller states. While a writer like Bookchin, referring to the old "Articles of Confederation" between the American states,[10] underscores the structural distinction between federalism and confederalism, the Greens as a whole are unclear about which approach they should take to European unification, though this process is now happening explicitly in a federalist rather than confederalist form, dominated by presidial elements constituted by the ministers of the individual national governments. The actual legislator of the European Community, following Article 145 of the Treaty for Foundation of the European Community, is the council of ministers in the particular regions of competency. It is the "organ" of European unification.[11] This institution, constituted by the state and governing leaders of the member nations combined with the presidents of the European Community (EC) Commission, arose from the demand of individual governments (the "Luxembourg Compromise") for a consensus format for decisions on structural changes. Each national government has insisted on retaining direct executive control in order to cope with the basic issues of EC foreign policy and of European political cooperation.[12]

Given this degree of executive privilege, the historic formation of nation-states in early modernity can serve as a model in many respects for understanding contemporary European unification. In Barrington Moore's terms, we see the "dictatorial" rather than "democratic" mode of state building;[13] or thinking in the terms of Geoff Eley and David Blackbourn's contributions to German history, we see the Bismarckian model of unification of the German Reich, a top-down federalism of the princes, or creation of hegemony over the individual principalities, dukedoms, and kingdoms that constituted the specific path to Germany's modernity as opposed to the more liberal-democratic path followed by England.[14] This Prussian model, as much a "path" to modernity as the English model, is, as M. Rainer Lepsius notes, the best past event for understanding the present terms of European unification. The "EC institutional order," he notes, "is . . . the core of a new political entity analogous to the 1871 German Reich. Then as now, sovereignty lay with the contracting states, even though the people elected a parliament limited in its ability to initiate legislation and to control the budget."[15] In this sense, the "expansion of EC legislation increasingly subordinates the courts and the citizens of the member states to legal norms originating outside national legislation. Its various legal systems are not determined democratically." The people are sovereign only in terms of their representative nation-state governments, while they are only subjects in the EC.[16]

A libertarian confederalist perspective contrasts group concepts based on the idea of sovereignty with those based on the idea of solidarity. Instead of domination by force and protection, friendship, social ties, fellowship, and comradeship characterize the psychological ties among individuals. The conception of rule or sovereignty as rooted in the princes was advocated by conservative medieval Christians and taken up by Jean Bodin and the liberal social contract thinkers. It is a concept based on the feudal system and its overarching discourse of servitude, on the one hand, and the development of the nation-state and mercantilism, on the other. The rise of Roman law, the doctrine of absolutism ("supervisory and tutelary state"), a *homogeneous* conception of sovereignty, and the contract state all figure in this modern discourse. In Otto Gierke's terms, this path of modernity is that of the *Anstalt* as a tutelary principle of rule and the federation of ruled principalities in contrast to that of *Genossenschaft* as a form of association and federations of *Genossenschaften*. This distinguishes the concept of a social contract of interests such as that understood by modern private law or modern concepts of citizenship from that constituted by participation and collective ownership.[17] The former tutelary model served as the basis for the formation of the modern nation-state, especially in the eastern portions of Europe, while collective ownership is the principle of the league or federation of cities, the Hansa federation, or that of the Netherlands, Northern Italy, or Switzerland, as opposed to the absolutist model of the nation-state.

The anstalt form of corporation and contract underlying modern legality served as the basis for German unification, as a model of individual principalities negotiating a unity under claims of military dominance; it is, as Max Weber emphasizes, a relationship *compulsory* in nature,[18] whether this legal relation is expressed in relation to the market or the state. While Moore emphasizes the historic difference between nation-states built on the basis of feudal subservience or dependence on a class of agrarian capitalists (Junkers) and those built on the basis of free-holding farmers, Blackbourn and Eley emphasize that the latter served as an authoritarian path to modernity as logical as the other. This Prussian model of state building ascendant in Eastern Europe during modernization is being followed today in the process of European unification, a "neo-Absolutist grey zone"[19] in the European Community, an "aristocratic system."[20]

Evidence of both the difficulties of unification and the fact that it is occurring on the model of princely rule from above has reappeared in the *Frankfurter Allgemeine Zeitung*'s representation of the Maastricht Treaty process. The newspaper compares European unification to contestations among the German *Länder,* who "are behaving like faithless vassals in a Germanic heroic epic."[21] While leaders of the individual states complain about lost competence in education, health, and domestic or legal policy, three of Germany's most prominent jurists, from a spectrum of political positions (Konrad Hesse, Ernst Benda, and Helmut Simon), criticized unification as unconstitutional, above all as a violation of principles of "popular sovereignty." While constitutional critique of Maastricht occurs from all sides,[22] the *Frankfurter Allgemeine* has developed increasingly the conservative position that Maastricht is unconstitutional, characterizes the people in cultural-nationalist imagery, and spurs anxiety about the loss of national *sovereignty.*

While we can criticize the process of European unification from many perspectives, an antistatism uncritically endorsing every kind of popular antiunity perspective carries with it many risks. Paul Piccone, for example, supports regionalisms such as the Italian "Northern League" largely on the basis of Carl Schmitt's conception of federalism and the libertarian conviction that movements advocating popular-local sovereignty are thereby safe from development of distasteful ethnic, xenophobic, or ressentiment-laden attitudes.[23] That Piccone endorses Schmitt and Pierre-Joseph Proudhon (who supported the South in the U.S. Civil War for antistatist, federalist reasons) in his defense of the new regionalisms makes us realize that in the wake of the Eastern Bloc collapse, there are many possible positions on "decentralization." Those supporting regional or ethnic particularity have a national or conservative focus (i.e., on retaining the riches of local industrially strong regions).[24]

While Piccone is impressed by Schmitt's argument that the units of a federation must all be like one another, he fails to note that the main federated body Schmitt addresses in homogeneous terms are *national* "units," and this kind of discourse has an intrinsically "ethno-pluralist" tendency.[25] That such typical ethno-pluralist right-wing journals, such as *Nation Europa,* edited by the neo-Nazi August von Thadden, regard the *Lega nord* as a decisive part of the New Right suggests problems with a neo-Schmittian federalist endorsement of the northern leagues. The very fact that failure of European unification, no matter how bureaucratic, would benefit the case of racists and nationalists throughout Europe means that it is difficult to question in principle.[26] A Green concept of confederalism emphasizing empowerment and ecological balance based on a *reformist* orientation, which does not reject the role of the nation-state or larger institutions, is preferable to one whose antistatism supports movements for regional autonomy in *potentially nationalist* form.

A reformist conception of federalism with some acceptance of tutelary elements modeled on the work of Johannes Althusius and Otto Gierke is preferable to the regionalist league version of federalism held by left-Schmittians like Piccone.[27] Assuming this, opposition to European unification, despite the unfortunately centralistic and absolutist paths taken up to 1995, should not be endorsed despite increasing popular opposition to Maastricht. One commentator in the *Tageszeitung* noted with regard to letting the German people vote on Maastricht: "The question will be posed to Germans once again as to whether they are civilised Europeans or warloving nationalists. This question is one which in my view ought to be decided by parliament."[28] Even from libertarians and decentralists, antipathy to the nation-state is so strong that it has engendered a search for both new forms opposed to Maastricht centralism and skepticism even to the idea of introducing *ius soli,* or "law of land" basis for individual citizenship. At the same time, with the danger of the New Right and the potential of a successful antiunification vision of an ethno-pluralist Europe of ethnically homogeneous or "cleansed" nations so present,[29] a popular front attitude for unity is the only possible stance. Since the invention of the nation-state, there has been a devastating war in Europe every century and a quarter (Thirty Years War, Napoleon, World Wars I and II); thus, the desire to seek an end for this characteristic of European modernity is well directed. Rightist and regionalist politics can easily become *unübersichtlich* (unsurveyable)[30] and weak in an American fashion with the successful federalization of Europe, fragmented and disparate enough that they cannot seriously affect the central federal institutions.

The *necessity* for European unification, despite the displeasing elitist and centralist mode, is evident as well in the *general* tension between differentiation, on the one hand, and participation in universal forms, on the other. Differentiation, for example, can mean the separation of powers as a federal project (multiple states) or a *functional* project (differing powers of government). These do not necessarily overlap. For example, in the issue of "One Big Central Bank" for Europe, critics of all sorts note that the currency crisis forced a federalist *Bundesbank* monetary policy, which is the model for the EC, to "an open debate on whether democratic Europe can afford to surrender its economic fate to the hands of a few bankers—or indeed whether it can afford not to."[31] On the one hand, a banking system's *independence* from government has been linked, as Alberto Alesin notes,[32] to low inflation. On the other, surrendering monetary policy to one council of bankers is extremely undemocratic. Functional differentiation is combined with intense spatial centralization and homogenization of territory.

This opposition is part of a larger tension in the theory of federalism between differentiation and universality, a tension that all federalist theory must address. To what extent do modern states demand "homogenization" of the population? To what extent are modern states "differentiated" into various and distinct "subsystems"? Which forms of integration require homogeneity and which plurality? Interestingly, while Jürgen Habermas and his followers have routinely attacked neo-Aristotelians and civic republicans for their "particularist" presuppositions, the problem of a democratic universalism based on *institutional homogeneity* is always in tension with the differentiation of society. Here we see a key historic shift between a Gierkean organic pluralism and the introduction of a mechanist language for funtionalism in Durkheim as we follow the development of theories of group association.[33]

On the one hand, as left-Schmittian advocates of "integral federalism" (Piccone, Ulmen) point out, Schmitt argued that federations, just like nation-states, will never be composed of cities or communities with particularistic forms of life, because *federations are always federations of like units*.[34] While this indeed constitutes an independent contribution by this right-wing thinker, Schmitt (as these left-Schmittians *fail* to point out) used this same demand of *homogeneity* for his explanation of the federations between ethnically distinct but *homogeneous* units. Schmitt thus in the end supports a right-wing conception of ethnic politics that dovetails dangerously with support for regionalism like that found today in South Tirol, Lombardy, and Tessia. On the other hand, by constantly attacking as particularistic the *universal* concept of a confederated, city-state republicanism, the Habermasians consistently occlude the manner in which the construction of the modern state and national economy they defend is as much an immense process of dedifferentiation and ethnic homogenization carrying with it a huge ballast of unresolved antagonisms. The homogeneity presupposed by the modern they insist upon is the breeding ground for the contemporary nationalist and regionalist particularisms that so concern them. Nationalist "imaginaries" can be constructed where civic personalities are interrupted or nonactive, and a concept of (national-popular) sovereignty that refuses to see itself as specifically located in institutional bodies politic will tend to privilege the existing, national bodies politic.[35] Functional differentiation combined with confederal state institutions at the center may be preferable in this respect to a vision of federations of similar, homogeneous units (attacking the nation-state).[36]

Further, though unification has occurred thus far in top-down form and according to the more authoritarian precedents drawn from European constitutional history, this need not be the case in the future. As Stephan Leibfried remarks, "the field for great institutional transformations is wide open, and one finds within the member states, especially on the periphery of the EC, actors who are proposing alternative paths of development and seeking to systematically contribute to present structural changes." These actors include strong previously extant interest organizations (growers, unions, employer organizations) who are present at the EC level, as well as new social movements.[37] Certainly while the question of the room to maneuver for social movements and left forces is the premise of a serious discussion of federalism, the *potentiality* of the possible actors is much more incalculable than the *possibility* of changing the mode of European unification. Nonetheless, given the perils of both misguided federalism and (mega-)state building, it is also imperative that we consider a position on Europe. Particularly since the fall of the Eastern Bloc, social movements have had difficulty formulating strategies for addressing the new themes with their toolkit.

• • •

The contribution of the new social movements and the Greens to European politics has been minimal, especially during the early period. The obvious reason is that despite their dislike for states, their decentralist and basic democratic perspective make it hard for them to offer a program on Europe or to support one managed as a centralist, bureaucratic market-oriented enterprise. The Greens in the European Parliament are caught in the paradox of having to defend traditional-ecological community forms (like the highly subsidized and largely conservative agricultural sector) most intransigent to European unity.[38] At the same time, the Greens must maintain liberal views opposed to national interest and xenophobia. In the Green faction in the European Parliament, the fundamentalist wing represented especially by Anton Wächter, Gianfranco Amendola, Sara Parkin (and such intellectuals as Arne Naess, Paul Ehrlich, and Edward Wilson) focuses on biodiversity[39] with a tendency toward a "population bomber" and antisocial, biocentric, or biologistic views of regionalism.[40] Since such views play an increasingly important role in the United States and Europe, it is important to work out the details of a democratic federalism and to address the benefits and dangers of a *populist* discourse of survival, localism, regionalism,[41] or even landscapes.[42]

Further, the divide between more ecofundamentalist and left Green views in the European Parliament faction, in the opinions of many (Jean Lambert, Friedrich Bahringdorf, Frieder-Otto Wolf) hinders the party from effective contributions to European policy. The Green left is more concerned with the question of a new "fortress Europe" sealed against foreigners[43] and with conceptions of an ecological *Umbau* or ecological rebuilding of industrial society.[44] The fundamentalists are concerned with regionalism, species preservation, and biodiversity. Though the fundamentalists had a political majority of parliamentary deputies until 1994, the views of the Green left tend de facto to be more influential; along the lines of the German Greens, whose electoral influence continues to grow in comparison with other European Green parties, the realist positions tend to get closest to central economic and political policy. Nonetheless, the European Parliamentary Greens split over the issue of how to formulate opposition to Fortress Europe and the new core/periphery form of international capitalism. Attempts to prohibit leftist views in the faction have occurred over issues of third world and World Bank policies.[45] The overarching contradiction between the accumulation dynamic and the ecological balance means, however, that in either case (left or fundamentalist), the European Greens are faced with a struggle against "really existing capitalism" in order to achieve their aims.

The "grow or die" logic of capitalism, whether liberal productivist[46] or otherwise, runs diametrically opposed to ecological principles of balance, diversity, and ecological stability.[47] In this respect, they reflect a common petit bourgeois opposition on environmental issues that nonetheless seriously affects the capital goods sector, regardless of verbal lack of support for left social policy.[48] While green politics tends de facto to be opposed to the law of value even when it openly advocates capitalist solutions, there is no doubt that the increasing influence of "green-greens," "deep greens," fundamentalist greens from England, France, and Italy, combined with the increasing influence of the "Realist" Greens in Germany, have weakened the "left" green social critique of the European Greens seriously, even though such an approach has deleterious, even disastrous, electoral effects.[49] In the wake of the 1994 Europarliament elections, some of these parties nearly disintegrated, while greens evolved in the new federal states in Germany, Austria, and Switzerland, those areas where a left-green, "citizen-native" or "red-green" component has retained its voice. Characteristically with regard to European unification, just as earlier with German unification, the Greens have had difficulty adjusting their old orientations to new issues. Greens have had little elaborate conception of European politics, which is not surprising given the contradictions between localism and regionalism, on the one hand, and the need for a universal answer to the New Right, on the other—between the fear of nationalism and dislike of state and market.

Even though they would seem to have less influence at present than in earlier mobilizations, through representation such as the Greens in the European Parliament, new social movement issues play a role, because their advocates have competence in areas where there is relatively little political or intellectual experience coming from traditional areas of society but where the potential for influencing lives is extremely large, such as on nuclear or water policies. Thus, Green parliamentarians' focus on rain forests, energy, or the human genome reflects areas of specialization where movement groups have developed important competencies.[50] Alternative institutes and organizations, such as the Darmstadt/Freiburg Eco-Institute, which have emerged from the alternative scene in opposition to the established and unmovable institutions (like newspapers and publications, polling organizations, institutes, and financial associations), have established their reputations, setting the discourse of arguments in their field and receiving important publicity.[51]

In the German Greens, Cohn-Bendit—though he has shown himself liberal enough in the past few years, if not positively right-wing in his own party through support of capitalist and entrepreneurial measures—has been important on the question of liberal immigration policies. But in terms of Europeanization, his focus on turning the cities into privileged subjects is open to an objection—offered most prominently in Germany by Habermas and his followers—of an excessive particularism that arises inherently out of a community- rather than a society-oriented position. While the overarching idea of a "commune of communes" is an idea from the libertarian tradition,[52] without a coherent federalist concept, the traditional warnings about particularism appear more pertinent in a period of fervently increasing and deadly nationalisms, ethnic particularities, and religious fundamentalisms.

• • •

A libertarian confederalism that can answer these objections can learn much from the theory of plural or multiple sovereignty best articulated by the late nineteenth-century legal historian, Otto Gierke. Gierke focused on German law, the Middle Ages, and not surprisingly on the period of the rise of the city-state in northern Europe—especially in the Netherlands in the early modern period of the fifteenth and sixteenth centuries. Most decisive in this respect is Gierke's revival of the ideas of a legal scholar from the Friesian islands named Johannes Althusius. Althusius is the only major thinker to develop natural law into a theory of *pluralized* rather than *homogeneous* and *unified* sovereignty; he developed this notion of plural sovereignty in opposition to the nation-state absolutism emerging in England and France, with its single point of sovereignty.

This most fruitful tradition of federalism includes an assortment of legal scholars influenced by the Dutch-German legal professor Althusius. Of particular note is his influence on the meticulous legal historian and advocate of the genossenschaft, Gierke, but he also influenced Ernst Troeltsch, John Figgis, F. W. Maitland, Fredrick Pollock, and G. D. H. Cole, the "guild socialist," and their "pluralist" followers, to use a term from Melvin Laski.[53] Althusius and Gierke offer a communal federalism based on the theory of *groups;* such groups are understood not just as a community of rights or goods but as encompassing life in a larger sense.[54] On the one hand, this Gierkean view mixed work and participation in politics and leisure insofar as "fellowship" or genossenschaft organizations, like guilds, were not just "interest organizations." These communities socialized and regulated life in manifold aspects, including work and work administration, security of family and town, and public events in general. Althusius understood such a unity in psychological terms as that between heart and understanding, but he also saw it in terms of the organic qualities of a division of labor and its complex web of interdependency, in the sense of mutual aid or a cooperative, "nature-rightly" attitude.

Althusius and Gierke's ideas are federalist not because of this syndicalist component alone but also because they understood this group as one among a complex institutional layer of bound or federated organizations and degrees of community. Each layer, from the greater, like *universitas*, to the smaller, like corporations, collegium, partnerships, and associations that existed below it, bears its own ethic or ethos that comes not merely from recognition of shared interests but from a continued participation or *practice* in the organization, each of which in itself becomes a distinct *loci* of sovereignty over a distinctive portion of human activity.[55] Hence, we have a participatory conception of distributed, plural, or multiple sovereignty in which city, syndicate, family, school, church, country, and federation all play a role.[56] Althusius called this web of interwoven associations a *corpus symbioticum* (symbiotic body), governed by an *ius symbioticum* (symbiotic right).

A fellowship-based conception of a federal participatory form of government fits into the ideals of a libertarian, such as Proudhon or Bookchin, since it arises historically from the federations of free cities, which were founded in early modernity in Northern Germany, the Netherlands, Northern Italy, and Switzerland—in which strong guilds played central roles.[57] Plural sovereignty grants the civic order its own universal status; this connection of material interest and civic good is still evident in the *political* roots of the term "community," as commune or city government in the Romance languages. It is also evident in the German word for community, gemeinschaft, from *Gemein*, meaning together or common in the sense of *Gemeinwesen* (commonwealth), as well as gemeinschaft (community) or *Gemeinde* (county government). In this respect, such forms allow for what Bookchin rightly calls notions of "confederation" or a "greater whole" that is "conceived as a form of participatory administration."[58]

Maitland and Pollock note that universitas in early English legal history referred to the independent legal status that was distinct from that of the sum of its members. The distinction, in this regard, between universitas (the whole) and *societas* (the allies) was by no means certain, even on the continent during the Middle Ages, since both were subordinate to a fellowship conception that included both public and private components. "We can find in our law books no such terms as *corporation, body corporate,* or *body politic,* though we read much of *convenants, chapters,* and *communities.* The largest term in general use is *community, commonality,* or *commune,* in Latin, *communitas* or *communa.*"[59] Commune in this sense fits Gierke's concept of community precisely, since it treats life as a whole, including both heart and mind, public and private. Universitas in thirteenth-century Oxford, says Maitland, had a dual sense: a corporation "as much within the sphere of the public as within the sphere of the private."[60]

These are juridical associations but only in the sense that community or fellowship rather than violence, domination, or *Herrschaft* is the organizing principle. A genossenschaft conception explicitly rejects the Roman law idea of private corporation based on compulsion and interest, instead privileging the free city over kingship. The "glue" of community is not a common fear of government or recognition of material interests but *concord* (fellowship). *Concordia* in Althusius's work refers to relationships of friendship that each has at various levels (and invokes the Aristotle of the *Ethics,* rather than of the *Politics,* who considers "community" as a term of all different kinds of partnerships, clubs, and modes of association). The political order is like a *scala natura* of participatory associations in the political order, ranging from shared religious community to city, work, play, and family. (And since Althusius is a Calvinist,[61] like many modern figures, he sees the family also as a realm or kind of fellowship, not unlike the Aristotelian moralist, Jane Austen, at a later date.) Friendship as the glue of community appears not only in the genossenschaft tradition but also in the idea of mutualism found in Proudhon or Kropotkin's idea of civic communism through mutual aid: in all cases we can see equality as participation in civic affairs, economic comparability to one another as the precondition for friendship, and friendship as the mode of association.[62] The group is formed as a community or city by active members rather than as a society formed where status is shared anonymously and passively by subjects or individuals, subordinate to the structural or mechanical and quantitative "laws" of supply and demand or support for parliamentary candidates.[63]

Gierke and Althusius follow Aristotle's thinking as well regarding the biological naturalism characteristic of the latter thinker. Aristotle as marine biologist assumed an overall teleology based on the scala natura, the gradated emergence of mind out of nature and the formation of organization, the regulation of the body, as a central metaphor in his science as a whole. On the one hand, he sees the development of associations starting with the smaller forms of *koinia* or community, above all the family, and on the other, he sees all of these forms of associations as organic wholes regulated by their own principles, as well as those of their placement in the system or its overall teleology.[64] By the same token, Althusius, writes Gierke, avoids a "superficial" anthropomorphism. Aristotle's (civic) world, in opposition to one constituted by the "media" of money and power, market economy and state, is assembled via the interchange of friends, the sea of social, mannered, or amiable ties binding or bathing the virtues.

This conception is taken up by Althusius and Gierke in the idea of fellowship, *Genoße*, or comrade. Gierke's organicism "worked into the principle that the essence of the State consists in a unity of common life which, as in the case of natural organisms, results from the harmonious coherence of the parts, which are properly differentiated, disposed and vested with special functions." Community was understood as an organic unity of diversity in which differentiated individuals are members of the living collective body. This body was composed of overlapping networks of institutions, with each institution constituting a mix between the individual and the universal, and each institution a "necessary articulation" of a constitution that unites the many into one, an expression of constitutional power as organic function.[65] As did Ernst Troeltsch later, Gierke emphasizes the Aristotelian notion of different layers or *entelechia* in development and group formation, such that a federalist formation (of varying overlapping levels of group or fellowship-based sovereign spheres or competences) appears.[66]

For Gierke, as for Althusius before him, the political community as a whole is characterized by a multiplicity of levels and layers, all sharing their portions and capacities of sovereignty. Gierke finds German law packed with circumstances where the terminology makes plain that we are dealing with multiple forms of the interplay between particular and universal (i.e., the interplay of "singular and plural forms" with one another). This is, as Gierke notes, reminiscent of Antigone's conflict with the city, the "opposition of collective tribal and particular rights."[67] We find this in expressions such as *Gemeinde, Gemeinheit, Gemeinschaft, gemeine Gemeinheit (meene meente), gemeine Menge, gesammteheit der Nachbarn, Leute, Genossen, universitas, communitas, communio, communia, communis, congregation, consocium, conventus, multitudo commarchionum*, and so on. In each, we see this characteristic dialectic between "particular and universal, tribe and other, individual and general, *communiter et divisim, universaliter et singulariter.*"[68]

This federalism of multiple layers of unity in diversity or interlocking cooperative relations and competencies was for Gierke always a "radical democratic" idea (to use contemporary language) in that it rested on the irreducible quality of sovereignty as *presence*. It sought to negate all *abstracting* conceptions of right deriving from the Roman sense of "fictive" or abstract individual or "private person." Decision-making assemblies of members constitute each federative element, whether familial, professional, collegial, civic, or political[69]—one of the features, besides the jury system, that Maitland praises in early English law in all its German purity.[70] (The law of fellowship, *Genossenschafts-recht*, the general or organizing principle of German law, rests on the right not of the individual against individual but on the right of the fellowship via its members.) For Gierke, official positions inside any given fellowship or association are open to election, and the members who serve in the federative offices are recallable from below.[71]

The federalist conception of organization in groups is Aristotelian since it does not begin with an abstract conception of the political organization or the individual. Each appears in relation to one another. The character and psychological aspects of the individual or a person's personality appear as an outcome of the form of group life and group practices in which they live. A communal- or fellowship-based conception of the human being is thus not the result of human nature but the character or "nature"—accumulated (collective) practices—of human associations inculcating this attitude. In this sense, it shares a political psychology and ethics with the "tradition" in political theory, the historical doctrine of natural law, or more precisely, with an Aristotelian rather than a Hobbesian, Kantian, or utilitarian conception of the moral and political self. Thus, the community federalism of Gierke and Althusius and the conception of genossenschaft as an ius symbioticum shares a conception of self, of community formed by participation, and of friendship among equals as the glue in the Aristotelian or civic republican conception (Machiavelli, Rousseau, and Arendt). The communitarian federalism, while emphasizing the role of free cities and federations of free cities in its model, does not limit the group characterized by the ethos of comradeship, equality, and participation to the civic form. Althusius gives political shape to subpolitical forms (guilds, private organizations) on the one hand, and to superpolitical orders and federations, complete with their own membership identities, on the other. While civic life is a central form of universal group organization, a primary universitas, it is embedded in a net of associations and groups both above and below it.

During the late Middle Ages and early modernity, says Gierke, we find only exceptional cases on the coast and in the mountains where there is a development of a communal constitution and political independence on the basis of territorial communes, which then aspire (like and along with the cities) to unite with one another to form a truly federal state. Switzerland is one of the few places where the territorial commune became "fully developed."[72] Here, as earlier in the Northern German Hansa confederation, a "real state without an intermediary supreme territorial power" is created. The civic communes, the unit of such confederations, along with guilds, alliances, and brotherhoods, developed the "most ancient state association in German law on the basis of self-government and consensual justice."[73]

This conception merits comparison with the idea of "libertarian municipalism" advanced by Murray Bookchin, who writes the history of modernity as a pincer of state building and expansion of the "self-regulating" capitalist market. In such a context, the space of *political* life gets increasing devoured or colonized by the market and the private sphere ethos of *business* on the one hand and the bureaucratic discipline of *statecraft* on the other. Bookchin underscores the difference between civic republican institutions and the modern state, by emphasizing the difference between the modern and the Aristotelian distinction between state and society or public and private. (Aristotle called the kind of pure executive rule or domination of a state or bureaucracy a kind of "domestic" rule, with Persia as his model.) Bookchin's position is essentialist, however, insofar as it proposes the transfer of institutional life from the two outer spheres of modern organizational life—those of bureaucratic management and capitalist markets—into the center sphere of the municipality, city life, the civic or public space where politics is done. Here, Bookchin, like the libertarian tradition in general, insists on the role of participation in administrative conceptions or political praxis. But he does not elaborate an institutional model of such participatory administration beyond the civic level (just as such figures as Rousseau and Kropotkin also failed to do.)[74] This perspective tends to locate political life in one (local) institutional locus. Broader, extra-civic forms of political life are excluded almost per se, given the face-to-face requirement of politics in the first person.

Civic republicans are traditionally reproached for insensitivity to the politics of private life, or those things that tend to fall outside of the public sphere. Gierke, through his reading of Althusius, circumvents this reduction to one primary sphere of politics insofar as his theory of groups offers a more dispersed, federal conception by *deepening* associate ties both below and above the locus of the city and the governing institutions of a nation-state. In the case of the city, the spheres of associations below the polity—especially professional and labor organizations—play a larger role, as do spheres of organizations above the level of the polity (leagues, federations, and larger "universal" groups). Gierke thus grants a much stronger institutional role to federal organizations that transcend the polity and that are oriented by considerations arising from broader groups and organizations. Gierke's reading of the tradition of natural law, emphasizing Althusius (and Grotius) rather than Hobbes or Bodin, is unique among modern conceptions of sovereignty. Like those conceptions stemming from civic republican sources such as Aristotle and Marcellus of Padua, Gierke's reading systematically de-emphasizes, even opposes, territorial concepts of polity, or those based on ascribed "national" characteristics such as ethnicity, race, or confession.[75] His concept is not homogeneous and unified, geographically limited and based on force, like that of Hobbes, Bodin, and their followers (e.g., Kantians and utilitarians).

Althusius is both an important locus of Aristotelian and communitarian thought in early modernity and the central advocate of a conception of multiple or plural sovereignty. Political thought in the Middle Ages is caught in a conflict between notions of divine monarchical or princely authority, on the one hand, and popular sovereignty, on the other—two versions as it were of the "great chain of being."[76] This antagonism, argues Gierke, reappears in modern political thought in the opposition between the thinking of someone like Bodin and Hobbes, on the one hand, and Althusius, on the other; the upward directed federative conception of a popular medieval great chain of being is redeveloped in a conception of civic federations in the former case, while the formal dominance of the ruling monarch in the feudal-princely conception gets transferred into an absolutist model of the new nation-state.

We can understand Gierke's antagonism to Roman law and its theory of abstraction, of an abstract or fictive legal subject in the context of modern state building. In Gierke's view, this subject embodied an individual concept of right set up to justify hierarchy and slavery, in principle capable only of developing fully as (modern) private law. It is based on the individual and is fixed or absolute in form.[77] German law, Gierke argues, takes a "diametrical form" opposed to Roman law in two ways. German law is (1) a much later and less complete *abstraction* from within an unending diversity of wealth and forms of concrete relationships, and (2) the more complete, broader predisposition (*Anlage*). German law demonstrates a long and progressive elaboration of the concept of person not simply as a legal individual in private contracts; it remained for millennia without abstraction, allowing for concrete distinctions between legal subjects without losing a view of the species unity.

In this respect, notes Gierke, the complete establishment of the Roman abstraction of the differences of legal subjects and their subsumption under a colorless concept of species (*Gattungsbegriff*) never occurred in Germany until the reception of Roman law, as is evident in the absence of German terms for "person" or "legal subject."[78] Unlike Roman law, German law could not begin with the opposition of an absolute order of the will of the state and the sum of sovereign individual wills. Rather, its starting point was a unified conception of will marked by freedom under confines including both "being for itself and being for another," the individual and the communal together. Roman law, starting with the abstract idea of the equality of subjects, was the basis of the development of individual freedoms allowing for the expansion of business on the basis of its abstracted conception of the individual acting according to self-interest.[79] This principle of Roman law was crucial to the development of modern capitalism,[80] as well as being the model of sovereignty upon which thinkers like Bodin and Hobbes developed their new concept of the state and its relation to the social individual abstracted out from all other associations.

As both Gierke and Maitland emphasize, sovereignty itself was not a clearly defined concept in the medieval world. This term is ultimately only established with the hegemonic dominance of the Hobbesian-Bodin conception of state and law, or what Gierke calls the exaltation to the last degree of sovereignty on the part of Bodin and Hobbes.[81] An anstalt or tutelary conception of associative life, as social life, derives in large measure from the generalization not only of the Roman legal subject but more originally from the concept of *patria potestas*. This became the basis for a theory of subordination and natural inequality in private law, which multiplied and assumed manifold new forms with the development of the modern state and capitalist economy.[82]

The development of the Roman idea of the legal subject was by no means complete in the Middle Ages throughout Europe. Gierke notes:

> Professional lawyers of the Middle Ages were already operating—and sometimes in a very precise fashion—with the concept of the ideal "right-subjectivity" of the State. But the concept that they were using was . . . the "juristic person" of the Civil-Canonist theory of corporations, an instrument produced in the workshop of private law, which was ever more commonly regarded as a creature of pure thought ("persona repraesentata"), a fiction ("persona ficta") set up by an artificium iuris, and, with whatever differences of interpretation, was connected in a purely external and mechanical fashion with the aggregate of real persons.[83]

This purely mechanical concept in political theory, tied with the idea of society as the sphere where people meet as abstract, private individuals develops with the increasing penetration of Roman law into Europe, with emerging capitalism, and with the new concepts of sovereignty seen in Bodin and Hobbes.[84] Gierke notes that Hobbes viewed state-personality as "nothing more than the ruler's personality of the old doctrine, made absolute and mechanical." Hobbes is an individualist through and through, and this individualism is the source of his conception of the "right subjectivity" of corporations and the state. To be sure, in the picture of the great Leviathan, Hobbes represents the state as a gigantic body and works out in detail the analogy with a living body, but the supposed organism turns out to be nothing but a mere automaton.[85] This conveys an image of the individual related mechanically to the whole in a system of equal right or exchange, which becomes the model for the individual's relation to both the modern nation-state and the market.

What we see theoretically in Hobbes or Locke—namely the colonization of all the various spheres of life by society—parallels the colonization of the world by capitalist markets and the state. Ultimately, says Gierke, this leads to a Prussian view of society that "like the theory of the state derived from it was given an individualist and mechanical form." When this theory of the state "wiped out all sharp distinctions between '*societas*' and '*universitas*,'" it amounted inwardly to the idea of the social contract as a *bond of obligation* between individuals, and outwardly to the realm of the 'moral person' which makes the sum total of individuals a collective unity."[86] Societas is the root of the joint-stock company and partnership is "a kind of Contract, and Contract as a kind of Obligation"—and as Maitland notes, societas can really only be translated as contract.[87] Moreover, in modern *social* contract theory, the relationship becomes increasingly the model of the modern state as well. The individual is isolated between the impersonal law of the state, on one hand, and the market, on the other. Thus, despite the attempts at a different conception of sovereignty and legality, the major course of modernity is, as Maitland observes, a "river gaining in strength and depth and lucidity as it sweeps onward towards the Leviathan," a course "away from organization and toward mechanical construction, away from biology and towards dynamics, away from corporateness and towards contractual obligation."[88]

Gierke contrasts Althusius to this Hobbesian-Prussian perspective: Althusius "differs altogether from the prevailing view as represented chiefly by Bodin. Expressing the ideas of a small minority he ascribes the rights of sovereignty not to the ruler but wholly and solely to the people. The rights of sovereignty belong necessarily and exclusively to the social body (*'corpus symbioticum'*). They are its spirit, its soul, the breath of its life; only when it possesses them does it live; when it loses them it perishes or at any rate forfeits the name of 'Respublica.'"[89]

Gierke's understanding of modernity as a struggle between the genossenschaft and the principality for political hegemony parallels Murray Bookchin's libertarian reading in terms of the rise of capitalism. For Gierke, the rise of the nation-state and the subjection of the free cities and their genossenschaftsformen appears in the history of political philosophy as the colonization of all other associative spheres by the gesellschaft or societas—or in Marxist terms, the rise of civil society, the self-regulating market, the modern capitalist political economy. Societas, during the medieval and early modern period, was only one of several forms of association. With the advent of the modern and the contract, society or civil society became an increasingly and universally used abstract term: on the one hand, for the whole; on the other, it denotes the legal sense of association or private society. The Roman law concept of corporation or private law contract, as societas, erodes other forms of community and replaces them with an abstract individual immediately related to the new realm of market or state, both of which follow a mechanical logic.

Gierke makes it clear that the dualism between the individual and the state was both "modern" and done at the expense of all "intermediate groups." The centralizing, absolutist tendency of modern natural law (Hobbes, Locke, Hugo Grotius, Samuel Pufendorf, Francisco Suarez) was an intrinsic movement in the denial of public authority to associations, a theory in Hobbes or Suarez corresponding to the rise of society as a description of human forms of life. Society, societas, and gesellschaft arise as terms for the *absence* of mediation, the absence of associative life between individual and state (e.g., that right of *collega et corpora* is only a matter of ius societas, a simple "business partnership of individuals united by private contract").[90] Society emerges as the state erodes community and the associative and guild life of the free cities, replacing it on the one hand with state institutions (Roman institutes, anstaltsrecht) and the ever-widening market in goods and labor, on the other.

Understood as the history of the forms of groups, Gierke broke down the periods of European history into an early period of folkmoot equality up to 800 C.E. (and even longer in England, as Maitland notes).[91] This was succeeded, particularly on the continent, by feudalism and its overarching discourse of servitude. The country, in the form of feudal princes and lords, dominates the city. Feudalism provided a context for the emergence of free cities between 1200 and 1525. This period, capped by the intense energies of the radical reformation, marks the appearance of political freedom in Europe in the form of federated cities: "while the feudal state and hierarchical structure collapses irretrievably, the principle of *union* creates the most magnificent organisation from below by means of *freely chosen* fellowships (*Genossenschaften*)."[92] By the time of the disastrous battle of White Mountain at the latest (outside of the Netherlands and Switzerland), this period of civic and associative freedom had come to an end.[93]

The advent of modernity is thus marked by the destruction of civic freedom via state and capitalist markets, or the rise of "society": the development of Empire and nation-state, mercantilism and sovereignty, and the rapid movement of unemployed migrants into cities. Civic freedom was threatened by the fact that it always remained an urban affair in contradiction to agrarian interests. While political life in the towns and unions flourished, circumstances remained authoritarian in the countryside. The formation of a territorial state based on a purely communal constitution was impossible in Germany since none of the rural population had any part in the union movement, resulting in their sinking "ever deeper into servitude."[94]

Libertarian thinkers such as Bookchin read modernity as a struggle between two incipient forms of organizations replacing feudalism: federations of independent free cities and new nation-states with absolutist institutions. If the former project failed in Northern Italy and Germany, it largely succeeded in the Netherlands and Switzerland— at least insofar as these countries' histories suggest an alternative path. During the nineteenth century, Gierke supported the labor federation or genossenschaft movement along the lines of this earlier civic model; while he probably did not have as pessimistic an assessment as later observers, he opposed the introduction of Roman law, societas, and the private contract as the new dominant forms of productive and political relations. Bookchin, writing a century later, views the federative project as a failure, although he invokes it, in Walter Benjamin's style, as a *memory* to be actualized in revolutionary form, by conceiving the social movements and locus of political organization as the contest between the cities and the state on the model of the earlier federations of free cities.[95] In this model, the city is largely the sole seat of sovereignty, though associated with treaties; it determines the division of labor with an eco-communist logic. In Gierke's conception, there are multiple levels of sovereignty, though the historical precondition is the federated civic form.

• • •

Given the weaknesses and contradictions in a Green conception of European unification (despite the fact that they are still the general trendsetters of the left),[96] the conception of plural sovereignty and federalism developed by Althusius and Gierke suggests several ways of conceiving European unity and of addressing the paradoxes of the Green perspective. While the Althusius/Gierke conception of group personality and communal equality retains the idea of civic virtue and participation inherited from an Aristotelian or premodern view of community, it overcomes the tendency toward parochialism latent in a communitarian and/or civic republican perspective. Gierke recognizes the role of the city as the locus of political freedom, nonetheless offering a conception of federalism both deeper and broader than that developed by traditional republicanism. This capacity for constitutional extension, for spreading and deepening sovereignty into syndicate and professional organizations, on the one hand, and federal institutions above city and state, on the other, suggests an approach to unification amenable to reform while maintaining participatory democratic and anticapitalist principles. Gierke's concept of genossenschaft democracy, since it insists on organizational forms with a logic of usufruct rather than exchange and rejects the Roman law concept of the individual, remains a classically Aristotelian, anticapitalist concept of association.[97] Yet its interest in *more* levels of political organization allows us to consider federalist institutions and established paths of reform such as the European Parliament.

The contrast between the version of confederation offered by Althusius or Gierke and the present course of the EC couldn't be more dramatic. Indeed, the process of unification from Gierke's perspective would be another decisive historic victory for the anstalt or herrschaft form of association that has characterized the modern innovations of state and society. This historical presentation of the genossenschaft form and the free city as the basis of associational life took several centuries to develop; development in our time has rather continued the process of weakening the communes and strengthening the state. A Gierkean perspective makes dismally evident the present deficit in mobilization of social movements. There is no evident participatory alternative to Prussian unification.[98] We see no significant *counter-institutional* voice advancing confederal and participatory conjoinment and not merely "federal" unification of extant nation-states.[99] Despite overall pessimistic estimations of libertarian confederalism's potential, the outlines of a democratic but developed theory of federalism can only improve a discussion that has until now focused on agricultural subsidies and the end of purity restrictions on malt beer or wheat pasta. As a consideration of federalist options from a civic and democratic standpoint, Gierke's model is capable of transcending the civic sphere without sacrificing its predominance.

Considering such libertarian federalist views, however, underscores the need to find popular forms of protest on themes salient to a *confederal* Europe. The various Green manifestos and positions on European and foreign policy issues support the ideas of a democratically controlled federation but leave open the *institutional* question of the capacity to organize this, except insofar as they address important pan-European and international issues of redistribution.[100] The institutional question involves not just devolving increased power and competence to smaller professional groups (especially those focusing on new ecologically sound forms of production), citizen groups, neighborhood assemblies, and the civic sphere as a whole. The demand of more power for the cities and unions and for alternative organization of European institutions is the opening for a Gierkean democratic-federalist approach to reform. It is particularly important in view of the notion of "subsidarity" from *this* perspective. Interjected by Jacques Delores into the unification discussion, subsidiarity stems from Catholic sources and means help or assistance to those who cannot help themselves. In a libertarian federalist view, it means the *preeminence of the civic division of labor*.[101] This should be combined with a strategy that demands the reestablishment of local sovereignty over an entire panoply of issues relating to ecological balance and the quality of life, a process that should strengthen neighborhood and local assemblies as a counterpart to the transfer of more power to professional associations with democratic-syndicalist constitutions and that in turn parallels the extension of sovereignty beyond the civic level in terms of intercivic and confederational connections.

Gierke's perspective provides a view of functional differentiation in relation to spheres of social action and disciplines of knowledge. While the followers of Habermas reproach civic republicans for particularism, the leftist followers of Carl Schmitt advocate radical federalism on the basis of a "homogeneous" ethno-territorial concept of local rule. Moreover, the *universality* demanded by the Habermasians presupposes a distinctive institutional and disembodied *homogeneity* that must be reconciled with the "differentiation of society." Gierke offers a confederalist view of differentiation contrasting to the homogeneous Kantian one that Habermas shares with Hans Kelsen, Weber, and the modern views of the state. Gierke's conception is not a functionalist system with one medium of rule or a uniform concept of power.[102] It does not view the institutions of law as professionally staffed and driven, which organize "validity" for the "facticity" generated by system irrationalities, an image of bureaucratic and professional crisis management.[103] His view allows political competency over human affairs at various layers in the association of groups and organizations while insisting that "function" fits with "form" and "end" in the goal-directed model of the living organism. Such consociational confederalism suggests a possible polity and society in a manner that can adapt and contain this development democratically (and hence *politically*) in each differentiated "subsystem," because each "system" insisted on the proper mix of shared work, shared ownership, and shared practice in group self-government, which gives each group and its members a *living* personality organized by the practices and commitments of cooperative administration and the shared competencies of teleologically related skills and vocational abilities determined by the vocational orientation of a vocational association. While Habermas's positivist perspective based on Weber's concept of power and state is de facto a tutelary one, Gierke's view is divided first among different professions or sciences in a manner that regards each division both internally and publicly in participatory terms—through respective shares in the overall sovereignty.

To see Gierke's genossenschaft idea in post-Fordist terms, it helps to compare it not with Habermas but with the view of Ulrich Beck. Beck notes that the necessary differentiation of professional life that has come with late industrial technology is administered more and more by an intellectual class educated in specialized scientific disciplines. This differentiation accompanies the expansion of productive technologies into areas of marketability (e.g., genetic technology) where normal parliamentary institutions can no longer exert control. In such circumstances, Beck's proposal to develop democratic councils within each productive and research field with panels of specialists expressing differing political views suggests a mode that fits with Gierke's conception of federation and genossenschaft and offers a green approach to social differentiation. Beck's view of council-syndicate style control of new differentiated regions also fits with Michael Piorés and Charles Sabel's view of craft-industrialism and its present potential as a successful model in terms of small-scale firms with high levels of education, specialization, and collaboration among colleagues.[104] Democratization of the division of labor via syndical planning groups combined with local decision making over production and environmental policy means that we also need mediatory organs between the civic division of labor and the various lower but syndicated professional organizations.

Notes

1. Gerhard Meyer-Vorfelder, "Welches Europa wollen wir?" (ZEIT-umfrage), *Die Zeit* no. 26 (1992).

2. Frieder-Otto Wolf, "Alternative Zukunft: Europa," *Stachilige Argument: Zeitung der Alternative Liste Berlin*, no. 2 (May 1993): 44.

3. Daniel Cohn-Bendit, quoted in Mayer-Vorfelder, "Welches Europa wollen wir?"

4. In any case, such ideas are widely distributed among European Greens of various political perspectives. See *The Guiding Principles of the European Greens* (Brussels: The European Greens, 1993), par. 3.3; Frieder-Otto Wolf, "Es gibt eine grüne Alternative zur Maastrichter Währungsunion," in *Kein leichter Weg nach Eurotopia*, ed. Reinhild Hugenroth (Berlin: Pahl-Rugenstein, 1993), 91.

5. Murray Bookchin, "Toward a Libertarian Municipalism," *Our Generation* 16, no. 3–4 (1985); "Municipalization: Community Ownership of the Economy," *Green Program Project*, no. 1 (Burlington, Vt.: Green Perspectives, 1986); "The Transition to the Ecological Society: The Meaning of Confederalism," *Society and Nature* 3 (1993).

6. See Bookchin, "Self-Management and the New Technology," in *Toward an Ecological Society* (Montreal: Black Rose, 1980). Or, as Theodor Adorno once remarked sarcastically, if Marx had had his way, he would have turned the whole world into a workhouse. See Martin Jay, *The Dialectical Imagination* (New York: Little Brown, 1973), 259.

7. On the topic in general, see Helmut Rüdiger, *Föderalismus: Beitrag zu Geschichte der Freiheit* (1947; rpt. Berlin: Ahde, 1979); Ernst Deuerlein, *Föderalismus: Die historischen und philosophichen Grundlagen des föderativen Prinzips* (Munich: Paul List, 1972); Daniel Elazar, *Exploring Federalism* (Tuscaloosa: University of Alabama Press, 1987); *Telos* (Special Issue on Federalism) no. 91 (1992). While all of these texts develop the differences between federal states and federations of states, they are less clear on the importance of civic versus ethnic and cultural grounds for political membership in a given federation.

8. Udo Knapp has since become a Social Democrat. In general, we can see the "social democratization" of civic republican ideas, at least in the German context, in the increasing replacement of interest in the work of Arendt and Castoriadis with interest in Michael Walzer's work. This change, in my view, will also tend to strengthen ethnic and national readings of communitarianism. The disturbing emergence of identity politics (the topic of the 1993 annual meeting of the American Political Science Association) suggests this as well. While civic republicans must evaluate their own weaknesses at recognizing and supporting the emancipatory aspects of new identity politics—feminism, queer politics, minority rights—the more disturbing fact is that the term "identity," probably stemming from the influence of humanist psychology on the self-transformation movements of the sixties and seventies, is probably congenitally incapable of distinguishing between those identities that are ascriptive and those resulting from emancipatory political practice and good, useful work. Like most important concepts—such as values and interests—the

term "identity" is everywhere in use with virtually no genealogical reflection on its origins or meaning.

9. M. Rainer Lepsius, "Beyond the Nation-State: The Multinational State as the Model for the European Community," *Telos* no. 91 (1992): 59.

10. Bookchin, *The Rise of Urbanization and the Decline of Citizenship* (San Francisco: Sierra Club Books, 1987), 147–59, 163–72; see also Sheldon Wolin, "Two People's Bodies," *Democracy* 1, no. 1 (1981).

11. Klaus Busch, *Umbruch in Europa* (Cologne: Bund-Verlag, 1991), 29.

12. Jochen Struwe, *EG 92—Europa der Unternehmer?* (Frankfurt: Fischer, 1991), 19ff.

13. Barrington Moore, *The Origins of Dictatorship and Democracy* (Boston: Beacon Press, 1966), 414ff.

14. Geoff Eley and David Blackbourn, *The Peculiarities of German History* (Oxford: Oxford University Press, 1984), 54ff.

15. Lepsius, "Beyond the Nation-State," 58.

16. Ibid., 68f.

17. Otto Gierke distinguishes between association and (compulsory) institution, between genossenschaft and anstalt or the *Körperschaft* and anstalt, fellowship and tutelary forms of political or group organization. This underscores the difference between a Roman law conception of association—on which figures like Thomas Aquinas and Jean Bodin defined their concepts of principality and domination—and a German law conception of fellowship formed by confederated tribes, cities, and guilds. This distinction clarifies the difference between associations as a form of community and those that are corporations in the modern sense. See Gierke, *Das deutsche Genossenschaftsrecht,* 4 vols. (Berlin: Weidmannische Buchgesellschaft, 1868–1913), 1:638ff., 1030ff.; 2:39ff. See also Anthony Black's introduction to *Community in Historical Perspective,* an abridged English edition to vol. 1 of Gierke's *Genossenschaftsrecht* (Cambridge: Cambridge University Press, 1989), xvff.

18. Max Weber, *Economy and Society* (1908; rpt. Berkeley: University of California Press, 1978), 1:52f.

19. Andrea Fischer, "Die Grenzen der EG überschreiten: Ein Plädoyer für eine neue gesamteuropäische EG-Politik der Grünen," in *Grüne Aussenpolitik: Aspekte einer Debatte,* ed. Hans-Peter Hubert/BAG Frieden und Internationalismus der Grünen (Göttigen: Verlag die Werkstatt, 1993), 172.

20. Thomas Mayer, "Europa: Mit oder ohne Demokratie?" in Hugenroth, *Kein leichter Weg nach Eurotopia,* 115.

21. "Ministerpräsident Teufel kritisiert die Debatten um die Rechte der Länder in der Europapolitik," *Frankfurter Allgemeine Zeitung,* July 1, 1992. More recently, declining French influence in the European Council after Jacques Delores's tenure has led to a spat between Yves-Thibault de Silguy, in charge of the Economic and Monetary Affairs portfolio in the Council, and Edith Cresson, Commissioner of the Research and Development budget. A Cresson aid pledged to "emasculate" de Silguy, who in turn conspired to foil Cresson's ascendancy to ceremonial positions in the Commission. The dispute, writes

Lionel Barber in the *Financial Times*, was "more suited to the court of Louis XIV" ("The French Divide in Europe," Apr. 10, 1995).

22. See Christine Rath, "Die europäische Union und das Grundgesetz," in Hugeroth, *Kein leichter Weg nach Eurotopia*, 25ff.

23. Paul Piccone, "The Crisis of Liberalism and the Emergence of Federal Populism," *Telos* no. 89 (1991); "Federal Populism in Italy," *Telos* no. 90 (1991–92): 14ff. See also G. L. Ulmen, "What Is Integral Federalism?" *Telos* no. 91 (1992).

24. Piccone, "Federal Populism in Italy," 17f.

25. See Paul Piccone and Alphonse D'amico, "The Future of Federalism," *Telos* no. 91 (1992): 11f.; G. L. Ulmen, "Schmitt and Federalism," *Telos* no. 91 (1992): 21f.

26. This commonly noted argument is also rejected by some who oppose Maastricht for ecological reasons, such as Wilfried Telkämper ("Die Strukturen der EG, der Unterschied zwischen Binnenmarkt und Maastricht-Europa," in *Grüne Aussenpolitik*, 148ff.).

27. Piccone's deployment of Schmitt's theory of federalism—"doctrine" would be a better translation—fails not merely to navigate around the nationalist concept of agonistically competitive national states. Schmitt, the great Catholic reactionary, based his federalism, like his theory of rule or the political in general, on an agonist notion of the so-called "friend-enemy" distinction. It is in large measure a conservative, land-based, estate-oriented concept of the private or legal personality that fits harmoniously with the picture of the Austrian Middle Ages and its feudal structures as presented by Otto Brunner in *Land and Lordship* (Philadelphia: University of Pennsylvania Press, 1992). Schmitt's concept of *Land* and *Landnahme* as the basis of legal relations defines itself as a *territorial* and *homogeneous* unit. As Walter Ullmann has pointed out in his studies of the medieval civic republican, Marcellus of Padua, and as Gierke notes of the Middle Ages in general, the cities had notions of political rule virtually excluding or functionally subordinating the theme of territory. See Ullmann, "Personality and Territoriality in the 'Defensor Pacis': The Problem of Political Humanism," in *Law and Jurisdiction in the Middle Ages* (London: Valorium, 1988), and Otto Gierke, *Das deutsche Genossenschaftsrecht*, 1:575ff., 860ff.

28. Cited in Robert Leicht, "Das Bund mit dem zwölf Siegeln," *Die Zeit* no. 40 (1992).

29. Ethno-pluralism is a term coined by the right-wing ideologue Henning Eichberg. It refers to an idea characteristic throughout the New Right: the image of Europe broken into independent and (ethnically) homogeneous, pure and peaceful nation-states with traditions of rule and obedience. In general, see Thomas Jahn, *Ökologie von Rechts* (Frankfurt am Main: Campus, 1990).

30. Jürgen Habermas, *Die Neue Unübersichtlichkeit* (Frankfurt am Main: Suhrkamp,1985).

31. Peter Passell, "A Continent Considers One Big Bank," *New York Times*, Sept. 22, 1992.

32. Alberto Alesin, cited in ibid.

33. Émile Durkheim, *The Division of Labor in Society* (New York: Macmillan, 1933), chaps. 1 and 2.

34. Carl Schmitt, "The Constitutional Theory of Federation" (from the *Verfassungslehre*, 1928), in *Telos* no. 91 (1992): 33–37; Piccone, "Federal Populism."

35. See Habermas, "Volkssoveränität als Verfahren," in *Faktizität und Geltung* (Frankfurt am Main: Suhrkamp, 1992), 612–16. For a critique of Habermas and his followers on this point, see my "The Politics of 'Civil Society,'" *Telos* no. 93 (1992): 173ff.

36. Homogeneity can quickly become, even in a regional part of a nation or *ethnos*, constructed as a form of nationalistic particularism, especially where, as in the case of South Tirol, we already find a linguistic divide.

37. Stephan Leibfried, "Europäische Integration zwischen Marktbürger und Marktfreiheit: Über die Chancen und Risiken eines Wohlfahrtsstaats," *Frankfurter Rundschau* (Dokumentation), Aug. 4, 1992. In general on the problem of social movements and Europe, see Detlef Jahn, "Die Situation neuer sozialer Bewegungen im 'neuen Europa': Einige Reflexionen," *Forschungsjournal neue soziale Bewegungen* no. 1 (1993).

38. Friedrich Bahringdorf, "Quadratur des Kreises," *Die Tageszeitung*, May 23, 1991.

39. Anton Wächter, Bilan d'activités, May 1990, cited in Jean Lambert, "Impact of the Green Group in the European Parliament," paper presented at the European Consortium for Political Research, University of Essex, Colchester, 1991.

40. This biodiversity approach is combined with neo-Malthusian viewpoints in the American organization Earth First! On E. O. Wilson, see William K. Stevens, "A Strategy to Survey the Vast Unknowns of Life on the Earth," *New York Times*, Sept. 22, 1992.

41. Wächter gave one of the most significant reports of the faction on regional policy, Doc. A3-245/90, cited in Lambert.

42. Such social Darwinist views are evident not only in biologists like E. O. Wilson but also in conservative eco-philosophers like Vittorio Hösle or Peter Klossoski. Particularly in a middle European context, versions of bioregionalism could take a right-wing tenor. On Germany, see Peter Bierl, "Feindbild Mensch: Ökofaschismus und New Age," *Schwarzer Faden* 14, no. 2 (1993): 13ff.

43. Johann Galtung, "Supermacht im werden," *Die Tageszeitung*, Apr. 4, 1991.

44. Pierre Juquin, Frieder-Otto Wolf, Wilfried Telkämper, Isabelle Stengers, *Für eine grüne Alternative in Europa* (Hamburg: Argument, 1990), 81ff.

45. See Lambert, "Impact of the Green Group," on the document by Juquin et al., *Für eine grüne Alternative in Europa*. See also Rainer Falk, "Neue Armut und Verschärfung der globalen sozialen Konflikte: Thesen zur Perspektive des Südens in der Neue Weltordung," in Hubert, ed., *Grüne Aussenpolitik*; Andrea Lederer and Joachim Schmidt, "Die 'Gemeinsame Außen-und Sicherheitspolitik': Die EG auf dem Wege zu einer Großmacht mit militärischen Muskeln," in *Kein leichter Weg nach Eurotopia*, ed. Hugenroth.

46. See Alain Lipietz, "Démocratie après le Fordisme," *Les Temps moderns*, no. 524 (1990).

47. Lambert, "Impact of the Green Group"; Juquin et al., *Für eine grüne Alternative in Europa*, 82f.

48. On this phenomenon in Los Angeles, see Mike Davis, *City of Quartz* (London: Verso, 1988), and in Frankfurt, see Martin Wenz (Walter Prigge), ed., *Stadt-Raum* (Frankfurt: Campus, 1991).

49. See *Guiding Principles of the European Greens* (par. 1.3), which advocates an "ecological and socially regulated market economy." On the "green-green" or "left green" split, see Mark Franklin and Wolfgang Rüdig, "The Green Voter and the 1989 European Elections," *Environmental Politics* 1, no. 4 (1994). For a promarket and biocentric sort of fundamentalist view of green economics, see Robyn Eckersley, "Green vs. Ecosocialist Economic Programmes: The Market Rules, OK?" *Political Studies* 40, no. 2 (1992).

50. Lambert, "Impact of the Green Group."

51. See my "Alternative Economics in the Federal Republic of Germany: From the New Social Movements to the Ecological Reconstruction of Industrial Society," *Faultline: A Journal of Interdisciplinary German Studies* 1, no. 2 (1993).

52. This is even used by the Social Democratic defenders of the "civil society." See my "Politics of 'Civil Society.'"

53. See Melvin Laski, "The Pluralist State" (1917), in *The Pluralist Theory of the State: Selected Writings of G. D. H. Cole, J. N. Figgis, and H. J. Laski*, edited by Paul Q. Hirst (London and New York: Routledge, 1989), 83–94, 9–12.

54. Peter Winters, *Die "Politik" von Johannes Althusius* (Freiburg: Verlag Rombach, 1963), 179.

55. This focus on *practice* means that Althusius and Gierke, in the civic republican tradition, de-emphasize territorial concepts of politics and ascriptive features of community, which, for example, is a notable problem with the tendentially Catholic communitarianism of Charles Taylor, the Protestant communitarianism of Robert Bellah and Harry Boyte, and the Jewish communitarianism of Michael Walzer.

56. Gierke, *Das deutsche Genossenschaftsrecht*, 1:165ff.; 2:66ff.

57. Bookchin, *Urbanization and the Decline of Citizenship*, 87–122 (though Bookchin is also critical of guilds as institutions). In general, see Rüdiger, *Föderalismus*.

58. Bookchin, *Urbanization*, 95.

59. Frederic William Maitland and Frederic Pollock, *History of English Law*, 2 vols. (Cambridge: Cambridge University Press, 1893), 478.

60. Ibid., 493.

61. Winters, *Die "Politik,"* 37ff.

62. In this sense, both the Althusian-Gierkean conception of fellowship and later libertarian traditions are Aristotelian in their emphasis on friendship. See Aristotle's *Ethics*, bk. 8. As Richard Mulgan observes, *koinon* is used by Aristotle in the *Ethics* to cover "all the various forms of friendship, including father and son, fellow soldiers, hosts, guests and kinsmen, members of phratries or

priestly colleges, those involved in all the various exchange relationships such as a doctor and a farmer, or a builder and shoemaker" ("Aristotle and Political Participation," *Political Theory* 18, no. 2 [1990]: 214).

63. Althusius's conception of federation is decisively different from many modern conceptions because it is a *communitarian* conception based on the Aristotelian view that the nature or kind of individual exists in relation to the kind of institutional world in which they live, as well as through their practices. Like Aristotle or Rousseau, Althusius and Gierke conceive of political life as education or transformation of "subjects" into citizens via a notion of the relation of the participating part to the associative whole, or the idea, in Gierke's terms, of "group personality." The virtues of the citizen or the civic personality correspond as a micro-cosmos to the virtues of the polity and associational forms. This view considers the kind of personality, or the "human nature," of individuals in relation to the kind of political society. It is an *ethos* conception of individual ethics rather than an abstract individual definition based on interest and/or relativism. As Anthony Black, one of Gierke's editors remarks, Gierke is interested in a close study of the "way people are connected" rather than a study of individuals or structures (Black, preface to Gierke, *Community in Historical Perspective*, xiv). For Gierke as for the civic republican tradition, states are too large. Only lesser associations of a civic or syndical nature allow individuals to develop as political beings and allow the sense of belonging through partipation or the virtues of membership and the public virtues of citizenship.

64. In this sense, Gierke draws on a medieval conception of federalism as a harmoniously articulated organism of the universe filled with a divine spirit. "This forms a unity which is neither absolute nor exclusive, but forms the over-arching dome of a social structure organized as an independent whole. And this principle is repeated in its various gradations down to the smallest local, vocational and domestic groups. . . . Everywhere in the church and in the state the unitary total body consists of living member-bodies, each of which, though itself a whole, necessarily requires connection with a larger whole. . . . Between the highest universality or 'All-Community' and the essential unity of the individual there is a series of intermediate unities, in each of which lesser and lower unities are comprised and combined." In this manner, argues Gierke, Althusius enlarges on "the Aristotelian gradation of communities" (Gierke, *Development of Political Theory*, 257f.).

65. Ibid., 149.

66. Ernst Troeltsch, *The Social Teaching of the Christian Churches*, vol. 1 (New York: Macmillan, 1931). In this respect, the ecologically important image of the scala naturae or the gradated emergence of mind out of nature fits with federative notions of ius symbiotica, since in this respect such ideas are part of both an Aristotelian and a libertarian-ecological orientation. See R. G. R Mure, *Aristotle* (1932; rpt. Oxford: Oxford University Press, 1964), 102, 195, and chaps. 4–8; Peter Kropotkin, *Mutual Aid* (1914; rpt. Montreal: Black Rose, 1992); Murray Bookchin, *The Ecology of Freedom* (Palo Alto: Cheshire, 1982), 280ff.

67. Otto Gierke, *Das deutsche Genossenschaftsrecht*, 2:49.

68. Ibid., 2:50.

69. Ibid., 2:51.

70. F. W. Maitland, *A Constitutional History of England* (Cambridge: Cambridge University Press, 1908), 5. The genossenschaft in its English form can define the interests of its members in terms of usufruct, as organic participation, as a part in the whole. As Stubbs (*Constitutional History*, vol. 2, cited in Maitland, 85) observes, "the commons are the communities or the *universitates*, the organized bodies of free men of the shires and towns, and the estate of the commons is the *communitas communitatum*, the general body into which for the puposes of parliament these communities are combined." Representatives in Parliament were, continues Stubbs, not "inorganic collections of individuals but represented shires and boroughs."

71. Gierke, *Das deutsche Genossenschaftsrecht*, 2:54.

72. Gierke, *Community in Historical Perspective*, 80.

73. Ibid., 96.

74. Bookchin, "Toward a Libertarian Municipalism."

75. Which, by the way, makes it principally opposed to the territorial-based, homogeneous, volk-nation version of the political advocated by the followers of Carl Schmitt.

76. Gierke, *Political Theory of the Middle Ages*, ed. Maitland (1900; rpt. Boston: Beacon, 1958), 37ff.; Gierke, *The Development of Political Theory* (New York: W. W. Norton, 1939), 143; James Bryce, *Studies in History and Jurisprudence* (Oxford: Oxford University Press, 1901), 527ff.

77. Gierke, *Das deutsche Genoßenschaftsrecht*, 2:29.

78. Ibid., 2:30.

79. Ibid., 2:34ff.

80. Franz Neumann, *Die Herrschaft des Gesetzes* (Frankfurt: Suhrkamp, 1980), 105ff.; Jürgen Habermas, *Theorie des kommunikativen Handelns* (Frankfurt: Suhrkamp, 1981), 2:466ff.

81. Gierke, *Development of Political Theory*, 169; Maitland, introduction to Otto Gierke, *Political Theory of the Middle Ages*, xliii.

82. Henry Maine, *Ancient Law* (1861; rpt. Dorset Press, 1986), 126: "The family as held together by *patria potestas* is the nidus out of which the entire Law of Persons has germinated."

83. Gierke, *Development of Political Theory*, 150.

84. Or, worded differently, the *development* of sovereignty insofar as the term has today a largely and exclusively modern meaning deriving from the idea of jurisdiction in a territorially ordered national state.

85. Gierke, *Development of Political Theory*, 185.

86. Ibid., 275f.

87. Maitland, introduction to Gierke, *Political Theories of the Middle Ages*, xxiif.

88. Ibid., xliii.

89. Ibid.

90. Gierke, *Das deutsche Genoßenschaftsrecht*, 4, 276–313. See also Ernest Barker, ed., *Natural Law and the Theory of Society* (Cambridge: Cambridge University Press, 1958), 68n.

91. Maitland, *Constitutional History*, 14ff.

92. Gierke, *Community in Historical Perspective*, 10.

93. Ernst Forsthoff, *Verfassungsgeschichte*, 168; Otto Kimminich, *Deutsche Vervassungsgeschichte* (Baden-Baden: Nomos, 1987); C. J. Friedrich, preface to Althusius, *Politics*, ed. Carny, ix.

94. Gierke, *Community in Historical Perspective*, 75.

95. Walter Benjamin, "Theses on the Philosophy of History," in *Illuminations* (New York: Schocken, 1969).

96. See, e.g., Andrei Markovits, "The German Left between Crisis of Identity and Orthodoxy," *New Political Science* no. 15 (1993).

97. Aristotle argues a politics of virtue that limits the prospect of making money rather than making goods on the model of scale and the prevention of *excess*. See *Politics*, edited by Ernest Barker (Oxford: Oxford University Press, 1958), 1:9. Kantian and utilitarian conceptions of morality, on the other hand, presuppose a concept of "society" unmediated in this sense, or mediated by market fetishism.

98. Compare with Joscha Schmierer, *Die neue alte Weltordnung* (Frankfurt am Main: Wiser Verlag, 1993).

99. In this sense, we can see the outlook on European unification as part of a world dominated by "capitalism without an alternative," to use Joachim Hirsch's characterization of a regulationist premise for understanding the array of possible new post-Fordist regimes. See Hirsch, *Kapitalismus ohne Alternative?* (Hamburg: VSA-Verlag, 1990).

100. Frieder-Otto Wolf, "Es gibt eine grüne Alternative zur Maastrichter Währungsunion," in *Kein leichter Weg nach Eurotopia*, ed. Hugenroth; Andreas Fisher, "Die Grenzen der EG überschreiten: Ein Plädoyer für eine neue gesamteuropäische EG-Politik der Grünen," in *Grüne Aussenpolitik*, ed. Hubert, 170ff.

101. Peter Kropotkin, "Municipal Socialism," *Freedom* no. 172 (1902), reprinted in *Act for Yourselves* (London: Freedom Press, 1988); Bookchin, *Rise of Urbanization*.

102. This contrasts above all with Habermas, *Theorie des kommunikativen Handelns*, 470ff.

103. Habermas, *Faktizität und Geltung* (Frankfurt am Main: Suhrkamp, 1991).

104. Michael Pioré and Charles Sabel, *The Second Industrial Divide* (New York: Basic, 1994). Robert Putnam, in *Making Democracy Work: Civic Traditions in Modern Italy* (Princeton, N.J.: Princeton University Press, 1993), underscores the historic influence of northern Italian civic republicanism in this development. See also Paul Hirst, *Associative Democracy* (Amherst: University of Massachusetts Press, 1992).

Contributors

Michael Crozier is a lecturer in political science at the University of Melbourne and an editor of the journal *Thesis Eleven*.

John Ely teaches in the program in Culture, Ideas, and Values at Stanford University and is the author of *The Greens of West Germany: An Alternative Modernity* (forthcoming) and coeditor of *The German Greens: Paradox between Movement and Party* (1993).

Ferenc Fehér, prior to his death in 1994, was a professor of liberal studies on the graduate faculty at the New School for Social Research and a fellow of the Hungarian Academy of Sciences. His most recent works include *From Yalta to Glasnost* (1991), *The Grandeur and Twilight of Radical Universalism* (1991), and *The Frozen Revolution* (1987).

Paul R. Harrison, a senior lecturer in sociology at the Queensland University of Technology, Australia, is the author of *The Disenchantment of Reason* (1994).

Barry Hindess, a professor in the Research School of Social Science at the Australian National University, Canberra, is the author of *Political Choice and Social Structure* (1989) and *Choice, Rationality and Social Theory* (1988).

Dick Howard, a professor of philosophy at the State University of New York at Stony Brook, is the author of *The Birth of American Political Thought* (1989) and *Defining the Political* (1989).

Peter Murphy is a senior lecturer in politics at the University of Ballarat, Australia, and an editor of the journal *Thesis Eleven*.

Gillian Robinson is a lecturer in politics at Monash University, Australia, and coeditor of *Between Totalitarianism and Postmodernity* (1992) and *Reason and Imagination* (1993).

Barry Smart, a professor of sociology at the University of Auckland, is the author of *Foucault, Marxism and Critique* (1983) and *Michel Foucault* (1985).

Index

Absolutism, 25
Affects, 94
Afghanistan, 17
Alberti, Leon Battista, 80
Algeria, 16
Althusius, Johannes, 184, 189, 191–95
   passim, 197, 199
Ambivalence, 54, 71
Amendola, Gianfranco, 187
American Republic, 6
Ancient Greece, 29, 35, 99, 128
Ancient Rome, 25, 29, 96, 113, 128
Antigone, 192
Arendt, Hannah, 29, 80, 106, 118, 122,
   131, 132, 140–55 passim, 180, 181
Aristotelianism, 23
Aristotle, 91, 119, 130, 141, 142, 150,
   151, 153, 180, 181, 191, 193–95
Asian-Pacific integration, 87
Associations, 190, 198
Athens, 29, 113, 114
Atlantic Ocean, 4
Augustan England, 25
Australia, 4, 9
Autonomy, 27, 110, 114, 115, 116, 121,
   122, 125, 127, 154, 155

Bahringdorf, Friedrich, 187
Balance, 30, 128, 129, 180, 184
Balkans, 13

Baroque, 72
Bauman, Zygmunt, 49, 52, 55, 59, 66–
   68, 70, 71, 73, 75–78, 80
Beauty, 35, 133, 134, 135
Beck, Ulrich, 202
Benda, Ernst, 183
Benjamin, Walter, 199
Bentham, Jeremy, 72
Bloch, Ernst, 32
Bodin, Jean, 171, 182, 195–97
Body, 71
Bookchin, Murray, 180, 181, 190, 194,
   198
Borders, 87, 100
Braudel, Ferdinand, 87
Bridgeman, Charles, 79
Britain, 9
Brown, Lancelot ("Capability"), 79
Brussels, 12, 87
Buchanan, Patrick, 8, 15
Bureaucracy, 22
Bush, George, 8, 15

Cairo, 4
Canovan, Margaret, 150
Capitalism, 4, 18, 19, 168, 171, 172, 174,
   197
Cartesianism, 72, 129–30
Castoriadis, Cornelius, 35, 180
Central Europe, 14

Chaos, 49, 52, 58
Chaos theory, 70, 73, 75
Checks and balances, 86
China, 3
Choice, 9, 14, 15, 121, 130, 131
Citizenship, 21–24 passim, 29, 100, 109,
    112, 114, 115, 123, 154
City, 5, 26, 28, 29, 119, 123, 145, 183,
    192, 193, 198, 199
City leagues, 13
City-state, 3, 6, 25, 27, 30, 186
Civic humanism, 23
Civic ideal, 23–26 passim, 29, 118, 128
Civic life, 6
Civilization, 6, 68, 122, 123
Class, 8, 119, 120, 121
Classicism, 128
Cohn-Bendit, Daniel, 180, 181, 189
Colbert, Jean-Baptiste, 72
Cole, G. D. H., 189
Colonialism, 16, 17, 116
Columbia, 16
Communism, 2, 3, 15, 16, 21, 24, 36,
    128, 162, 168
Communitarianism, 179
Community, 3, 5, 11, 17, 20, 59, 96,
    106, 112–16 passim, 121, 191, 192
Complexity, 24, 72
Conflict, 6, 19
Confucianism, 3, 15
Conscience, 149, 154, 155
Consent, 106, 107, 111
Conservatism, 2, 8, 14, 15, 17, 20, 24
Consistency, 27
Constitutionalism, 12, 13
Consumerism, 2, 7, 24
Contemplation, 140, 141, 142
Contestation, 16, 29, 133
Contingency, 24, 27, 40, 52, 53, 54, 59,
    71, 72, 122, 124
Corporations, 7, 10, 191
Corporatism, 7, 14, 21
Cosmopolitanism, 28, 29, 113
Cosmos, 76
Cultural patterns, 19, 67
Cynicism, 5, 17
Czechoslovakia, 163

Debt, 7–8
Decentering, 26

Decentralization, 179–80
Decision-making, 8, 107, 131
Delores, Jacques, 12, 201
Democracy, 7, 18, 20–23 passim, 162,
    163, 164, 168, 169, 171, 174, 202
Descartes, René, 89
Destiny, 53, 59
Deterritorialization, 87
Difference, 60
Differend, 130
Discontinuity, 51
Disenchantment, 43
Dissatisfaction, 38, 52, 54
Diversity, 60
Durkheim, Émile, 185
Dutch East India Company, 88
Dutch Republic, 28, 86, 97
Dutscke, Rudi, 163
Dynamism, 3, 5, 7, 12, 14, 15, 18, 20, 30

East Asia, 7, 17
Eastern Europe, 1, 100
Eco-fundamentalism, 187
Economic growth, 10
Economic recession, 11, 19
Egypt, 15
Ehrlich, Paul, 187
Electorates, 11
Elias, Norbert, 90
Employment, 8–11 passim, 123
English Constitution, 25
English Whigs, 30
Enlightenment, 44, 50, 68
Epicureanism, 31
Equality, 8, 119
Equilibrium, 30, 35, 128
Ethnic cleansing, 32, 185
Ethnicity, 27, 28, 35, 100, 115, 201
Ethnic wars, 13
Europe, 87, 181
European Commission on Human
    Rights, 12
European Parliament, 187–88
European Union, 12, 13, 28, 179, 181,
    182
Excellence, 7, 119, 134

Falklands War, 11, 15
Fascism, 21
Fear, 31, 34, 57

Federalism, 13, 28, 116, 179–202 passim
Fehér, Ferenc, 49, 52, 55, 59, 60
Fellowship, 189–93 passim, 199
Figgis, John, 189
Fiji, 17
Foucault, Michel, 49, 50–52, 55, 59, 66, 111
France, 11, 12
Freedom, 15, 80, 97, 99, 119, 120, 122, 133, 141
Free trade, 17
French Revolution, 68, 170
Friendship, 123, 180, 191, 193
Functionalism, 20

Garden(s): landscape, 26; human universal, 65; wild vs. garden cultures, 66, 71; garden state, 68; Dutch, 72; eighteenth-century English landscape, 77, 79; naturalistic, 79
Gellner, Ernest, 66
Georgia (former U.S.S.R.), 16
German Social Democratic party, 179
Germany, 7, 12, 13, 14, 173, 183, 184, 199
Gibbs, James, 79
Giddens, Anthony, 47, 49, 51, 52, 55, 59, 105
Gierke, Otto, 182, 184, 185, 189, 191–99 passim, 201, 202
Globalization, 87
Goethe, Johann Wolfgang von, 31
Goodman, Paul, 180
Goodness, 144
Government expenditure, 14, 15
Gramsci, Antonio, 109
Green politics, 179–202 passim
Gulag, 32

Habermas, Jürgen, 48, 110, 181, 185, 189, 201
Hansa Confederation, 194
Harmony, 35, 128, 134
Hauff, Volker, 179
Hawke, Robert ("Bob"), 9, 11
Hegel, Georg Wilhelm Friedrich, 165, 167
Heidegger, Martin, 32, 40, 151, 152
Heller, Agnes, 49, 52, 55, 59, 60
Helsinki Accords, 173

Heraclitus, 134
Hesse, Conrad, 183
Hierarchy, 7, 8, 13, 17, 120
History, end of, 18
Hobbes, Thomas, 88, 91, 97, 104–6, 112, 114, 195–97
Hofstadter, Richard, 164
Holocaust, 32
Homer, 134
Hong Kong, 3
Hope, 2, 27; radical utopia, 32; rational, 40; self-contradictory, 40
Howard, Ebenezer, 180
Hoy, David, 50
Human condition, 140
Humanism, 30
Human rights, 16
Hume, David, 130, 131
Hussein, Sadam, 15

Identity, 12, 28
Ideology, 18
Imagination, 46, 93, 94, 132
Immortality, 140–41
Indonesia, 17
Industrialization, 3, 10, 19, 20, 24
Intellectuals, 69, 70
Interpretation, 73, 91, 92, 98, 119
Iran, 15
Iraq, 15
Irish Republic, 12
Irrationalism, 27
Islam, 16, 17
Italy, 28, 199

Jacobins, 67, 80
Japan, 3, 5, 13
Jasper, Karl, 122
Jefferson, Thomas, 30
Judgment, 6, 118, 127, 134, 135
Justice, 127–30 passim, 136

Kampuchea, 17
Kant, Immanuel, 71, 119, 121, 122
Kateb, George, 150
Keating, Paul, 9, 11
Kelsen, Hans, 201
Kent, William, 79
Keynesianism, 24
Knapp, Udo, 181

Knowledge, 69
Kretschmann, Winifried, 181
Kropotkin, Peter, 180, 194
Kuwait, 15

Labor party (Australia), 9
Labour party (U.K.), 9
Lambert, Jean, 187
Laski, Melvin, 189
Latin America, 15
Law, 108, 134, 189, 190, 195, 196
Learning, 123
Lefort, Claude, 170, 172, 173
Le Goff, Jacques, 77, 78
Le Nôtre, Andre, 72
Liberalism, 2, 7, 11, 14–18 passim, 20,
    23, 24, 29, 121, 165, 173
Libertarianism, 179, 194, 199
Limits, 27, 128, 135
Locke, John, 96, 107–9
Lukes, Steven, 105, 109, 110
Luxemburg, Rosa, 162–67 passim, 169,
    172
Lyotard, Jean-François, 122, 130

Maastricht Treaty, 12, 179, 180, 183, 184
Machiavelli, Niccolò, 180, 181
Madison, James, 6, 30, 122, 169–72
    passim
Maitland, Frederic William, 189, 190,
    193, 196, 197
Malaysia, 16
Mandelbrot, Benoit, 73, 74, 80
Marcellus of Padua, 195
Marcuse, Herbert, 39
Marx, Karl, 50, 164–66, 170, 171
Marxism, 18, 19, 110, 163, 167, 172,
    175, 180
Masculinity, 113
Mathematical topology, 74
McCarthy, Thomas, 48
Meaning, 3, 29, 45, 46, 65, 118, 123,
    133
Mediterranean, 25, 26, 29, 128
Messianism, 39
Middle Ages, 76, 78
Middle East, 15
Military, 14, 15
Moderation, 27
Modernism, 17, 124, 129, 130, 131

Modernity, 3, 4, 5, 12, 37, 38, 40, 43, 48,
    55, 57, 58, 67, 167, 198, 199
Modernization, 12, 15, 24, 183
Monarchy, 25
Montesquieu, Charles Louis de Secondat,
    baron de, 25, 96, 122
Morality, 27, 123, 125, 127, 128
Moses, 96
Multiculturalism, 113, 116
Multipolarity, 87
Mumford, Lewis, 180
Music, 133, 134
Mysticism, 39

Naess, Arne, 187
Nagorno-Karabakh, 100
Nationalism, 7, 11, 12, 18, 28, 90
Nation-state, 5, 7, 13, 22, 28, 67, 100,
    182, 183, 184, 186, 189, 194, 195
Natural rights, 97
Nature, 180
Neo-Aristotelianism, 181, 185
Netherlands, 28, 199
New Left, 39, 164, 172
New World, 13, 16, 31
New York, 87
Nietzsche, Friedrich W., 36, 47
North America, 4
North Vietnam, 105

Obedience, 97
Opinion, 108, 109, 114, 129, 147, 148
Oppositions, 128
Ovid, 64

Pacific Ocean, 4
Pakistan, 16
Palladio, Andrea, 79
Parkin, Sara, 187
Parsons, Talcott, 106
Pascal, Blaise, 74, 168
Paternalism, 107–8
Patriarchy, 7
Patrimony, 7, 17, 21, 28
Patriotism, 11, 12, 13, 96
Pericles, 29, 113
Perrault, Charles, 72
Persian Gulf War, 15
Philippines, 15
Philosophy, 140, 141, 144, 146, 152, 153

Piccone, Paul, 183, 184
Piores, Michael, 202
Plato, 141–44 passim, 147, 149, 150, 151, 153
Pleasure, 134
Pluralism, 30, 122, 123, 124, 141, 153, 189
Polanyi, Karl, 165
Political, 80, 136
Political community, 18, 28
Political languages, 18, 20
Pollock, Frederick, 189, 190
Pomona, 64
Pope, Alexander, 37
Postmodernism, 16, 25, 33, 48, 55, 56, 58, 69
Power, 94, 96, 104–12 passim
Pragmatism, 29
Productivism, 25
Professionals, 10
Progress, 3, 4, 39
Protectionism, 17
Proudhon, Pierre-Joseph, 184
Psyche, 5
Public, 6, 7, 22, 23, 29, 123, 126, 133, 140, 150
Pufendorf, Samuel, 198
Pyrrhonianism, 76
Pythagoras, 134
Pythagoreanism, 128

Race, 8
Rationality, 9, 15, 129; reason, 27, 91; practical reason, 118
Rationalization, 4, 5, 10, 11, 14, 17, 18, 20, 21, 47, 48
Reagan, Ronald, 11, 14, 15
Reflexivity, 6, 59
Religion, 4, 6, 7, 8, 15, 44, 46, 68, 77, 78, 87–92 passim, 95, 98, 99, 100
Renaissance, 6, 25, 26, 28
Republicanism, 22, 23, 28, 30, 80, 180, 194
Republican party (U.S.), 8
Resident aliens, 113, 116
Respect, 16
Revolution, 163
Rights, 23, 120, 165, 166, 170, 172
Risk, 57
Romanticism, 16, 25, 76, 77, 79

Rousseau, Jean Jacques, 71, 96, 180, 181, 194

Sabel, Charles, 202
São Paolo, 4
Schmitt, Carl, 183, 184, 186, 201
Schumpeter, Joseph, 165
Security, 14, 15, 24, 58, 99
Self-determination, 29, 53, 54, 59, 120, 122, 124
Self-management, 19
Simon, Helmut, 183
Singer(s), 133, 134
Skepticism, 68, 130, 131, 132
Slavery, 113, 116, 143
Social contract, 28, 197, 198
Socialism, 20, 21, 23, 24, 56, 162
Social labor, 19
Social movements, 186, 187
Social question, 40
Socrates, 145, 147–49, 151–53
Solidarity, 59, 60
South Korea, 3
Sovereignty, 21, 28, 89, 90, 95, 97, 99, 103, 106, 108, 111, 170, 182, 183, 190, 195–98 passim
Soviet Union, 1, 17, 87, 100; collapse of (1989), 1, 19, 25, 35, 162
Spain, 86, 87
Spartakus League, 163, 164, 166
Spectator, 132–35 passim
Spinoza, Baruch, 28, 31, 86–89, 91–93, 95, 96, 98
Stalinism, 2
State of nature, 98
St. Augustine of Hippo, 44
St. Jerome, 78
Stoicism, 27, 31
Strasser, Johanno, 179
Suarez, Francisco, 198
Sublime, 79
Surveillance, 67, 69
Switzerland, 28, 194, 199
Syndicalism, 180

Taiwan, 3
Taste, 129, 131, 132
Thadden, August von, 184
Thatcher, Margaret, 9, 11, 15

Theater, 135
Thinking, 152, 153, 154
Thompson, Edward P., 165
Thucydides, 112
Tocqueville, Alexis de, 167–69
Tokyo, 87
Tolerance, 59, 100
Totalitarianism, 18, 168, 169, 171, 173
Toulmin, Stephen, 89
Touraine, Alain, 19
Tradition, 5, 7, 13, 20, 170
Troeltsch, Ernst, 189, 192
Truth, 147, 148, 152
Tyranny, 15, 97, 107

Ukraine, 16
Underclass, 10
United States of America, 2, 11, 14, 15, 25, 87, 105
Utilitarianism, 118
Universal history, 16
Universalism, 16, 119, 120, 124–25
Utopia, 19, 60

Values, 122, 123, 124, 126, 128, 132, 135
Vanbrugh, Sir John, 79

Versailles, 72
Vertumnus, 64
Virtue, 11, 119
Vita activa, 142, 143, 145, 151
Vocation, 124, 126, 127
Voting, 8

Wächter, Anton, 187
Walpole, Horace, 71, 79
War of Independence (U.S.), 86
Weber, Max, 43–45, 90, 122, 130, 201, 202
Weil, Simone, 139, 181
Welfare state, 7, 9
Western society, 1, 2, 17, 26, 118, 140, 174
Wilderness, 76, 78, 79; desert wilderness, 77
Will, 120, 125, 152
Wilson, Edward, 187
Wolf, Frieder-Otto, 179, 187
Women, 8, 107, 113, 116, 165
Wonder, 149
Workers' movement, 19

Yeltsin, Boris, 2
Yemen, 16
Yugoslavia, 16